Reconceiving Writing,
Rethinking Writing Instruction

Reconceiving Writing, Rethinking Writing Instruction

Edited by

Joseph Petraglia
Georgia Institute of Technology

 LAWRENCE ERLBAUM ASSOCIATES, PUBLISHERS
1995   Mahwah, New Jersey

Lawrence Erlbaum Associates, Inc., Publishers
10 Industrial Avenue
Mahwah, New Jersey 07430

Cover design by Mairav Salomon-Dekel

Library of Congress Cataloging-in-Publication Data

Reconceiving writing, rethinking writing instruction / edited by
   Joseph Petraglia
          p. cm.
     Includes bibliographical references and index.
     ISBN 0-8058-1691-7 (alk. paper). — ISBN 0-8058-1692-5
(pbk. : alk. paper)
     1. English language—Rhetoric—Study and teaching. I.
Petraglia, Joseph.
PE1408.R383 1995
808'.042'07—dc20   95-5787
                                              CIP

Books published by Lawrence Erlbaum Associates are printed on
acid-free paper, and their bindings are chosen for strength and
durability.

Printed in the United States of America
10 9 8 7 6 5 4 3 2 1

Contents

List of Contributors

Charles Bazerman is Professor of English at the University of California at Santa Barbara. He has written and edited several books on the psychosocial dynamics of writing, the rhetoric of science and technology, and rhetorical theory, as well as textbooks. Currently he is completing two projects: a new first-year textbook entitled *Involved: Writing for College* and an analysis of the textual and social construction of the incandescent light entitled *The Languages of Edison's Light*.

Lil Brannon is Professor of English and Director of the Center for Excellence in Teaching and Learning at the University of Albany, SUNY. She is co-author of *Critical Teaching and the Idea of Literacy and Rhetorical Traditions* and *Teaching of Writing* with C. H. Knoblauch (Boynton/Cook) and *Writers Writing* with Vara Neverow-Turk and Melinda Knight (Boynton/Cook). She has also published essays in the journals *CCC, College English, Journal of Basic Writing,* and *Freshmen English News,* among others.

Robert J. Connors is Associate Professor of English and Director of the Writing Center at the University of New Hampshire. He has published extensively in rhetoric and writing journals and has co-authored and edited several books and textbooks on writing with Lisa Ede, Cheryl Glenn, and Andrea Lunsford. His most recent project, a monograph on the history of composition studies, is forthcoming from the University of Pittsburgh Press.

Patricia L. Dunmire is Assistant Professor of English at Kent State University. In addition to composition studies, her research interests include language and argument of scholarship and public affairs. Her dissertation, entitled *Events, Social Identities, Speaker Roles: A Critical Discourse Analysis of the 1990 Persian Gulf Conflict*, explores the linguistic and rhetorical construction of political events.

Aviva Freedman is Professor of Lingustics and Applied Language Studies at Carleton University. Her research has focused on the acquisition and development of writing abilities from the school years to skilled maturity, and on variation in discourse genres. Her recent work includes two co-edited collections on genre: *Learning and Teaching Genre* (Heinemann Boynton/Cook) and *Genre in the New Rhetoric* (Taylor & Francis).

Cheryl Geisler is Associate Professor of Rhetoric and Composition at Rensselaer Polytechnic Institute, where she teaches graduate courses in literacy and directs the Writing Intensive Program. Her research on writing in the academic professions has been published in *Academic Literacy and the Nature of Expertise: Reading, Writing, and Knowing in Academic Philosphy* (1994) from Lawrence Erlbaum Associates.

Maureen Daly Goggin is Assistant Professor of Rhetoric and Composition in the English Department at Arizona State University. She has published on the history of rhetoric and on the emergence of rhetoric and composition as a discipline.

Charles A. Hill is Assistant Professor of English and Director of the Writing Center at the University of Wisconsin at Oshkosh. He has published collaboratively in *Computers and Composition* and *Written Communication*. His current interests include argumentation pedagogy and curricular issues in writing.

David A. Jolliffe is Associate Professor of English and Director of the Writing Center at DePaul University. Recent publications include *Scenarios for Teaching Writing* (NCTE) and *Rhetoric: Concepts, Definitions, Boundaries* (Allyn & Bacon).

David S. Kaufer is Professor and Head of the English Department at Carnegie Mellon University. His research interests include written composition, critical thinking, and computers and writing.

*N*ow there are varieties of *gifts*,
but the same *spirit*;
and there are varieties of *service*,
but the same *Lord*;
and there are varieties of *working*,

but it is the same *God* who inspires
them all *in everyone.*

1 Cor. 12:4-6

activity/invention
theory/invention

without directing student
towards writing that
holds meaning and motive —

template | engaging students in new
and motive of genre

rather than academic discourse

preparing students to write
in one genre

· adequate writing

interaction w/ text
more to than demonstrating
knowledge
more than teacher as audience

Fred Kemp is Associate Professor of English and Rhetoric at Texas Technological University and is director of both the department's Composition and Rhetoric Program and its Computer-Based Writing Project. He is co-director of the National Alliance for Computers and Writing and the list owner of the electronic discussion list Megabyte University (MBU-L). Research interests include writing about networked computer-based writing instruction and classroom applications for the Internet.

Joseph Petraglia is Assistant Professor of Rhetoric and Writing at the Georgia Institute of Technology. He has written on affect and cognition and issues of social construction as they relate to rhetoric and writing instruction. His book, *Reality by Design*, on the rhetoric and technology of authenticity in education is forthcoming from Lawrence Erlbaum Associates.

Lauren Resnick is Professor of Psychology and Director of the Learning Research and Development Center at the University of Pittsburgh. She has written extensively on literacy development both in and out of school and is a past president of the American Educational Research Association.

Daniel J. Royer is Assistant Professor of English at Grand Valley State University in Allendale, Michigan. His other publications include discussions of philosophical issues in rhetoric and composition studies and articles on African American literature.

David R. Russell is Associate Professor of English at Iowa State University, where he teaches in the PhD program in Rhetoric and Professional Communication. His publications include *Writing in the Academic Disciplines, 1970–1990: A Curricular History* (SIU Press) and a recently co-edited (with Charles Bazerman) volume entitled *Landmark Essays in Writing Across the Curriculum* (Hermagoras). He is currently writing a book on activity theory and genre acquisition and collaborating on a multimedia program to simulate writing activities in the disciplines.

Introduction:
General Writing Skills Instruction and Its Discontents

Joseph Petraglia
Georgia Institute of Technology

The introduction-to-academic-anthology is a fairly staid genre. Its predictable purpose is to introduce the theme of the collection and suggest how each chapter provides coverage of that theme. In addition to serving those important functions here, however, I would like to draw the reader's attention to what I think of as the especially polemic value of this anthology, for although each of the chapters has the typical research aim of illuminating a theoretical framework, genre, context, or process, the volume also aims to be provocative. Taken together, these chapters are meant to focus our attention on the weak relationship of writing research and theory to writing instruction, or perhaps more accurately, to a particular framework for writing instruction: something that might be labeled *general writing skills instruction* (GWSI).

DEFINING THE OBJECT OF INQUIRY

Although the acronym is freshly minted, GWSI is undoubtedly familiar to everyone who has taught writing, for practically every contemporary approach to writing instruction from current-traditionalism and expressivism to "cognitivist" and "constructionist" curricula has, at its core, the idea that writing is a set of rhetorical skills that can be mastered through formal instruction. These skills include the general ability to develop and organize ideas, use techniques for inventing topics worthy of investigation, adapt one's purpose to an audience, and anticipate reader response. Conversely, although GWSI encompasses much of what we call *composition,* it is not synonymous with all writing instruction; it does not characterize writing instruction in the forms of basic writing, technical writing, writing-intensive content courses, or creative writing. For instance, instead of teaching writing as a set of generative rhetorical skills, courses in basic and technical writing are intended, respectively, to either lead up to, or build on, a broader writing ability, and thus have a specialized content and limited rhetorical scope. Writing-intensive content courses do not usually fall within the purview of GWSI, for in such courses, writing is seen as the means to the end of learning a content material, and composition instructors would probably concur that the skills learned in the context of most creative writing curricula are not generic writing skills that are intended to be applicable to writing in general.

Unlike these other writing-based curricula, general writing skills instruction sets for itself the objective of teaching students "to write," to give them skills that transcend any particular content and context in much the same way that Plato's Gorgias conceives of oratory as a transcendent ability that can be applied to any sphere of human activity. Although this sketch of GWSI is highly abbreviated, it is no strawman; it is a curriculum that an overwhelming majority of writing instructors is paid to teach, that practically every composition textbook is written to support, and the instruction for which English departments are given resources to deliver.

Now there is a problem in asking, as I have, that the reader consider a critique of GWSI provocative, for the vulnerability of GWSI is hardly a secret among writing professionals and its intellectual fragility has been felt for years and manifested in several ways: in the persistently low status of composition as a study both within and outside of English departments, in professional journal articles and conference presentations that are growing both in theoretical sophistication and irrelevance to the composition classroom, and in the rhetoric and writing field's ever-increasing attention to nontraditional sites of writing behavior. But, to date, there has been relatively little concerted discussion within the writing field that focuses specifically on the fundamentally awkward relationship of writing theory and most writing instruction. Of course, occasionally the awkwardness becomes excruciating and, even if only for a moment, the tensions pitting research and theory against the practice of GWSI push their way to the surface. However, in the past, eruptions of discontent with the general enterprise of freshman writing disappear as quickly as they arise (see Connors, chap. 1, and Goggin, chap. 2, this volume) and our field's usual long-term response to such outbursts is to politely pretend we did not notice. This collection asks that we forget our manners and consider the variety of ways in which the very idea of general writing skills instruction runs afoul of the discipline's theory and research as well as our own common sense.

THE CHAPTERS

Although it can be said that contributors to this anthology hold in common a sense of GWSI's inadequacy, that inadequacy's shape and perceived severity varies from writer to writer; whereas some of the contributors included here recommend that we turn our backs on the very idea of the general skills composition classroom, most hold out the hope that a reformed notion of writing instruction can be made to work. From a methodological perspective, as well, many different questions motivate the chapters contained herein. For instance, some contributors ask, "historically, how and why has GWSI attained and retained its pre-eminence as the pedagogical flagship of the writing field?" More social scientifically, other contributors question whether the "skills" students learn in their composition courses are those that will enable them to perform successfully in the academy and the workplace (or even in next semester's composition class). More theoretically, still other contributors speculate on whether our increasing understanding of what it means to be a rhetor and a writer make adherence to a GWSI framework intellectually defensible. More pragmatically, many of us wonder whether GWSI—if it is not defensible on theoretical grounds—can be counted on to provide the relatively secure "space" in academia it currently affords and further, if it cannot, whether the rhetoric and writing field should be proactive in creating spaces that are more in line with our theory and research.

The anthology opens with Connors' account of what has been called the "New Abolitionism." As he makes clear, dissatisfaction with GWSI, especially as manifested in freshman composition, is hardly a modern phenomenon. What is new, however, is the source and quality of the contemporary criticisms. Connors argues that whereas composition's earlier detractors had largely risen from the ranks of literature faculty in English departments, the New Abolitionist movement is being generated within the writing field and, as a result, has become a more potent, "insider's" critique. In this and several other ways, Connors' essay (prepared as a conference presentation long before I asked him to contribute to this anthology) actually foreshadows this project in many respects and provides something of a historical context for chapters that follow even though the term *abolitionism* is, most contributors might argue, an inaccurate characterization of their positions. Like Connors, Goggin's chapter traces the history of dissatisfaction within the ranks of English studies. Unlike Connors, Goggin does not focus on the differences that arise between the fields of literature and composition, but instead explores the schism separating composition as a professional enterprise and rhetoric as an intellectual tradition. Her historiographic reading of this schism illuminates some of the important sources of the paradox to which I alluded earlier: that GWSI is, at the same time, the writing field's principal raison d'être and albatross.

The second group of chapters analyzes the writing classroom from frameworks drawn from the literatures of social and cognitive psychology, linguistics, and education. Russell's contribution is the first to offer an extended application of activity theory to the practice of writing and, more specifically, to the practices of the composition classroom. From an activity theory perspective, Russell analyzes the conflicted nature of general composition courses and suggests reasons why writing across the curriculum and courses about writing provide a more coherent alternative to the space GWSI currently occupies. In this same vein, my own chapter is rooted in cognitivist investigations into school writing as a particular (and peculiar) variety of writing. I argue that if we accept that the purpose of writing instruction is to train students to be rhetorically sensitive, the context of GWSI can be shown to be inimical to these ends. This is not to say that school writing is somehow oxymoronic, however, and in the final section of the chapter I suggest how, if we are willing to adapt writing assignments to the functional context of formal education, schools may provide perfectly legitimate occasions for writing and rhetorical exploration.

In this same section, Geisler, Freedman, and Hill and Resnick share a focus on the practices of literacy in school and outside it. Geisler's chapter uses the research literatures of composition and education to show that the classroom is inhospitable to the goals many writing instructors purport to have for their students. Although the field at large is motivated by the desire to inculcate in our students a sense of "knowledge transformation," Geisler illustrates how the purposes for which students write and the assignments students receive place writing instruction and this enriched notion of learning at cross purposes. We are tacitly reminded, with the inclusion of Freedman's chapter, that the cross purposes associated with GWSI are, to a great degree, stamped "Made in USA." At Canadian universities, writing for writing's sake is the exception rather than the rule and for this reason Freedman's contribution provides a welcome view from abroad. Her chapter assembles the socio- and psycholinguistic frameworks that lead her to the conclusion that writing is better taught in the context of the disciplines rather than by designated "writing instructors." I believe Freedman's chapter also illustrates the point that a rejection of GWSI does nothing to diminish an abiding intellectual and professional concern with writing.

In their chapter, Hill and Resnick call our attention to a simple fact that is too often elided in discussions of writing curriculum: We teach writing in the classroom to support writing outside of the classroom—specifically, writing in the workplace (not to be confused with technical writing). The workplace has recently received a great deal of attention both in psychology and writing, for one of the implications of situated cognition is that of *apprenticeship*: the traditional method by which learners are enculturated into their professional communities. Hill and Resnick note that creating apprenticeship within the confines of a classroom poses a variety of problems and suggest, instead, that writing professionals may have to go to where the "real" writers are—out into the world of work.

But just as writing can be investigated and analyzed as a behavior and a social practice, it is also an idea in the purest sense of that word. For this reason, the third part of the anthology is set aside for two chapters that might be characterized as more philosophically oriented. Royer, principally drawing on the work of Whitehead, argues that the issue of invention—as understood and objectified by both modernist and postmodernist teachers of writing—reflects a failed metaphysics. In its place, Royer introduces a "guided phenomenology" that views creativity as growing out of lived experience. From this vantage point, he argues that invention on demand (one of the foundations on which GWSI is built) is untenable as it arbitrarily isolates creativity from the rest of human experience. This "commodification" of invention is, to a large extent, based on certain presumptions of writing's temporal fixedness and physicality, presumptions that lie at the center of Kemp's chapter. In it, Kemp suggests that the advent of electronic text demands a postmodern conceptualization of what it means "to write," which in turn disabuses us of notions of written texts as vessels carrying static meaning. In place of the vessel metaphor, Kemp outlines how he has used networked classrooms to engage students in "written conversation," a metaphor that he believes complements the nature of textual instability and rhetorical dynamism.

Although every chapter in this collection suggests ways in which theory and research can directly inform our approach to writing instruction, the final group of contributors perhaps most fully articulates alternatives to the traditional writing classroom. Jolliffe's essay on interdiscursivity takes subject matter as its subject matter. Jolliffe argues that GWSI courses have traditionally opted for either assigning students topics on which to write (a practice that has always been an easy target for criticism) or allowing students to write on what they know (a more difficult target, perhaps, but one that he demonstrates is just as theoretically unsatisfactory). He suggests how an analysis of interdiscursivity can enable an instructor to draw up an "inquiry contract" that requires students to reflect on the embeddedness of their ideas in broader social and rhetorical frameworks. Jolliffe, perhaps to a greater degree than other contributors, suggests that the GWSI classroom can be made theoretically sound, but only if teachers consider the multivocal and intereferential nature of discourse.

An interest in seeing students recognize the social and public dimensions of the composing act is also accentuated by Kaufer and Dunmire, who believe that writing courses can be the site of broader rhetorical education if students are challenged to be knowledge designers. They draw on their experience at Carnegie Mellon to promote a pedagogy that makes use of curricular space devoted to GWSI in English departments, but that differs radically in its assumptions and objectives. However, whereas Kaufer and Dunmire propose "upgrading" writing within its traditional space, several of the contributors to this anthology come to a very different conclusion: If writing is to be taught in schools, it must be taught across the curriculum. Whereas other contributors provide theoretical and empirical rationales for WAC, Brannon's essay provides an eyewitness account of the situation at SUNY–Albany, where a mandate for critical literacy continues to take root throughout the university. With a combination of writing-intensive courses and an enhanced role for the Writing Center, Brannon reports that SUNY has successfully made writing a concern of the entire faculty rather than a discrete and purely "functional" responsibility assigned to a few instructors.

But even with the efforts contributors devote to arguing for writing as an important dimension of every learner's life, there is little doubt that radically modifying (and perhaps forsaking) GWSI will be traumatic for the writing field; as Connors' and Goggin's histories of disciplinary concerns make clear, this curricular framework has been the source of the writing field's identity since its inception. Indeed, for many in the field as well as within the larger academic community, GWSI is synonymous with writing instruction, and thus calling into question the legitimacy of GWSI may, to some, be equated with questioning the viability of the discipline. To complicate such a simple equation, Bazerman was asked to write a critical response to this collection as an observer who (like many readers, perhaps) is sensitive to any threat to the hard-won intellectual and pedagogical space occupied by GWSI. Although I do not summarize or comment on his criticisms here, Bazerman's response to the collection is meant to signal our collective awareness that this volume is but a single contribution to an ongoing conversation. Each contributor understands both that GWSI cannot be dismissed without exacting some cost to the field, and that the project of reconceiving writing and rethinking writing instruction is one under perpetual revision.

CONCLUSION

I close these introductory remarks by reiterating that this anthology presents neither a monolithic argument against GWSI nor any recommendation for the abolition of writing instruction. As much as all of the contributors share misgivings about our field's current shape and curricular mission, there is a great deal of disagreement and divergence of perspectives among us, reflecting the diversity of our methodological, pedagogical, and ideological commitments, commitments that, as the reader will see, prompt very different responses. Even if this collection's constituent chapters lead us in different directions, however, I believe each of them performs the important function of leading us away from a conception of writing instruction that has ill served teachers, the discipline, and ultimately, students of writing for generations.

I

The Tension Between Writing and Writing Instruction: Historical Perspectives

The New Abolitionism: Toward a Historical Background*

Robert J. Connors
University of New Hampshire

Since the required course in freshman composition was conceived at Harvard in 1885 and quickly adopted by most U.S. colleges and universities, it has been at the heart of a continuing series of arguments about its worth and standing. Arthur Applebee (1974) characterized the history of English teaching in the United States as being marked by periods of tradition and reform, and in this chapter I want to borrow one of his terms and, changing its meaning rather seriously, claim that the history of American higher education in composition over the last century has been marked by alternating periods of what I call *reformism* and *abolitionism*. During reformist periods, freshman comp, although problematical, is seen as the thin red line protecting the very life of literacy. Abolitionist periods are times during which at least some English teachers call for the end of freshman composition, declaring the large sums expended on this all-but-ubiquitous course a gross waste.

There is a sense in which these arguments about the required comp course are metonymic representations of other more general questions facing American culture. We see reformist periods of deep interest in improving composition—some of which are called literacy crises—and abolitionist periods, when some teachers declared it too hopeless to reform, repeat themselves several times across the last 10 decades. Each reformist or abolition period is to some degree unique, of course, but they do have certain elements in common, and they ebb and flow according to patterns that we may learn from. As this volume suggests, we are now involved in

---

*This chapter is a longer and more fully developed version of a paper given at the 1993 Crisis and Change conference at Miami University of Ohio. A condensed version of the essay appears in the volume of papers from that conference, *Composition in the Twenty-First Century: Crisis and Change*, edited by Lynn Z. Bloom, Donald Daiker, and Edward White.

the end of a reformist period and in a new period of abolitionist sentiment. Contributors to this anthology represent a growing number of writing professionals asking us to reconsider the theoretical integrity and practical utility of required composition as manifested in general writing skills instruction (GWSI) for over the last century. By way of introducing the collection gathered here, it may be worthwhile to ask how or whether this New Abolitionism is like the older ones, and whether the current movement will go the way of the older ones. To understand the New Abolitionists in context, we need to look back.

REQUIRED FRESHMAN COMPOSITION: THE FIRST REFORM AND ITS ANTAGONISTS

The required freshman composition course itself is the product of a reformist period. It was created in direct response to the literacy crisis of the period 1875 to 1885. This is a story that has been told many times by historians, and we need only outline it here. Harvard College, roused by popular debates on literacy and linguistic correctness, had by 1870 become uncomfortably aware that students entering from the academies that served as its feeders were having problems with its demanding classical courses. In response, Harvard instituted its first entrance examinations in written English in 1874. To the horror of professors, parents, and the American intellectual culture as a whole, more than half the students taking the exam failed it. What had been a vague disquiet crystallized into a sharp alarm. Large numbers of American boys from the best schools were incapable of correct writing, and something had to be done. This first crisis might be called the "Illiteracy of American Boys" crisis, after the best known article written about it.

The Harvard exam and the continuing problems students had with it (and with the host of similar writing examinations quickly set up by the many colleges that took Harvard for a model) created the first American college literacy crisis and the first experiments in basic writing instruction on the college level. The Harvard examiners began quickly to agitate for better training on the secondary level and for more effective writing instruction on the college level.

A. S. Hill, Boylston Professor of Rhetoric, had argued strongly as early as 1879 that the sophomore rhetoric course be more oriented toward correctness and composition and be made a required course for freshmen: "The next best step [after improving secondary schools] would be to give to English two hours or more a week during the Freshman year. Could the study be taken up at the threshold of college life, the schools would be made to feel that their labors in this direction were going to tell upon a pupil's standing in college" (Hill, 1896, p. 12). At first no room could be found for such a requirement during freshman year, but the exam results kept the pressure on and in 1885 a basic freshman course, "English A," was offered at Harvard. Its structure solidified quickly. By 1894 the only required courses for freshmen were English A and a modern language (Rudolph, 1962). By 1897 the only required course at Harvard for any student was English A. Many other colleges took Harvard's lead on all educational issues, and by 1890 the majority of U.S. colleges and universities had established required freshman composition courses. The formation of these courses nationwide was a great paroxysm of reformist work, a large-scale curricular endeavor that has no parallel in U.S. college history.

Yet it was very soon after 1890 that the first widespread movement to disestablish these new course requirements arose. This first group of abolitionists consisted primarily of literature teachers in what were then newly established English departments. Their dislike of required composition courses was based in their affiliation with Arnoldian idealism, but their essential rationale for abolishing freshman requirements was based on two more practical claims about college composition: First, the required freshman course was never meant as a permanent English offering, but was instead a temporary stop-gap until the secondary schools could improve; and second, the teaching of required composition was tiresome, labor-intensive, and a bad use of trained literary scholars.

That the early freshman course was considered a temporary remedial measure and was bitterly resented by college faculty members is clear from the few published comments that exist on it. "The instruction in English which we are forced to give to Freshmen and perhaps to Sophomores should all be finished in the preparatory schools," wrote Hurlbut (1896). "It is absurd that a college should be obliged to teach spelling, pronunciation, grammar, construction of sentences and of paragraphs" (p. 49). Only if reforms were made on the elementary and secondary levels, argued Hurlbut, would the student acquire there "the training in English composition which is now given in college, and the college student will be able to devote himself to university work" (p. 53). Up until the mid-1890s, in other words, it was assumed by many that freshman composition courses were a stop-gap remedial measure, a temporary aberration, to be dispensed with after the great propaganda war in favor of more secondary school composition had been won.

We see a good deal of this attitude in William Morton Payne's (1895) interesting collection, *English in American Universities*, which contains 20 reports on the teaching of college English at different institutions that had originally appeared in *The Dial* in 1894. Although most of the reports detail both literature and composition courses being offered, several are fervid in their triumph at having dispensed with required freshman writing altogether. Payne himself, the editor of *The Dial*, was entirely sympathetic to this movement, and his introduction makes clear why; he was a classic exponent of literature teaching who was in favor of the most stringent entrance requirements possible. He was very doubtful about the Eastern colleges' reliance on the freshman course. "As we go West, we do better and better" (p. v) he said, noting that Indiana, Nebraska, and Stanford had all abolished freshman composition in favor of strong entrance requirements.

Examining the reports from those schools, however, it was clear that liberal culture is not the only reason for the abolition. Martin Sampson (1895) of Indiana wrote that "There are no recitations in 'rhetoric.' The bugbear known generally in our colleges as Freshman English is now a part of our entrance requirements" (p. 93). Melville Anderson's (1895) report on English at Stanford gives us a genuine feel for the earliest abolitionist sentiments. Stanford, he said, had abolished Freshman English: "Had this salutary innovation not been accomplished, all the literary courses would have been swept away by the rapidly growing inundation of Freshman themes, and all our strength and courage would have been dissipated in preparing our students to do respectable work at more happily equipped Universities" (p. 52). We see here the expected liberal culture attitudes, of course, but more strongly we see pure self-protection on the part of the tenured faculty. They did not want to teach theme writing, and killing the requirement was the easiest way out of it. Anderson wrote a bit later that Stanford would be hiring two "instructors" the following year to give the two unfortunate composition professors a break, because "however great a man's enthusiasm for such work may be, it is incident to human nature that no man can read themes efficiently for more than three hours at a stretch" (p. 52).

THOMAS LOUNSBURY AND LIBERAL-CULTURE ABOLITIONISM

The first wave of abolitionism ebbed after 1900, and Anderson's attitude gives us a key to the reasons why: the growing willingness of universities and colleges to draw on lecturers, instructors, and graduate students to teach their required freshman courses. As discussed in more detail in Connors (1991), the rise of academic specialization and the modern hierarchy of ranks in English departments meant that between 1880 and 1900 most tenured professors were gradually relieved of composition duties by younger and less powerful colleagues or by graduate students. Thus the earliest wave of abolitionism, which had been caused by overwork panic among faculty members, receded because the Andersons and Sampsons no longer had to worry themselves about having to teach freshman composition. This was fortunate for these senior professors, because the requirement of the course had hardly been touched by their arguments in most places (Stanford, for example, reinstituted English A in 1907; Greenbaum, 1969). The years between 1885 and 1915 saw a tremendous number of critiques of the freshman course launched, but most of them were oriented toward reforming the course. Not until the end of that period was there a resurgence of the abolitionist sentiment, in the famous article "Compulsory Composition in Colleges" by Thomas Lounsbury (1911). David Russell (1988) did groundbreaking work on Lounsbury and some of the attitudes that have underlain the early forms of abolitionist argument. Russell described Lounsbury's abolitionist sentiment as a product of a specific kind of educational idealism that sounds today like liberal culture literary elitism, tinged throughout by Lounsbury's thinly concealed opinion that undergraduate students were ignorant barbarians.

To Lounsbury, the idea that expression could be taught was idiotic, the conception that college students could know anything worth writing about silly, and the position that writing teachers could respond usefully to student writing unlikely. Wrote Lounsbury (1911), "I [am] thoroughly convinced that altogether undue importance is attached to exercises in English composition, especially compulsory exercises; that the benefits to be derived from the general practice in schools is (sic) vastly overrated" (p. 869). His answer to the problem of literacy was more or less to let it take care of itself, to make composition completely elective, thus making certain that only those students who wanted to write—a minority compared to that "large body of students who have not the slightest desire to write a line" (p. 876)—took it. The enthusiasm of the students would make the course so much more satisfying to teach that it would again attract experienced and effective teachers.

Despite his romantic elitism, Lounsbury (1911) made some telling points against compulsory composition. He was correct in his assessment that "the average student loathes it," that "under the compulsory system now prevailing the task of reading and correcting themes is one of deadly dullness," in which "more and more does the business of correcting and criticizing themes tend steadily to fall into the hands of those who . . . have themselves little experience in the practice of composition" (pp. 870–871). But Lounsbury was an outsider. His claim to have 25 years' experience correcting themes had never actually included required freshman composition, which Yale did not have, and he was senior enough to have avoided the most punishing junior composition teaching assignments. Thus his sympathy for teachers was mostly forced, because he considered most of them "incompetent to do anything much better," and for students hardly existent; they are "crude," "thoughtless and indifferent," "immature," and clearly in need of a stiff dose of Milton. Lounsbury presented an early but completely recognizable version of E. D. Hirsch's cultural literacy argument: Writing could not be taught as pure practice-based skill without content. His real and obvious sympathy was with those who had a "cultivated taste begotten of familiarity with the great masterpieces of our literature" (p. 876), and until students' minds were thus furnished, they need not apply, to him at least.

This article caused a small sensation in the English teaching world, and especially in the still-active circle of composition enthusiasts. Lounsbury had repeated several times in his essay that his was an unpopular minority position, but it was taken very seriously. His article was not followed up in *Harper's,* but it created a long discussion in the *Educational Review (ER)* in 1913, and we see here the whole modern reformist–abolitionist debate for the first time.

Although some of the *ER* correspondents agreed with Lounsbury, the majority did not. Some commentators saw no problem in the freshman course at all, and they actively praised the course as they had experienced it. We also see in this discussion the first wave of what might be called status quo or modern reformism. These correspondents took the position, as all reformists later would, that the course was imperfect but necessary, and that it would be much improved by the author's suggestions. N. A. Stedman (1913) of the University of Texas admitted that freshman English was useful and yielded some good results, but he saw that its "technical" nature created in students "a distaste for English" (p. 53), and proposed that the course be reformed to create more interest in English. Lucile Shepherd (1913) of the University of Missouri believed that "the course on the whole is admirable," and that with more humanism and a few tinkerings it would be better still (p. 189).

Lounsbury had some clear allies. Carl Zigrosser (1913) of Columbia wrote that, "in my estimation prescribed work in English is unnecessary" (p. 188), and George Strong (1913) of North Carolina huffed that, "My own experience with these courses was profitless. It was, in fact, enough to discourage me from continuing the study of English. I failed to derive any benefit whatever from them. . . . Away with such work! I should rather live an ignoramus all my life than to endure again such a burden as I did in English I and English II" (p. 189). We begin in these responses to Lounsbury to see proposals for that brand of abolitionism later called *writing across the curriculum.* Preston W. Slosson (1913) proposed that "The real way to make sure that every Columbia graduate, whatever his other failings, can write whatever it may be necessary for him to write as briefly, logically, and effectively as possible, is not to compel him as a freshman to write stated themes on nothing-in-particular but to insist on constant training in expression in every college course" (p. 408).

Finally, the Lounsbury-based discussion petered out sometime around 1915, after having never attained a solid enough base of agreement from the abolitionists. Charles G. Osgood (1915) writing in *English Journal,* titled his article "No Set Requirement of English Composition in the Freshman Year," and suspected that the suggestion made by his title "is not a popular opinion, and that in holding it I am one of a small minority" (p. 231). Osgood went on to make a case for literature rather than composition in the freshman year, and to praise the small-group preceptorial system used at Princeton, but his attitude was that of a man who did not expect to win. Reformism began to dominate the professional discussion.

At least part of the reason for the failure of abolitionism and the segue into a clearly reformist period during the mid-1910s had to do with the growing influence of the ideas of John Dewey. Some of the more widely read teachers of composition were beginning to realize that freshman composition could be more than a mere enforcement of mechanical rules. Helen Mahin (1915), one of Fred Newton Scott's graduate students, wrote that she was moved to action by Lounsbury. "Stirred to an indignant curiosity by the vigorous denunciation of compulsory composition in colleges by a learned professor of English," she asked her freshman students if they would take the course without the requirement. Their answers made her realize that "nearly two-thirds of these Freshmen, many of who had entered the course unwillingly, realized before the end of the first semester that their lives had grown in some way broader and fuller then they had been before" (p. 446). This result, Mahin said, controverted Lounsbury's claims. Required composition could be taught, and should be taught, in such a way that students realize that "writing means simply living and expressing life":

> From the testimony of the Freshmen themselves and from the actual results shown in their work the conclusion is very well justified that the student of writing who does not in the course of his study, if that study is rightly guided, become a happier, bigger, and more socially efficient being is the student who, unless he is subnormal in intellect, deliberately sets himself against progress. (p. 450)

This concept of "English for life skills" and the "more socially efficient being" is instantly recognizable as based in Dewey's ideas. This concept, that writing skills were humane learning and inherently broadening, was to become a staple claim of reformism for decades.

The reformist movement was set even more strongly on the road by the victory in Europe in World War I and the millennial ideas many intellectuals held immediately after the war. The United States had lost thousands of men, but it had not been ravaged as Europe had, and many educators saw the war victory as the gateway into a shining new world. Horace Ainsworth Eaton (1919) looked forward to a new birth of democratic spirit in the world, to be created by committed teachers: "The war is won—marvelously and completely won—and we stand on a new

Pisgah looking into the future. . . . In composition we must, I believe, even more than in literature, work in the new spirit. The first and most important thing is to awaken the pupil to think and then to help him to express his thought effectively. . . . Ideas come first, ideas expressively and effectively phrased; impeccable spelling and faultless punctuation are sorry substitutes" (pp. 310–312). Used to seeing the postwar era through the eyes of Dos Passos and Hemingway, we can sometimes forget that for many Americans it was a glorious time of dreaming world rebirth. In this atmosphere, and abetted by Dewey's educational ideas, many English teachers began to work hard toward reforming the freshman course in the direction of more social experience, more practical kinds of writing, and more creative expression.

The period following the war was, then, a classic period of reformism that saw the end of Lounsburian grousing and a halt to talk of abolitionism. The Central Division Modern Language Association (Fred N. Scott's home base) commissioned a Special Committee on Freshman English in 1916, and the report of this committee (which was made up of Scott's former students) gave no credence at all to abolishing the course. It proposed that there were two ways of thinking about freshman composition, "merely elementary drill" or "a subject in which the student is given a maturer and more largely significant training in thinking and in expression," and, not surprisingly, came out strongly for the latter. "The present committee . . . when it remembers the increasing number of students whose contact with a liberal type of training is virtually confined to this one course, does not doubt that the second and more ambitious conception of Freshman English is the only one which a university can afford to adopt" (Scott, Thomas, & Manchester, 1918, p. 592). The committee recommended, in fact, a second required composition course for those students who did not do well in the first.

The reformist period that began after World War I lasted throughout the 1920s. Examining the professional articles of that period, one finds any number of proposals for improving the required course but none that make any version of the abolitionist case. This is not to say that reform periods contain no grumbling or that no teachers existed during them who wished to see freshman composition done away with. However, abolitionism is submerged during reform periods because the mission of the course comes to seem so important that more of value would be lost than gained by cutting the requirement altogether, and so it was during the 1920s. The 1920s were filled with criticism of the course itself, which by that time had become a standardized institution immediately recognizable to anyone who had ever attended college. Many agreed with Bernard DeVoto (1928), who had taught at Northwestern, that "nothing in the colleges is more grotesquely taught. . . . It is universally loathed by those who teach it and those who take it. . . . And yet, for all this, it generally gets results. Students do usually write a little better when they have finished it than they did when they began" (pp. 205–206). DeVoto was no friend of English composition, but like many critics he did not feel it could be done away with.

A DECADE OF DEBATE: THE 1930S

By the end of the 1920s, college demographics were shifting strongly. Enrollments had almost doubled between 1920 and 1930, from 598,000 students to more than 1.1 million, and they were beginning to place a strain on the single course that had to serve all students (*Digest of Educational Statistics*, 1974, p. 84). As so often occurs, demographic changes in the student body seemed to create strains leading to powerful proposals—either radical reformism or some kind of abolitionism. When abolitionism appeared again after the 1920s, however, it came from a place that Scott would not have suspected: the educational research community, which by 1930 was finding a serious voice within English studies. The debate erupted at the National Council of Teachers of English (NCTE) meeting of 1931, in which Alvin C. Eurich (1932) of the University of Minnesota reported findings of a study conducted there in the late 1920s. In one of the earliest horse race experiments conducted of freshman composition, pretest and posttest compositions were required of 54 freshmen passing through the Minnesota course. These essays were rated using the Van Wagenen English Composition Scales (one of the many rating scales devised during the first three decades of this century in the attempt to make essay grading "scientific"), and the results showed that "no measurable improvement in composition was apparent after three months of practice" (p. 211).

Eurich's essay looks surprisingly "modern" in the context of *English Journal* composition essays of the period, which were often informal, personal, and pedagogical. Eurich's was a research report, written with a complete footnoted literature survey, and he reported his conclusion, which was simply the fact that the problem with freshman composition rested on "the inadequacy of the administrative arrangement which is based upon the assumption that the life-long habits of expression can be modified in a relatively short time" (p. 213). To solve this problem, Eurich proposed a different form of writing across the curriculum, a sophisticated system in which English teachers would work with teachers in other fields on writing-based assignments—one of the most serious early writing across the curriculum programs.

Eurich's paper at NCTE was answered by one written by Warner Taylor (1932). Taylor's essay was an archetype of reformist objection to abolitionism. Should the course be abolished, he asked. It is problematical, he said, but, "As for me, I do not consider the course futile. I do consider it, in general, open to several changes for the better" (pp. 301–302). Taylor went on to discuss a survey he had done that showed freshman courses relying overwhelmingly on handbooks and rhetorics and making a claim that such methods were themselves to blame for the poor showing the course made in Eurich's research. Taylor really believed in the freshman course, rejecting Eurich's contention that cross-curricular writing was a good answer and claiming that it would make teachers mere grading assistants: "Is it to be a course correlated with history or economics? If so, watch your rights! Historians and economists are in the saddle now, riding hard and confidently. You may call in a partner only to find him your boss" (p. 311). He proposed instead a course that got rid of rhetorics and handbooks and mixed composition with literature.

In the spirited discussion following the delivery of these two papers there was no consensus of opinion, although in general Eurich's writing across the curriculum-based plan was looked on as radical. The discussion was joined by such major figures as Charles C. Fries, Edwin M. Hopkins, and Joseph V. Denney, but although the general tenor of the discussion was reformist, Eurich held his own. The short reports of the discussion make clear the degree to which the composition teachers and scholars of the early 1930s identified themselves with the freshman course and were much more willing to make claims for its potential and to work at reforming it than to abandon it for less specific teaching situations (Davidson, 1932). No one could say that Eurich's findings were false, but they were interpreted in widely different ways, usually based, like Taylor's, in a claim that the freshman course did not work because it needed reform.

This willingness to admit problems and propose reforms rather than agree to abolitionist ideas has been a continuing entropic strand in composition discourse from that time forward. It represents a sort of argumentative jujitsu, using the strength and cogency of any abolitionist argument against abolitionism as a position. "The freshman course is problematical, is hated, is boring, does not work? Absolutely true," reformists typically say, "and proof positive that it needs reform—needs, specifically, the reform I am about to propose." There is, of course, a certain amount of vested interest on the part of composition reformers. Even as early as 1930, there were teachers and scholars whose careers were primarily concerned with writing pedagogy, and these people associated freshman composition as a course very clearly with "their discipline." It would be almost unnatural for them to admit that the course that was their primary responsibility and interest was so hopelessly compromised and ineffective that abolishing it was the best solution. There is no doubt that reform rather than abolition served the professional needs of most composition specialists best.

The decade of the 1930s saw more lively discussion of reform and abolition than had ever occurred before. The great lions of *fin de siecle* composition, Scott, Genung, and Wendell, were all dead by 1930, but the edifice they had raised had become a huge industry, and the profession of English was filled with their intellectual descendants. The decade of *English Journal* numbers from the 1930s is filled with debates that sound almost incredibly contemporary—proposals for English as training for social experience, for Marxist critique in the classroom, for writing across the curriculum, for research-based reforms of various kinds, for more or less literary influence on composition, and for better conditions for teachers. When *The Teaching of College English*, the report of the NCTE Committee on College English (1935) appeared, for example, it strongly condemned the freshman composition course and recommended that required writing be delayed until the sophomore year. The release of this report set off a "symposium" of different opinions in *English Journal* that year, most of which agreed that the report was admirable and that the freshman course was a serious problem—but not one of which agreed with the Committee's recommendation. "Shall we kill Freshman English? Certainly not!" harrumphed Frank Clippinger (1935, p. 575) in the Symposium before going on to propose how turning the course into a modern literature course would solve its problems. Outside the pages of the journal, the Committee's recommendations fell on even stonier ground.

Oscar J. Campbell chaired that critical committee, and in 1939, the strong liberal culture side of the abolitionist argument popped up again in his now well-known article, "The Failure of Freshman English." D. Russell (1988) dealt very effectively with the major part of Campbell's position, and here we might merely note that literary elitism was not the entirety of Campbell's (1939) position. He, too put forward a writing across the curriculum agenda, at least tacitly, saying that:

> What your students need is not more instruction in writing but a few teachers of geology who are capable of describing not only geological phenomena but also of teaching their students how to think consecutively and logically about geology. . . . Since most teachers of geology, history, or economics find themselves incapable of it, they conceal the incompetence from themselves by shifting the responsibility of their failure upon the harried instructor in Freshman English, who labors valiantly to accomplish the impossible. (p. 181)

As Russell described, Campbell also made the familiar claim that composition cannot be taught apart from content, that it is intellectually dishonest as well as futile. He blamed freshman composition for teacher disaffection and for the blunting of the impact of literary education.

Campbell's position, although probably sympathetic to most literature teachers, received far less support than Lounsbury's had 25 years before.

Unlike Lounsbury, Campbell was facing a composition establishment that was already entrenched and was even building the beginnings of a scholarship and a discipline. Although Campbell was respected, he was not agreed with, and all the responses to his essay were essentially reformist. Only a few months after Campbell's essay, Fred A. Dudley (1939) replied to it: "Accepting much of what Professor Campbell so vigorously says in his essay by that title, we yet believe that Freshman English is succeeding—not perfectly, but better this year than five years ago; and we expect it to succeed still better five years from now" (p. 22). Andrew J. Green's (1941) "The Reform of Freshman English" took Campbell's arguments on directly, stating squarely that "Freshman English is ubiquitous, inevitable, and eternal" (p. 593).

Campbell also found himself in the unfortunate position of opening a battle immediately before the nation's attention became caught up in an all-consuming World War II. Instead of the debate that Campbell had no doubt hoped to produce, the entire issue of the worth of freshman composition slipped away, as did what had been other consuming issues of the 1930s—experience curriculum, social conditions, Marxism—in the intellectual conflagration that was the war effort. After 1941, his complaints seem to have been forgotten, and reformism itself was almost blunted for the duration of the war as the needs of the military came to the fore and stressing any U.S. problems seemed somewhat defeatist. Throughout the war years, overt criticism of the course almost disappeared as scholars betook themselves to serve the war effort by keeping up morale.

POSTWAR: THE TRIUMPH OF REFORMISM

The postwar world was a different place, one in which the debate that had been damped down during the war emerged in many forms. Particularly hotly debated was the question of the mission and purpose of liberal arts colleges, a question that was always tied in powerfully to the issue of required freshman composition. Ironically, it was not the abolition sentiment of the Campbells but a kind of accelerated reformism that had the greatest abolitionist effect after World War II. The General Education movement, which proposed that college curricula after the introduction of the elective system had become too specialized, was first widely enunciated in the Harvard Report of 1945, and, gaining power rapidly after 1948, it produced widespread withdrawal from the traditional freshman composition course.

The General Educationists wished to meld the "heritage" model of traditional education with the more recent pragmatic insights of the followers of Dewey and James (Harvard Committee, 1945, pp. 46–47), and to do so they proposed that the specialized introductory courses of the freshman and sophomore years be supplanted by much broader general courses, one each in the humanities, the social sciences, and the sciences. The Harvard Committee specifically proposed that the traditional course in freshman composition be replaced by more emphasis on writing in these new general education courses: "Since the responsibility for training in written communication is vested in the staff of English A, the other members of the faculty too often feel that they have little if any responsibility for the development of skill and facility in writing. This seems to us a serious weakness" (p. 199). In 1949, the proposed change was made. English A, which had been taken by Harvard freshmen since 1885, was dropped. Other schools followed similar lines, and the static acceptance of required freshman composition courses that had for so long been tacit educational policy was suddenly shaken as "communication" courses replaced the older composition model.

The Communication movement, which was the working out of General Education ideas in an English context, proposed to unify what had been separate fields of English and speech by rolling together all four of the "communications skills"—speaking, listening, reading, and writing—and creating a new course around them, the communication course. This movement began to take hold in earnest in the late 1940s and prospered through the mid-1950s, when it lost momentum. During that time, however, many traditional freshman writing courses were converted into communication courses, often team-taught by English and speech professors.

It is important to note several things about these communications courses. First, they were not part of anyone's abolitionist agenda. The General Education movement itself was not at all against required courses; it was essentially about widening and adding requirements, especially during the first 2 years of college. Although the communications movement proposed to add to the charge of the traditional composition course, the requirement was still there for freshmen. This was a specifically successful brand of reformism, perceiving the freshman course in need of change, rather than abolitionism, which perceived the course as hopeless or its change as impossible. Second, the changes that came down during these years came down from on high as part of a sweeping mandate reaching all the way from Harvard to the federal government. Traditional freshman courses were not transformed by liberal culture romantics of the old literary sort or even by the sort of writing across the curriculum-oriented attitude of Eurich, but rather by a temporary enthusiasm for a new sort of reform. It was a reform that changed the name and some of the methods of the traditional freshman composition class in many places but removed not a jot of requirement anywhere.

Throughout this postwar period, there continued a steady drumbeat of dissatisfaction with the freshman course in its various forms. Most faculty members outside of English continued in their optimistic belief that a semester or a year of composition (or communication) early in a student's career would inoculate him or her from any viral illiteracies. English teachers responded to these critiques with their traditional protests that no one course could accomplish all that the critics asked but that the freshman course was an invaluable training ground in the humanities even if it could not guarantee inviolate literacy. Despite the critiques, freshman composition and communications courses flourished throughout the early and mid-1950s. Only at the end of the decade did abolitionism resurge.

The most famous recent abolitionist statement was made in 1959 by Warner G. Rice, Chair of the Michigan Department of English, at the NCTE Convention of that year. Rice's (1960) essay, "A Proposal for the Abolition of Freshman English, As It Is Now Commonly Taught, from the College Curriculum," was a classic statement of its period; the late 1950s were for colleges a low-stress time during which fewer but much better prepared students were seeking admission. We might think of the period as the antithesis of a literacy crisis: There was no press of new student populations, test scores were rising every year, and there were fewer bachelor's degrees conferred in 1960 than in 1950 (*Digest of Educational Statistics*, 1974, p. 84). The postwar GI boom had not quite been succeeded by the baby boom in colleges, and thus at that moment the need for a required course to remedy freshman literacy problems seemed to many less pressing.

Rice's (1960) stance is by now familiar. He made the same claims that abolitionists had always made: Basic literacy should be a prerequisite for college; freshman composition in a semester or a year tries to accomplish the impossible and does not really "take"; students are ill motivated; the course is a financial drain on colleges; English teachers will be happier teaching other courses (pp. 361–362). What is surprising to someone reading Rice's essay in the historical context of other abolitionist essays is its aridity of spirit, its open English department self-concern, and its lack of interest in seeking creative answers to the problem of underprepared students. Rice was an almost direct throwback to the very first generation of abolitionists 70 years earlier; his attitude was that literacy issues were the responsibility of the high schools and that college should not be bothered. He did not wish to replace required composition with literature. Although he thought that all disciplines should take over their own responsibilities for correct writing, he did not believe that English professors should be involved in any sort of writing across the curriculum-based program. He was not overly concerned with students who simply could not "make the grade" and get into colleges. "It will be asked what will replace the

Freshman English now taught if, by various expedients, it proves possible to get along without it. The answer must be firm and emphatic: Nothing. College requirements should simply be reduced by whatever number of hours Freshman English now absorbs" (p. 365). Rice's was the voice of literary professional self-interest.

As Eurich had been answered by reformist Taylor at the NCTE Convention 28 years earlier, Rice was answered by reformist Albert R. Kitzhaber in 1959. Kitzhaber's (1960) essay, "Death—Or Transfiguration?" admitted immediately that "no one would want to make an unqualified defense of the present Freshman English course" (p. 347), and went on to catalog its shortcomings: overambitious aims, lack of agreement about course content, poor textbooks and methods, and impossibility of proving success. However, Kitzhaber then went on to state positive aspects of the course: It subsidized graduate study, let young teachers gain experience, and often got clearly positive results. He also believed that a writing-based course was worthwhile in and of itself. Kitzhaber contested Rice's main points, arguing that abolishing freshman composition would not be cheaper to colleges, that faculty in other disciplines would not take up any great part of literacy responsibilities, that the high schools were not equipped yet to handle the responsibilities themselves, and that a more rhetorically oriented Freshman English course would help solve the problem.

Strangely, Kitzhaber's reply to Rice sounds to today's reader almost as hopeless about the course as Rice's attack. In Kitzhaber's rejoinder, reformism gets as far away from concern with students as we ever see it; Kitzhaber was concerned with college finance, teacher morale, English departments, and high school curricula—but only tangentially, it seems, with college students. A large part of his essay was taken up with proposals for improving high school English. Except for his admission that "there must be some value in requiring all Freshman to take at least one course that has writing as its focus," Kitzhaber found little to be cheered by in the possibilities of freshman composition, and those seeking any sort of humanistic defense of writing as learning in his essay will be disappointed. Perhaps it was the period; except for the New Rhetoric that he hoped would arrive (as it did, on schedule, 3 years later), he had little sanguinity about required composition in the form it usually took. Perhaps it was Kitzhaber's own historicism; he had read too deeply in composition history to be cheerily hopeful about course reform proposals.

REFORMISM AND ABOLITIONISM IN THE MODERN ERA

With the eruption of the New Rhetoric in the early 1960s and the gradual growth of composition studies as a scholarly discipline with its own books and journals, its own disseminative and reproductive mechanisms, we enter a new era. It is an era in which reformism is immensely strengthened—becomes, indeed, the backbone of an ever-larger professional literature. Improving the freshman course (through the New Rhetoric, or invention, or classical rhetoric, or Christensen paragraphing, or sentence combining) becomes the essential purpose of the books and essays that appear in always greater numbers.

Abolition sentiment, however, does not die easily, and there was a short period during the late 1960s when the iconoclasm of that time caused the usual reformist consensus to be disrupted again by arguments against the required freshman course. Several of these are familiar liberal culture arguments that took advantage of the ferment of the times. Robert Russell (1968), chair of English at Franklin and Marshall, wrote of pressuring his faculty to vote against teaching composition. Because "we have a discipline, too. It is the study of literature," and because "the breadth, depth, power, and importance of literature is more than sufficient justification for a lifetime spent in its study," Russell "began the campaign to stop the drain on our time and energies imposed by the college's requirement in composition" (p. 174). The school abolishes required composition and, according to Russell, lives happily ever after; student literacy skills do not decay, and faculty members in other departments cheerfully shoulder their portion of the responsibility. This is a familiar strain of magical realism.

The most interesting abolitionist attack was made by Leonard Greenbaum (1969) in his article "The Tradition of Complaint." Greenbaum's essay is a piece of historical research on abolitionism written by an author who took pains to situate himself outside the field of English. (Thus his stance as an abolitionist himself is easier to understand, because he had no professional stake in reform.) In spite of the slapdash nature of Greenbaum's historical research and his tone of classic late-1960s snottiness, his essay is still worth reading, and his essential point goes beyond the liberal culture self-interest of many other abolitionists:

> Freshman English is a luxury that consumes time, money, and the intelligence of an army of young teachers and of younger teaching fellows. It imposes the standards of taste of a single discipline upon a freshman population whose command of language is sufficient to its purpose. It seldom solves the educational problems of the students with real inabilities to speak, to read, to write. . . . It would be better to stop what we are doing, to sit still, to rest in the sun, and then to search for the populations whose problems can be solved by our professional skills. (p. 187)

Greenbaum's position as an outsider to composition kept him from having any of the kind of background that could lead to more detailed ideas about what sort of writing instruction he could support.

Greenbaum seemed to expect no followers. As his historical survey had shown him, "Freshman English flourishes; its opponents die, retire, languish in exile" (p. 187). A number of people agreed with him, and for a few years after his essay, as the general cultural upheaval of the late 1960s and early 1970s produced more obvious dissatisfaction with the status quo in U.S. education than had been seen, one of the institutions interrogated most strongly was freshman composition. Ron Smith (1974) conducted a survey that found that the number of colleges and universities requiring some form of freshman English had dropped from 93.2% in 1967 to 76% in 1973. Regina Hoover (1974) published "Taps for Freshman English?," making the point that "Among the many confusing and often conflicting currents sweeping through considerations of the status of Freshman English these days is one that may make all the rest irrelevant: that the discipline is dying" (p. 149). (It is telling that even as late as 1973, Hoover could so completely identify "the discipline" with Freshman English.) Both Smith and Hoover were clear abolitionists in the sense that they perceived the required freshman course as it existed as unsalvageable. Hoover thought that every student should take a writing course but that the dying freshman course was the wrong answer:

> Is the demise a good thing? To the extent that we continue to think of Freshman English as a monolithic service course, into which all students are rather indiscriminately dumped, I must admit that I think it is good, and that the best thing we who really believe in the inherent values of writing as a humane activity can do about it is to hurry it along. (pp. 149–150)

Smith, who admired Greenbaum's positions, saw so many continuing changes in the world of academia—"uniform equivalency testing, *true* three-year degree programs, the general elimination or streamlining of lower-division requirements, systems approaches, performance- or competency-based instruction, open-admissions policies, adjustments to booming and then declining enrollments, and even 'accountability'" (p. 139)—that the trend toward deregulation of freshman composition would certainly continue. "The change that has occurred these past several years is not going to end very soon," he wrote in 1974. "All signs point to more schools dropping the composition requirement." (p. 148).

Look upon my works, ye mighty, and despair. In direct contradiction to Smith's forecast, we see no more abolitionism after the early 1970s. In the research for this essay, I could not find anything written between 1975 and 1990 in the field of composition that called for general abolition of the course. Now and then a teacher may write about why he or she does not want to teach it anymore, but the requirement itself seems little questioned in the professional literature, and it gradually grew back in the colleges. There can be found every flavor of reformism—the theorizing, the experimental pedagogies, the complaining, the throwing up of hands, the proffering of every sort of solution to the problems that always recur—what Greenbaum's sometimes rather cruel essay calls "the piano that never stops tinkling . . . the universal moaning, the innumerable innovations." (p. 187). But abolitionism petered out after 1974, much as it had done after both World Wars. Shaw (1974) spoke for many colleagues when he wrote in an antiabolitionist essay, "I am tired of colleagues who are less interested in the teaching of composition than in the preaching of decomposition" (p. 155).

Reasons for the change are complex. Some are culturally bound. The general military draft ended, and the Vietnam War wound down. The last great antiwar protests were rigorously quashed by the Nixon administration in 1971. The antiwar movement imploded into quarreling factions, and the sudden deflation of campus radicalism after 1972 left schools extremely quiet. (The class of 1973 was the last class to have seen the student strike of 1970, and after they graduated in Spring 1973 the great campus movement that fall was "streaking.") There was a gas crisis and an economic recession. It was not a propitious time for any proposal for change.

Professionally, the most obvious reason for the decay of abolitionist sentiment was, of course, the rise of open admissions, the movement of a whole new demographic sector into college classrooms, and the resulting "literacy crisis" of the middle 1970s. There is nothing like a new population or a perceived problem of lack of student preparation to put energy back into a composition requirement, and by 1976 we had both in plenty. The "Johnny Can't Write" furor of 1976 was at least as potent as the "Illiteracy of American Boys" furor had been 90 years before, and any chance that abolitionist ideas might have had in the early 1970s was swamped by mid-decade. The "Back to the Basics" movement, the rise of basic writing as a subdiscipline, even the writing process movement all presumed a required freshman course.

Just as important to the decline of abolitionism, I believe, was the maturation of the discipline of composition studies and its increasing ability to turn out doctoral specialists who could direct and defend programs. The natural tendency early on was for such specialists to talk reform and defend the course, but their very existence tempered the conditions that had made some literary specialists argue for abolition. The liberal culture abolitionists of the 1890s had largely lost interest in the battle when they themselves had been relieved of the duty of teaching required composition by graduate students and instructors. This left literary specialists only with the duty of overseeing the toilers in the writing vineyard, and nearly all liberal culture abolitionists had been either freshman directors or departmental chairs. With the increasing availability of a class of tenure-track composition specialists to handle oversight of the course, literary members of English departments could rest increasingly secure from ever having to do anything associated with composition unless they chose to. Those overseeing required courses had an increasing professional stake in them, and thus reform ideas came hard and fast—but not proposals for abolition. So things went, through the later 1970s and most of the 1980s.

THE NEW ABOLITIONISM

This dearth of abolitionist sentiment, by now lasting almost 20 years, makes the historian with even a slight tinge of Toynbeeism begin to expect that the wheel must turn again, and turn again toward abolitionism. True to form, we now must consider the New Abolitionism. A founding statement of the New Abolitionism was made by Sharon Crowley (1991), in her "A Personal Essay on Freshman English."

Crowley's thoughtful essay is something that had not been seen in the literature for many years: a nonreformist argument from a composition insider. It details her gradual realization, by way of her immersion in the creation and ongoing attempt at implementation of the Wyoming Resolution, that required freshman composition courses implicated her and all composition specialists with any program oversight in structures that could not be significantly reformed. The course is simply too tied up with institutional and professional baggage to be amenable to serious reform. "In short," she wrote, "I doubt whether it is possible to radicalize instruction in a course that is so thoroughly implicated in the maintenance of cultural and academic hierarchy" (p. 165). Crowley's solution was abolition, not of the course but of the requirement. "Please note," she wrote, "that I am NOT proposing the abolition of Freshman English. I am not so naive as to think that the course can be abolished. But it can be made elective. To deny the supposition that all students need to jump over the hurdle of Freshman English is to begin chipping away at the course's historical function as a repressive instrument of student (and teacher) legitimation" (p. 170). Crowley went on to argue that eliminating the requirement would get rid of admissions exams, prevent any sort of indoctrination of first-year students, offer administrative control over enrollments in freshman courses, and control teaching assistantships more effectively. She then took on what she considered good arguments—that is, student needs-based—and bad arguments—that is, institutionally or ideologically based—that could be made against her position.

Crowley's deliberately provocative essay led to the proposal of a roundtable session at the 1993 Conference on College Composition and Communication (CCCC) in San Diego titled "(Dis)missing the Universal Requirement." From the quick sketch I have given here of traditional responses to abolitionist arguments over the last century, we might have expected the standard response: reformism; reformism of a very high standard, no doubt, but, still, reformism: protests that the freshman requirement does more good than harm, or that its methods must be changed to fill-in-the-blank so that it can reach its potential, or that fill-in-the-blank will certainly arrive soon and make it all worthwhile.

But no. No Mahin or Taylor or Kitzhaber stood forth to disagree with Crowley. Instead, three of the most respected composition scholars and theorists rose and each one, in his or her own way, agreed with Crowley that the universal requirement should be rethought. Lil Brannon of SUNY–Albany reported that her university had abolished the standard freshman course in 1986 because "a group of faculty from across the curriculum successfully made the case that a 'skills' concept of writing—the very idea of writing that caused the faculty to require Freshman Composition—had no professional currency" (p. 1). David Jolliffe (1993) making an argument based on his historical study, asked whether such a "skills"-based course was a reflection of late 19th-century perceptions: "I wonder if freshman composition isn't a metaphor for a time long passed. I wonder if we shouldn't rethink the position of requiring all incoming students to be 'skilled' in this anachronistic fashion" (p. 1). Calling regular freshman courses "literacy calisthenics," Jolliffe went on to argue that they should be replaced with a writing-based sophomore-level elective course that would concentrate on writing about content of their choice. Charles Schuster (1993) spoke from the point of view of a practicing composition administrator, saying that freshman composition is the third world of English studies, "a bleak territory within which students have little power to choose" (p. 6), and in which faculty are underpaid and overworked. Teaching writing is foundational, said Schuster, but "either Freshman Composition has to matter to our departments, or we have to get rid of it—or get rid of our colleagues" (p. 6).

The discussion that followed these three presentations was spirited, and although there was by no means unanimity of opinion, many session attenders agreed with the central points made by the presenters. Within a few weeks, the grapevine of hallway conversations, telephone calls, workshop and presentation discussions, and electronic mail was buzzing with word of the session, and the issue even had its name: the New Abolitionism. The following year saw the predictable rejoinder from the reformist camp in a session at the Nashville CCCC called "Dissing Freshman Composition," at which Marjorie Roemer, Russell Durst, and several other University of Cincinnati teachers criticized the claims of Crowley, Jolliffe, and Brannon. Two full-scale debates on the subject took place at the 1995 CCCC in Washington, and this continuing conversation bids fair to become a prime dialectic in the field.

We have come a long way from 1893 to 1993, from the oldest to the newest abolitionism movements. Are there any conclusions we can draw from what we have learned? Can our understanding of the past inform our sense of the present, or even the future? Is the New Abolitionism any different from previous similar arguments?

The observer of abolition arguments cannot help noting some salient similarities. The New Abolitionism is like previous versions in its condemnation of the required course as often futile, as a disliked hinterland of English studies, as expensive to run, exhausting to teach, and alienating to administer. Some New Abolitionists are present and former course administrators, as were a large number of abolitionists throughout history. The alternatives proposed by many of the New Abolitionists are not too dissimilar to alternatives proposed by Slosson in 1913 and Eurich in 1932 and Campbell in 1939 and Russell in 1968: Make writing instruction the responsibility of the whole faculty.

The differences between the New Abolitionism and the older movements are, however, even more striking than the similarities. Most obviously different is the professional forum in which the argument is playing itself out. The New Abolitionism is a product of a newly scholarly and professionalized discipline of composition studies, one with many national journals and a constant and ongoing conversation. Writing specialists today are not just course administrators or pedagogy enthusiasts but are increasingly visible in English departments as scholars and researchers with their own claims to respect. The change of the discipline is revealed most clearly in the fact that this abolition conversation is not between liberal culture literary specialists and embattled teachers, as previous abolition conversations have been, but between serious and prepared experts on writing issues. Since the institutional beginning of the required composition course, the greatest number of abolition arguments have come from outsiders who despised the course as useless and mechanical—nearly always from what D. Russell (1988) called "romantics," people who did not believe that writing could be taught at all. The New Abolitionism is the work of insiders—people trained as writing specialists from an early point in their careers—and it is based on exactly the opposite conclusion: that the development of writing abilities can be facilitated within different situational contexts, and that experts can assist the student writer in navigating through these contexts, but that the required freshman course is not the most effective forum for attaining the ends we seek.

The intellectual and pedagogical backgrounds for the argument have shifted dramatically as a result of these changes in institutional and disciplinary cultures, and it is this background shift that may be the most important element in any success the New Abolitionism may have. From a very early point, abolitionists have been claiming that freshman composition should be replaced with one or another system that would take responsibility for literacy off English teachers and place it on all faculty members. These were voices crying in the wilderness through much of this century, however. There were no institutional structures that would have helped faculty members in other disciplines make writing more central to their courses, and there was no extant part of English studies with enough credible expertise to do such outreach work. All that has now changed radically with the advent of the writing across the curriculum movement. For the last decade and longer, writing professionals have, with the blessing and help of administrators, been forging professional links that never existed before with extradisciplinary colleagues, bringing contemporary knowledge of writing issues to content-area courses. This is a strong and broadly respected movement, one that is unlikely to go away, and it provides a practical base for the ideas of the New Abolitionism that no previous such movement had (witness the arguments presented by Brannon, chap. 12; Freedman, chap. 6; Petraglia, chap. 4; and Russell, chap. 3, all this volume). Writing across the curriculum has made R. Russell's (1968) challenge to other faculty members who wanted students trained in writing papers, "Then assign them!" something more than bad-tempered buck-passing.

The arguments we hear from proponents of the New Abolitionism are qualitatively different from those to be heard in previous avatars of the movement. New Abolitionists typically appeal first to student interests, and only secondarily to the interests of teachers, departments, and colleges. Even when previous abolitionists transcended liberal culture arguments, their calls for the end of the required course were often based in issues of self-interest—getting rid of the composition underclass, or allowing professors to teach courses they liked, or avoiding the criticism of colleagues who felt the course was ineffective. Today's abolitionists are arguing from their scholarly as well as their practical knowledge of writing issues that students are not as well served by the required freshman course as they could be by other kinds of writing instruction. They are ideologically informed in ways that even 1960s radicals like Greenbaum were not, and they are certainly sympathetic to both students and teachers in ways that few abolitionists have ever been. Most importantly, this change in the institutional base of the argument means that we may see fewer reformist claims based in the need to safeguard jobs, turf, and respectability.

Finally, and perhaps most importantly, the New Abolitionists are in positions to make their critique stick. Because most of them are administrators or advisors to administrators, they know the institutional situation surrounding composition programs, writing across the curriculum, and literary studies. They know what is possible, and they know how to get things done—not just whether they should be done. Because they are respected scholars and teachers, they can and do counter the predictable response from traditionalists and reformists by taking a position of informed sympathy mixed with telling argumentation. Because they are composition insiders, they can make their case from within the discourse of the field rather than complaining scornfully from without, as most abolitionists have done in the past.

It may just be, then, that the New Abolitionism will come to have a real effect. It may be that after a century we will begin to see some actual abolition of the required freshman course in favor of other methods of writing instruction. But as Eliot's Gerontion says, "Think now/History has many cunning passages, contrived corridors/And issues, deceives with whispering ambitions,/Guides us with vanities." None of our historical knowledge can really predict the outcome of the New Abolitionism movement. What we can learn, however, is what may promote or block such changes in entrenched curricular practices. My own position, if I have not already tipped my hand, is one of sympathy for the New Abolitionism. I still believe that we have more of a chance today than ever before to rethink in a serious and thoroughgoing way the best methods for working on student literacy issues, and that we can do so without harming the best interests of either our students or our colleagues. I look forward to a continuation of the debate and even—could it be?—to real changes in our world of teaching and thinking about writing.

REFERENCES

Anderson, M. B. (1895). The Leland Stanford, Junior, University. In W. M. Payne (Ed.), *English in American universities* (pp. 49–59). Boston: D. C. Heath.

Applebee, A. N. (1974). *Tradition and reform in the teaching of English: A history.* Urbana, IL: National Council of Teachers of English.

Brannon, L. (1993, March). *(Dis)missing freshman composition.* Presentation given at CCCC, San Diego, CA.

Campbell, O. J. (1939). The failure of freshman English. *English Journal, 28,* 177–185.

Committee on College English, NCTE. (1935). *The teaching of college English.* New York: Appleton-Century.

Connors, R. J. (1991). Rhetoric in the modern university: The creation of an underclass. In R. Bullock & J. Trimbur (Eds.), *The politics of writing instruction: Postsecondary* (pp. 55–84). Portsmouth, NH: Boynton/Cook.

Crowley, S. (1991). A personal essay on freshman English. *Pre/Text, 12,* 156–176.

Davidson, H. C. (1932). Report of the College Section meeting. *English Journal, 21,* 220–223.

DeVoto, B. (1928). Course A. *American Mercury, 13,* 204–212.

Digest of educational statistics. (1974). Washington, DC: U.S. Department of Health, Education, and Welfare, Education Division.

Dudley, F. A. (1939). The success of freshman English. *College English, 1,* 22–30.

Eaton, H. A. (1919). English problems after the war. *English Journal, 8,* 308–312.

Eurich, A. C. (1932). Should freshman composition be abolished? *English Journal, 21,* 211–219.

Green, A. J. (1941). The reform of freshman English. *College English, 2,* 593–602.

Greenbaum, L. (1969). The tradition of complaint. *College English, 31,* 174–187.

Harvard Committee on the Objectives of a General Education in a Free Society. (1945). *General education in a free society.* Cambridge, MA: Harvard University Press.

Hill, A. S. (1896). An answer to the cry for more English. In A. S. Hill (Ed.), *Twenty years of school and college English* (pp. 6–16). Cambridge, MA: Harvard University Press.

Hoover, R. M. (1974). Taps for freshman English? *College Composition and Communication, 25,* 149–154.

Hurlbut, B. S. (1896). College requirements in English. In A. S. Hill (Ed.), *Twenty years of school and college English* (pp. 46–53). Cambridge, MA: Harvard University Press.

Jolliffe, D. (1993, March). *Three arguments for sophomore English.* Presentation given at CCCC, San Diego, CA.

Kitzhaber, A. R. (1960). Death—Or transfiguration? *College English, 21,* 367–378.

Lounsbury, T. R. (1911, November). Compulsory composition in colleges. *Harper's Monthly, 123,* 866–880.

Mahin, H. O. (1915). The study of English composition as a means to fuller living. *English Journal, 4,* 445–450.

Osgood, C. G. (1915). No set requirement of English composition in the freshman year. *English Journal, 4,* 231–235.

Payne, W. M. (1895). *English in American universities.* Boston: D. C. Heath.

Rice, W. G. (1960). A proposal for the abolition of freshman English, as it is now commonly taught, from the college curriculum. *College English, 21,* 361–367.

Rudolph, F. (1962). *The American college and university: A history.* New York: Knopf.

Russell, D. R. (1988). Romantics on writing: Liberal culture and the abolition of composition courses. *Rhetoric Review, 6,* 132–148.

Russell, R. (1968). The question of composition: A record of a struggle. *College English, 30,* 171–177.

Sampson, M. W. (1895). The University of Indiana. In W. M. Payne (Ed.), *English in American universities* (pp. 92–98). Boston: D. C. Heath.

Schuster, C. (1993, March). *Toward abolishing composition.* Presentation given at CCCC, San Diego, CA.

Scott, F. W., Thomas, J. M., & Manchester, F. A. (1918). Preliminary report of the Special Committee on Freshman English. *English Journal, 7,* 592–599.

Shaw, P. W. (1974). Freshman English: To compose or decompose, that is the question. *College Composition and Communication, 25,* 155–159.

Shepherd, L. (1913). Discussions: Prescribed English in college. *Educational Review, 46,* 188–190.

Slosson, P. W. (1913). Discussions: Prescribed English in college. *Educational Review, 45,* 407–409.

Smith, R. (1974). The composition requirement today: A report on a nationwide survey of four-year colleges and universities. *College Composition and Communication, 25,* 138–148.

Stedman, N. A. (1913). Discussions: Prescribed English in college. *Educational Review, 46,* 52–57.

Strong, G. (1913). Discussions: Prescribed English in college. *Educational Review, 45,* 189.

Symposium on *The teaching of college English.* (1935). *English Journal, 24,* 573–586.

Taylor, W. (1932). Should freshman composition be abolished? *English Journal, 21,* 301–311.

Zigrosser, C. (1913). Discussions: Prescribed English in college. *Educational Review, 45,* 187–188.

2

The Disciplinary Instability of Composition

Maureen Daly Goggin
Arizona State University

The post-World War II emergence of the Conference on College Composition and Communication (CCCC) signaled the coming of age for those interested in rhetoric and composition as a serious academic enterprise. Hailing its formation, Charles Roberts (1950), the first editor of *College Composition and Communication*, explained, "we are no longer selling a pig in a poke; ours is an established organization, with annual meetings and an official publication" (p. 22). In the half century preceding its emergence, composition had been virtually unseen and unheard within scholarly circles, having been relegated to and scattered across localized composition programs and specific classrooms. In the decades following Roberts' declaration, and especially within the last decade, however, the proliferation of professional organizations, monographs, journals, graduate programs, and tenure-track positions devoted to the study and teaching of literate practices provides evidence of the disciplinary vitality of this field (Anson & Miller, 1988; Brown, Meyer, & Enos, 1994; Huber, 1992).

Yet although it may be argued that an academic field has finally emerged for rhetoric and composition, it is less clear that it has achieved the prestige and status for which its proponents have fought. Despite impressive strides, disciplinary practitioners continue to struggle on professional, academic, and institutional fronts against marginalization (T. Enos, 1990; Miller, 1991; Winterowd & Gillespie, 1994; Yoos, 1990). The purpose of this chapter is to explore some of the factors that contribute to this ongoing struggle. To this end, this chapter traces the historical relationship between the discipline of rhetoric and the pedagogical enterprise of writing instruction and argues that the current disciplinary instability is mainly a product of conflicting representations of the field held both by those situated outside and situated within the discipline.

The persistent struggle for status, prestige, and recognition is driven partly by external forces, largely having to do with the precarious place of rhetoric and composition within departments of English. That is to say, proponents of the field have made only limited progress toward defining an intellectual space for the field (e.g., objects of study, methods, discourses), and they have been even less successful in securing their own material space. As Winterowd and Gillespie (1994) argued, "compositionists reside in the literarist empire only as documented aliens, the courses they teach entitling them to green cards. The content of composition is, by and large, an institution so structured as to provide no territory for the discipline (as opposed to the practice)" (p. vii). They went on to note that:

> Almost all scholarly fields have identity and status within the institutions of higher education; there are departments of physics, history, education, and so on. The historian can wander into the departmental coffee room and find someone who is interested in his or her work, who reads the same journals, and who attends the same conventions. There is no such coffee room for the compositionist. (p. xi)

Indeed, most in our discipline must wander into English department coffee rooms, where the reception may range from, at best, a polite disinterest in, to, at worst, open hostility toward what we do and who we are (cf. Jarratt, 1993).

A great deal of scholarly ink has been spilt on the troublesome relationship between rhetoric and literature within departments of English.[1] Yet as powerful and as problematic as the relations between rhetoric and literature may be, the disciplinary instability of our field is also affected by internal forces, largely having to do with the divisive relations between the pedagogical enterprise of composition and the larger rhetorical tradition. Although this divide has often been characterized as a conflict between practice and theory,[2] the problem appears to run deeper and to be

---

[1]In general there have been two major responses to the schism. The first calls for an accommodation between the two and is best exemplified by the metaphor of *bridging the gap*, which can be found in the title of Horner's (1983) collection, *Composition and Literature: Bridging the Gap*. The second response calls for breaking with literary studies, and is best exemplified by the metaphor of *breaking our bonds*, which comes from the title of Maxine Hairston's (1985) seminal, and rather polemic, article "Breaking Our Bonds and Reaffirming Our Connections." For discussions on bridging the gap, see, for example, Raymond (1987), Schilb (1989), Shumway (1985), and Smith (1993). For those on breaking our bonds, see, for example, Phelps (1991), Stratton (1985), and Burhans (1983). Neither proposal, to my knowledge, has been successfully implemented on any large scale, although at a local level, a few institutions have followed one or another call. At Syracuse University, for example, writing is an autonomous department, separate from and equal to the English department.

[2]See, for example, Schilb (1991), who discussed some of the debates over the conflict between theory and practice in rhetoric and composition.

more complicated than a simple bifurcation of the applied and the theoretical. The schism seems to result from two incompatible conceptions of the nature of the discipline. This divide is manifested by the variety of names used to designate the field, many of which gather around the terms *composition* studies as opposed to *rhetoric and writing* studies. In this discussion, I refer to those who use the former term as *compositionists* and those who use the latter term as *rhetoricians*.

Although the external and internal forces, as I characterize them here, are undoubtedly inextricably bound up with each other, for the purposes of this discussion I want to unravel them to focus on the internal forces. This move is important because it seems to me that until we address the pressing internal conflicts, we will not be able to address the very real external and material ones.

RIVALING REPRESENTATIONS: COMPOSITIONISTS VERSUS RHETORICIANS

What disciplinary practitioners choose to call a field has enormous implications for its future situation within the academy. Definition is a political act. The different names used to signify our disciplinary enterprise reveal a substantive conflict over how we define ourselves and our work. Compositionists tend to conceive of our discipline as a subfield of English studies with composition (i.e., writing instruction, usually in first-year college composition) as its focus. For this group, first-year composition is a site of both knowledge production and dissemination. This position is well exemplified by Lauer's (1984) characterization of our discipline: "The field [of composition] sustains itself through a lifeline connected to the composition classroom where many of its problems for research are generated and to which its theory returns for implementation and testing" (p. 28). Under this view, the generation and distribution of disciplinary knowledge remains in a tight, closed circle circumscribed by the composition classroom.

By contrast, rhetoricians tend to define the discipline in broader terms with composition as one component, a pedagogical component, of the field. Vitanza (1987), for example, defined composition as "a subset of rhetoric" (p. 261). Drawing on a long and rich, although decidedly varied, intellectual tradition, rhetoricians include pedagogy among a full range of disciplinary elements. Under this view, rhetoric is understood as an interconnected system of theory, practice, product, and pedagogy, in which it is possible to recognize, as Yoos (1990) did, that "rhetorical theory and research . . . are inseparable from pedagogical considerations" (p. 11). In short, whereas compositionists tend to equate their enterprise with the teaching of writing only, rhetoricians situate the enterprise within a much larger, and richer, framework of theories and practices that have been concerned with the reciprocal relationship between discourse and social, political, and cultural contexts. The rhetoricians' conceptualization of the discipline is thus more inclusive than the compositionists'.

These rivaling conceptions of our field may be traced to the unique set of circumstances that gave rise to the disciplinary enterprise of rhetoric and composition.[3] Definition is not only a political act; it is also a historical product. The necessarily brief sketch of this history that follows is meant to contextualize and, thus, contribute to an understanding of our present disciplinary configuration.

POSITION TO COMPOSITION: A BRIEF HISTORY

R. Enos (1993) traced the formation of the study and practice of rhetoric to Sicily in early fifth century B.C.E., and demonstrated how various rhetorical systems were spread to Athens through Sicilian sophists such as Gorgias and Protagoras (see also Jarratt, 1991). His examination of the sophistic rhetorics demonstrates a "range of perspectives exhibited by these foreign [non-Athenian] sophists, from the poetic embellishment of Gorgias to the agnostic relativism of Protagoras" (p. 102). It was during these formative years that the elements of rhetoric as a system of theory, production, product, and pedagogy were forged. Nearly a century later in Greece, diverse rhetorical systems were also evident in the differences that distinguish Plato's rhetoric in terms of theory, practice, product and pedagogy from that of Isocrates (Goggin & Long, 1993), both of which differ from Aristotle's rhetoric (Cahn, 1993). The study of rhetoric, in its various guises, became central to the ancient Greek concept of *paideia* (intellectual excellence), and thus became central to the classical educational process of initiating young people into Greek culture. For the next 2,500 years, rhetoric formed the core of classical studies.[4]

Toward the end of the 19th century, however, the study of rhetoric fell into minor importance in departments of English, not to be revived for nearly a century. Two related developments, the rise of the modern university and the specialization of the college curriculum, contributed to its decline (Rudolph, 1962/1990, 1977; Veysey, 1965). The demise of the study of rhetoric within departments of English occurred as the classical

---

[3]Throughout this discussion I use the (admittedly cumbersome) term *rhetoric and composition* to signal where I am situated in the larger debate concerning the nature and roots of our discipline.

[4]For discussions concerning the centrality of rhetoric in education from the classical period up to the 20th century, see, for example, Conley (1990), Kennedy (1980), and Murphy (1990). Of course, for the purposes of this discussion, I am oversimplifying a complex history of appropriations of rhetoric through the ages; see, for example, Blair (1992), Jarratt (1991), and Welch (1990).

college yielded to dozens of other kinds of institutions, including research universities, liberal arts colleges, professional and technical schools, religious institutions, and 2-year colleges (Rudolph, 1977). Grounded in a modernist epistemology, the new curricula forged within these new settings typically reflected the growing prestige of science, technology, and the social and behavioral sciences. Among the victims of the resulting contests for time and space in higher education was the study of rhetoric, which in most places dwindled in size within departments of English to a single required course, first-year composition (Berlin, 1984, 1987; Crowley, 1990; Kitzhaber, 1953/1990; Russell, 1991).

Ironically, this transformation of rhetoric occurred at the very moment that strong calls to elevate the study of the vernacular were being sounded within and without academia, and particularly by those within English studies. Study of the vernacular was made all the more pressing, according to Hunt (1884), a professor of rhetoric and of the English language at the College of New Jersey, because this was "an era when the vernacular must be understood as never before" (p. 122). Hunt was all too correct in his observation. During the 19th century, sweeping cultural, technological, and socioeconomic changes radically altered concepts of and demands for literacy (Varnum, 1986). For one thing, industrialization created profound changes in the kinds of reading and writing skills necessary to enter the workforce. As Varnum (1986) pointed out, "as industry became large-scale and management grew more institutional and complex, routine administrative tasks were multiplied, and the growing corporate and government bureaucracies came to rely on heretofore unnecessary quantities of paper records" (p. 149). Suddenly what had constituted literacy in an earlier time, the ability to sign one's name and to recite passages from memory, was no longer adequate to the tasks necessary for the efficient running of corporations and government (D. P. Resnick & L. B. Resnick, 1977). The rising demand for a new literate workforce had an enormous impact on education, significantly increasing student enrollments at both the high school (Butts, 1978) and college levels (Veysey, 1965), which in turn created a new and larger reading public. Further, the rapidly growing middle class began to turn increasingly to reading materials to fill the newly available leisure hours created by industrialization. At the same time, new technologies for manufacturing paper and printing significantly reduced publishing costs and, thus flooded the market with books and other printed material (Kaufer & Carley, 1993).

In addition to these new pressing social, political, and economic demands for literacy, significant systemic changes in education at this time, specifically the rise of disciplines, created other demands on literacy and its teaching. Hoskin (1993) traced the formation of disciplinarity as a knowledge form to 18th-century innovations in educational practices that resulted in a radical change in how students learned how to learn. He identified three new educational settings—the seminar in Germany, the laboratory in France, and the classroom in Scotland—that gave rise to three specific pedagogical innovations: writing, examinations, and grading. Taken together, these innovative practices focused on writing to create what Hoskin called a "*grammatocentric* world." Hoskin explained that "under 'grammatocentrism,' everything centres on or tends toward writing. Everyone needs to learn not just to read but to write" (p. 295). By the mid-19th century, these new settings and pedagogical practices were adopted by academic institutions in the United States.

Given the enormous new demands for educational, work, and recreational literacy, one cannot help but ask why didn't rhetoric expand to fill those needs instead of contracting so sharply? The answer is far too complex, being well beyond the scope of this discussion, to explore in any depth here. However, part of the answer lies in how rhetoric was conceived during this time. In a persuasive account of the influence of the modernist epistemology on rhetoric, Crowley (1990) traced how the tenets of 17th-century thinkers such as Bacon, Descartes, the Port-Royal logicians, and Locke were incorporated into and came to dominate the 18th- and 19th-century views regarding rhetoric. She pointed out that "the allegiance of eighteenth-century discourse theory to psychology and logic permitted two relatively new features to emerge within rhetorical theory: the privileging of a single authorial mind, rather than community wisdom, as the source of invention and the concomitant privileging of texts as reflections of this sovereign authorial mind" (p. 12). The modernist conception of knowledge contributed to the demise of rhetoric and specifically to the dismantling of the five canons (invention, arrangement, style, memory, and delivery) that had traditionally formed the core of every rhetoric since the time of the ancient Greeks.

By the 19th century, all that remained within the province of rhetoric were arrangement and style, invention having been pulled from rhetoric, and memory and delivery having been abandoned as superfluous to writing. Rhetoric became defined as a managerial task of arranging in the best language that which was already known (Young, 1978). As Crowley (1990) pointed out, in this light, "the best to be hoped for from writing was that it could copy down whatever writers already knew. What writers knew, of course, was the really important stuff—but this was not the province of writing instruction" (p. 160). The modernist epistemology and its transformation of rhetoric had an enormous impact on pedagogy; under the view of mind as an innate quality impervious to outside influence, a teacher could do little to improve the quality of the mind, to improve on innate genius, apart from recommending certain exercises to strengthen the mind.

In a nutshell, learning to write by the late 19th century meant something very different than what the learning of discursive practices had meant under the classical system. To these late Victorians, writing served as a demonstration of knowledge; students were required to write down what they heard and learned as a means of becoming accountable to the material of the seminar, lab, or class. Writing as demonstration represented a clear departure from the ancient practice of engaging in rhetorical disputation as an epistemic process. By the 19th century, rhetoric had been reconceptualized in ways that led to a loss of its explanatory powers and thus a loss of its appeal.

It is important to recognize that in the turn-of-the-century scramble for curriculum space and funds, disciplines needed to demonstrate that they possessed a rigorous course of study worthy of those material goods. But measures of worth were narrowly defined along objective, rational lines. Crowley (1990) explained:

> Rational inquiry, which was associated exclusively with scientific and philosophical investigation in early modern thought, simply edged out the claims to knowledge made by other disciplines. Rhetoric, ethics, and aesthetics were identified with the nonrational (or irrational) faculties: the imagination, the will, and the passions. The results of inquiry gained by these means were assumed to be less universally applicable, less predictable, and hence less important, than those made available by science. (p. 57)

Thus, rhetoric provided little of interest for the modernist, and held little clout in the academic contest for space and time.

Interestingly enough, the forces that worked to transform educational practices, as Hoskin (1993) characterized them, also transformed rhetoric. There is paradox at work here: Writing became central to disciplinarity as a knowledge form at the very moment that modernist concepts of rhetoric made writing increasingly impoverished as a tool of knowledge. In sum, the transformation of rhetoric from potentially rich intellectual enterprise into a truncated and impoverished one was the result of a complex confluence of epistemic, social, cultural, and economic forces that had a profound effect on concepts of literacy and on literacy education. Within departments of English, a study of the vernacular came to mean a disciplined and critical study—not of rhetoric, but of literature.

A TRUNCATED RHETORIC: COMPOSITION

As disciplines (intellectual space) and departments (material space) were constructed within academia in the United States at the turn of the century, rhetoric, now narrowly conceived as a managerial practice, was dismissed, being denied both kinds of space. Within departments of English, rhetoric found a limited home where it became transformed into a marginalized pedagogical service enterprise. Increasingly it became identified with problems of teaching writing, as a subject of student attention, and virtually limited to the first-year required college composition course. Within English studies, only this pedagogical dimension of rhetoric was given consistent attention, a point that becomes clear when we examine the formation and growth of the Modern Language Association (MLA).

The MLA, founded in 1883, emerged as the first professional organization for English studies amid vigorous arguments about the role and purpose of English studies (Franklin, 1978, 1984). One goal that held the diverse, competing visions of English studies together was a vigorous struggle for achieving disciplinary status. This struggle was perhaps best articulated at the second MLA meeting in 1884 by A. Marshall Elliott (1889), Associate Professor of Romance Languages at Johns Hopkins and Founding Secretary of the MLA, when he called on the organization "to move with all possible energy towards the establishment and legitimate maintenance of the claims of the Modern studies for the same rights and privileges as are now enjoyed by the classics" (p. vii). In vying for a position within higher education, English studies had to demonstrate it possessed a serious subject and a rigorous methodology. The abandonment of rhetoric in this pursuit had both an intellectual and a political dimension. On the one hand, had early scholars in English conceived of rhetoric in different terms, they might have found it a worthy candidate. In the turmoil of defining its aims, however, the MLA chose instead to set its sights on "literary culture, philological scholarship, and linguistic discipline" (Parker, 1953, p. 20). By importing philology as a demonstrably viable method from the German universities, English studies could lay claim to intellectual rigor (Berlin, 1984; Kitzhaber, 1953/1990). On the other hand, given the competition between classics and English studies for curriculum time and departmental space, it seems probable that the neglect of rhetoric—long central to classical education, and much of it written in Greek and Latin—was also a political move.

Stewart's (1985) analysis of the early publications and proceedings of the MLA reveals that the only place where rhetoric (by then becoming increasingly conceived in narrow terms as composition) was given any serious consideration was in pedagogical discussions (see also Douglas, 1985). In 1894 issues of pedagogy were relegated to one of the handful of sections then comprising the MLA. Given the small number of sections, pedagogy then held a prominent place in the organization. Thus, when in 1903 the MLA disbanded its pedagogical section, the only one dealing consistently with any aspect of rhetoric, the impact on this subject was devastating. Between 1903 and 1910, papers concerning pedagogy appeared only sporadically in the *Publications of the Modern Language*

Association (PMLA) and on the MLA convention program, but by 1910, they disappeared entirely. By this point, the MLA had limited its interests exclusively to literary scholarship (Parker, 1953; Stewart, 1985; Ward, 1960).

In 1911, The National Council of Teachers of English (NCTE) was formed, in part, to fill the void left by the dismantling of the MLA pedagogical section. The NCTE defined as its central mission improving the teaching of English at all levels (Hatfield, 1959; Hook, 1979). In choosing to focus on the pedagogical, the NCTE defined itself against the scholarly orientation of the MLA (Vandenberg, 1993) and became the only viable institution for the truncated version of rhetoric as composition instruction. However, because the NCTE was created to deal with all issues in the teaching of English at all grade levels, college composition had to compete with a diverse range of topics and instruction levels and was, consequently, afforded very little space on convention programs and in the pages of the NCTE journals.

Although the appearance of *College English* in 1938 held the promise of opening up space, those interested in college composition still were afforded few pages. Of the articles published in *College English* between 1938 and 1970, 70% to 90% were concerned solely with literature (Goggin, 1994; Hook, 1979). Not only was space in professional organizations and journals severely limited for those interested in rhetoric and composition throughout much of the first half of the 20th century, but books and monographs were also generally discouraged by departments and scholarly publishers, although pedagogical projects (e.g., textbooks) in rhetoric and composition were usually tolerated (Nelms & Goggin, 1993). Because textbooks were not (and generally still are not) regarded for tenure and promotion in the same manner as scholarly monographs, the rewards for work in this field were kept small as compared with those for work in literary studies.

As a practical matter, then, within English departments, rhetoric was denied professional and disciplinary status during the first half of the 20th century (Combies, 1987) largely because, after it had been intellectually viscerated, it had almost no access to the kinds of instruments through which disciplines gain legitimate status—instruments such as professional organizations, learned societies, conferences, journals, monographs, and graduate programs (Becher, 1989; Freidson, 1986; Kultgen, 1988).

Frustration with such limited access eventually would lead to the formation of a professional organization devoted solely to college composition. In 1948, an NCTE session on first-year college English entitled "Three Views of Required English" stirred such interest that it filled the conference room and ran over time. Riding on the wave of a demonstrative enthusiasm, participants from that session issued and were granted a formal request for a 2-day spring conference. It was at this April 1949 conference that the first steps were taken to develop a permanent organization for rhetoric and composition, the Conference on College Composition and Communication (CCCC). The formation of the CCCC in 1949 and the appearance of its journal, CCC, in March 1950 marked a significant turning point for the field. After nearly a century of languishing at the margins of college English departments with virtually no access to the kinds of professional forums in which disciplinary practices are constituted and legitimated, the rise of this national organization held the promise of extending the political power and intellectual reach of those working within the rhetorical trenches of English departments.

COMPOSITION TO RECOMPOSITION

Phelps (1991) correctly noted that "the theoretical enterprise of rhetoric and composition originated in the impulse of practitioners to understand better the fundamental activities of writing and reading in order to teach them better" (p. 883). If we begin with the assumption that rhetoric had been truncated, and that within departments of English, it had been reduced almost exclusively to the teaching of writing, then it is not too surprising that interest in the pedagogical would become the means by which rhetoric would re-emerge. As the brief history already given begins to demonstrate, the only intellectual and material space afforded rhetoric was that which concerned the teaching of composition. In other words, practitioners in the field had been historically conditioned to define their enterprise within the boundaries of writing instruction.

This historical conditioning is evident in the CCCC's mission statement, which was written in 1949 and formally ratified in 1952: "To unite teachers of college composition and communication in an organization which can consider all matters relevant to their teaching, including teachers, subject matter, administration, methods, and students." Roberts (1955) captured the spirit of this mission and many of the journal articles printed in the 1950s and early 1960s, when he wrote of the CCCC: "Most of us, I am sure, come to these meetings [the CCCC] to find out how we can best help [our] students. The meetings are really worthwhile only insofar as they enable us to return to our desks and face that pile of themes with greater equanimity and greater confidence that we handle them properly. All else is sound and fury signifying nothing" (p. 193). Roberts, and the three editors of CCC who came after him, encouraged and published mainly practical, service-oriented essays that were largely based on an author's experience in a specific and local program and that were designed to help teachers "face that pile of themes on their desk" (Goggin, 1994).

The point is that few in the 1950s were arguing in the CCC as did Hackett (1955) that "what we need is a discipline" (p. 11). But by the end of the decade and the beginning of the 1960s, it was clear that some found the CCCC's mission statement too limited and limiting, and a struggle to redefine it emerged. In 1959 a committee was formed to make recommendations for the future direction of the CCCC. Gerber (1960), the chair, reported that "the Committee feels that the CCCC has outgrown this statement of purpose at least as it has been traditionally interpreted. It believes that the organization can be more effective *if its efforts are focused upon a discipline rather than upon a particular course or a particular group of teachers*" (italics added, p. 3). The committee proposed revising the mission statement; the changes, which were debated for over 2 years, generated a great deal of controversy with "little agreement about how the purpose of the organization should be described" (Gorrell, 1961, p. 14). At the 1961 CCCC Executive Committee Meeting in Washington, it was decided that the original mission statement would remain unchanged.

Although the proposed revisions were defeated, a growing group of scholars continued to push for professional and disciplinary status. At the 1964 MLA conference, Booth (1965) probably spoke for many of these when he delivered a moving call for recognizing rhetoric as a valid scholarly enterprise:

> My rhetorical point to a group of rhetoricians is two fold: first, that in a rhetorical age rhetorical studies should have a major, respected place in the training of all teachers at all levels; and secondly, that in such an age, specialization in rhetorical studies of all kinds, narrow and broad, should carry at least as much professional respectability as literary history or as literary criticism in non-rhetorical modes. Whether we restore the old chairs of Rhetoric by name or not, chairs like my own Pullman Professorship ought to exist in every department, to provide visible proof that to dirty one's hands in rhetorical studies is not a sure way to professional oblivion. (p. 12)

This concern for recognizing the professional and disciplinary worth of a more rhetoric-infused study of writing began to shape the directions of the academic journals in the field. A few years later Lloyd-Jones (1978) argued that "we need our journals not only to deal with what to do on Monday but to demonstrate our right to a central function in the academy" (p. 29). This notion represented a clear departure from the mission Roberts and the first few editors of CCC had defined for that journal and the mission members had defined for the CCCC. By this time, new journals, such as the *Rhetoric Society Quarterly* and *Research in the Teaching of English*, along with some established journals were turning away from trying to "deal with what to do on Monday" and toward a more rigorous understanding of literate practices as they occur in a variety of settings, from a variety of perspectives (Goggin, 1994).

Tate's experience with founding and editing *Freshman English News (FEN)* (recently renamed *Composition Studies/Freshman English News*) exemplifies the field's shift away from a service orientation toward a disciplinary one, and the subsequent tensions. In 1972 Tate created *Freshman English News* as the first unaffiliated journal in rhetoric and composition (i.e., a journal not sponsored by a professional organization). In the inaugural issue, a 12-page mimeographed newsletter that he and his wife had pasted up on their dining room table, Tate (1972) explained the goals of *FEN* in this way: "The primary aim of *Freshman English News* will be to provide a continuing report on the status of Freshman English throughout the country. . . . *What* has been tried and *how* it has been tried will be the central concerns of this newsletter" (p. 1). These goals were reminiscent of those set by the editors of *CCC* nearly two decades earlier. *FEN* defined the field within the boundaries of first-year college writing and was interested in publishing administrative and pedagogical material. The initial submission guidelines supported this pragmatic view: "theoretical and speculative articles should not be submitted," rather "the editors are interested in facts and news about Freshman English only." Within 2 years, however, the journal began to shift from this practical orientation toward a more scholarly one. The policy and guidelines were revised to encourage theoretical work in "freshman composition, rhetoric, linguistics and closely related subjects." These changes came about, according to Tate, largely in response to the kinds of submissions he was receiving. Recently he explained that "from the beginning . . . in spite of all my efforts—field editors, etc.—people insisted on sending in essays that contained more theory than news" (personal communication, April 16, 1994).

Yet despite the significant changes in the kinds of disciplinary projects undertaken by those in the field as revealed, for instance, by the range of submissions to *Freshman English News*, the CCCC has continued to define the field within a narrow set of parameters. In fact, 20 years following the first major debate concerning the CCCC's mission statement the issue of rewriting the statement came up again in 1977; however, a comparison between the original statement and the 1977 revision shows that the changes simply condensed the original mission statement without changing its intent:

> *Original CCCC Mission Statement* (1952): To unite teachers of college composition and communication in an organization which can consider all matters relevant to their teaching, including teachers, subject matter, administration, methods, and students. The specific objectives are: 1) to provide an opportunity for discussion of problems relating to the organization and teaching of college composition and communication courses, 2) to encourage studies and research in the field, and 3) to publish a

bulletin containing reports of conferences and articles of interest to teachers of composition and communication.

Revised Mission Statement (1977): The broad objective of CCCC is to unite teachers of college composition and communication in an organization which can consider all matters relevant to their teaching. The specific objectives are 1) to provide an opportunity for discussion of problems relating to the organization and teaching of college composition and communication courses; 2) to encourage studies and research in the field; 3) to publish a professional journal and other materials.

The 1977 revision merely deleted a few words (e.g., "including teachers, subject matter, administration, methods, and students") from the original first sentence, replaced the word *bulletin* (part of the original title of *CCC)* with the phrase *professional journal,* and collapsed the details "reports of conferences and articles of interest to teachers of composition and communication" into one phrase, "other materials." The revised mission statement (which remains in the CCCC constitution today) did little to move the field along a rhetorical path. That the mission statement has yet to be reformulated is both a symptom of instability within the field and a cause of the strong constituents in the field who continue to equate the discipline exclusively with the teaching of general writing skills. It is a symptom insofar as the membership has yet to agree to a new mission statement to reflect concerns outside of the college composition classroom. It is a cause insofar as those who enter the field are defined in part by the professional organizations they join and participate in.

Today, another 20 years later, a new debate concerning how the CCCC's mission should be framed has surfaced. The current debate turns on the same central question that fueled the earlier ones, namely, how should we define our disciplinary enterprise. In November 1993, the CCCC Executive Committee voted to approve a revision of the mission statement that would radically alter how the professional organization defines the discipline:

Proposed Revised Mission Statement (1993): CCCC is an organization of members with diverse missions united by a commitment to promote college composition and communication through teaching, research and other action. The objects are: 1) to sponsor forums for exchanging knowledge about the teaching, learning, and nature of composition and communication; 2) to publish a professional journal and other materials; 3) to support a wide range of studies in the field; 4) to enhance the professional development of all members; and 5) to act to improve English education nationally and internationally.

These proposed revisions are scheduled to be published in the February 1995 issue of *CCC*, discussed as Agenda Item 4C at the annual Business Meeting at the 1995 CCCC Convention in Washington, DC, and voted on by the entire CCCC membership in the summer of 1995 (Debbie Fox, personal communication, May 24, 1994). The new mission statement redefines CCCC members (and by extension, disciplinary practitioners), shifting them from *teachers* to *members with diverse missions* and identifies pedagogy as one area of interest, opening up a legitimate space for other kinds of knowledge pursuits and intellectual activities. In short, it more accurately captures how rhetoric and composition has been reflected within the professional journals since at least the 1970s (Goggin, 1994). At the same time, however, it poses a tremendous challenge to those who continue to conceive of our enterprise solely within the confines of first-year composition.

It remains to be seen whether these revisions will be ratified by CCCC members, for their adoption undoubtedly depends on some practitioners having to re-envision dramatically their conception of our disciplinary enterprise and its work. What is clear, however, is that the proposed changes raise a question concerning the relationship of the pedagogical enterprise of composition to the larger tradition of rhetoric. So completely were the rhetorical ties severed from the 19th century and throughout much of the 20th century that there are those who deny any relation between rhetoric and composition (e.g., Knoblauch & Brannon, 1984; Miller, 1991; North, 1987; Tate, 1993). This denial can be seen in those who refuse the term *rhetoric* and insist on calling the discipline *composition studies*. To the degree that the study of rhetoric was abandoned by many, although not all, departments of English (Nelms & Goggin, 1993), such denials make sense; but it does not bear up under historical scrutiny, and, as this chapter later argues, this denial helps to keep the discipline stagnant and, thus, marginalized.

THE GORDIAN KNOT: FIRST-YEAR COMPOSITION

The stagnation is evident when we recognize that the exigencies that prompted the formation of the CCCC have not been resolved. The CCCC emerged largely for political and material reasons. As Wilson (1967) explained, "aggrieved by the discrepancy between our status and our function, and impelled by our interest, we set out to change things: to shape programs and textbooks, to lighten loads and to make the budgets heavier" (p. 128; also see, e.g., Archer, 1955; Gerber, 1952, 1956; Hook, 1955). The truth is that today the political and material conditions of first-year composition programs are not much different than they were over a half century ago. Course loads have not been lightened and budgets have not become heavier; most English departments still rely on an underpaid, overworked, exploited underclass of part-time instructors and graduate students (Moglen, 1988; Robertson, Crowley, & Lentricchia, 1987;

Wyche-Smith & Rose, 1990). As Robertson and Slevin (1987) noted, "the status of writing teachers is dismal" (p. 193).

Textbooks have also remained, by and large, stubbornly the same (Berlin, 1982; Hamilton-Wieler, 1988; Stewart, 1978; Welch, 1987).[5] What Francis (1953) wrote about the condition of textbooks over 40 years ago remains virtually true today:

> In no reputable academic discipline is the gap between the pioneers of research and the pedagogical rank and file more shockingly great . . . [textbooks] continue to put forward for the instruction of innocent freshmen a hodgepodge of facts, theories, and prescriptions most of which are from fifty to two hundred years behind the findings of linguistic science. (p. 329)

It is not that all textbooks are uniformly atheoretical; clearly, they are not. But many represent variations on rhetorical themes that have been in vogue on and off since the 18th and 19th centuries (Berlin, 1982, 1984, 1987). Almost all of these support what Petraglia (chap. 4, this volume) termed a "general writing skills instruction" (GWSI) perspective on what it means to write. In calling attention to the stubborn persistence of these ineffectual texts, Crowley (1986) made the point most forcefully: "To read through Freshman English textbooks of any era is to journey through a dreary wasteland marked by the same ill-conceived pillars of wisdom, which are repackaged rather than re-thought when some new intellectual fad requires their surface conformity to its configurations" (p. 11).

The persistence of these ineffectual textbooks draws attention to the rueful fact that despite decades of scholarly focus on first-year composition, the institution has not been changed in any significant way during this century. Instead of systemic changes, it has been treated to a number of superficial ones, like so many layers of paint being applied to a crumbling building. My purpose here is not to dismiss a half century of dedicated and sincere efforts to rescue the system but rather my goal is to call attention to the point that the system itself has not been reconfigured in any substantial or wide-scale way. The reasons for this are no doubt complicated by real political and economic pressures within the institution of academia, but other reasons can be found by looking inside the disciplinary enterprise itself.

Textbooks are supposed to promote and infuse disciplinary perspectives, values, methods, and discourses (Kuhn, 1970; Toulmin, 1972). Drawing on Kuhn, Young (1978) noted that "textbooks elaborate and perpetuate established paradigms; they are one of the principal vehicles for

---

[5]Of course, there have been textbooks that have tried to promote a radically new view of composition (see, e.g, Young, Becker, and Pike's [1970] *Rhetoric: Discovery and Change* and Corbett's [1965] *Classical Rhetoric for the Modern Student)* but these have been rare.

the conduct of a discipline" (p. 31). That textbooks, as Crowley (1986) argued, have largely been "repackaged" rather than "rethought" underscores the unique problem at the heart of our disciplinary efforts. Unlike other disciplines, where the introductory undergraduate courses serve to acquaint students with the disciplinary ways of knowing, first-year composition has been grounded in a mechanical literacy that has virtually nothing to do with the aims of rhetoric and composition (Crowley, 1986). As Crowley (1986) noted, "since Freshman English originated as a response to perceived deficiencies in students' literate skills, rather than as an arena in which to study a body of received knowledge, the course has never appropriated an area of study for itself that would bring order to its teaching" (p. 11).

Understanding the problem in this light helps to explain why recent research on composition programs reveals a great fissure between the disciplinary enterprise of rhetoric and composition and the teaching and administering of first-year composition programs. Hartzog's (1986) study and Larson's (1994) survey found that research and scholarship in rhetoric and composition have had little to no impact on program design and administration. Local institutional and departmental politics evidently play far stronger roles in the management of such programs. Most first-year composition curriculums thus continue to be built on shaky ground, whether epistemological (Crowley, 1990), ideological (Berlin, 1987), or functional (Petraglia, 1995; Russell, 1993). If this is the case, then why are there those who insist on defining the discipline almost solely within the boundaries of first-year composition? After nearly a century of trying to untie the Gordian knot that is first-year composition, some scholars are suggesting that it may be time for those within the discipline, like the young Alexander the Great, to eliminate the knot.

NEW ABOLITIONISTS

The goal of teaching literate practices is important but the pedagogical framework of GWSI that we have inherited, and have remained fettered to, has simply not worked. Russell (1993) made this point most clearly when he argued that "after more than a century of search for a method, a conceptual scheme, there have been no knock-down successes, no dramatic break-throughs, not even any noticeable let-up in the complaints about poor student writing. It might be useful to call off the search" (p. 195). In posing this argument, Russell joined a long tradition within departments of English of calling for the elimination of composition from the college curriculum (Greenbaum, 1969; Rice, 1960; Russell, 1991). Yet Russell's call, which seems to echo what has recently been termed the *new abolitionist* call, paradoxically represents both a continuity and a discontinuity in this tradition of complaint.

Connors (chap. 1, this volume) argues that there is something different about the most recent call. For one thing, it comes now from those who are situated within rhetorical studies rather than within literary studies; second, given their training, knowledge, and recently gained disciplinary force, this new wave of abolitionists may succeed in constructing a new pedagogy of writing. Crowley, for example, argued for abandoning the requirement of first-year composition in favor of a range of elective courses in rhetoric and writing (Connors, 1993; Schilb, 1994). Her position calls for transforming the enterprise of writing instruction so that it emerges out of and is integral to the discipline of rhetoric and composition.

The new abolitionists' position, although attractive to some, is quite unacceptable to compositionists who continue to define the discipline solely within the boundaries of first-year composition. For them, abolishing the course amounts to professional suicide. Yet, the problem with this position is that although in some instances composition classrooms may serve to generate research problems and also serve as research sites, these instances represent just one strain of scholarship in the field. Restricting our disciplinary enterprise to the composition classroom severely restricts the kinds of problems, questions, and objects of study that we validate for study, and thus severely restricts the shape of the discipline. As Burke (1966) taught us, "a way of seeing is also a way of not seeing" (p. 44). And perhaps more seriously, restricting our inquiry to the composition class helps to keep us invested in the present system however ill-conceived it may be. Such investment, I would argue, blinds us to the systemic problems, and thus prevents us from reconceptualizing pedagogies and programs in literate practices.

I want to make it clear that, like the other contributors to this volume, I am not advocating that we abandon the teaching of literate practices. In fact, I am arguing just the opposite. What I am suggesting is that we abandon the GWSI system we inherited over 100 years ago in favor of a rhetorical one that would instruct students in the complexities and richness of literate practices as they occur in a variety of situations and for a variety of purposes. What I am finally suggesting is that we let our pedagogy emerge out of our discipline rather than let our discipline be ruled by an ill-conceived and rotting pedagogical structure. To put it another way, I am advocating that we put down the paintbrush and take up the sledgehammer.

If we are to accomplish genuine systemic change, however, we need to define our disciplinary enterprise in broader terms than the college composition classroom. As Phelps (1988) argued, the discipline "was restricted and unfulfilled as long as it was conceived only in terms of that fleeting moment in the classroom through which teachers struggled to affect a life-long growth process" (p. 193). To continue to equate our identity and our work solely with first-year composition as it is presently configured keeps us restricted and unfulfilled. By contrast, under the rhetoricians' concept, it is possible to imagine a rhetorical discipline and a set of courses in a broad range of literate practices.[6] Rhetoric then may provide the sledgehammer that will enable us to reconfigure the discipline and reconstruct, in meaningful ways, the study and teaching of literate practices.

ACKNOWLEDGMENTS

I want to acknowledge Richard Young, David Shumway, and David Fowler for their generous contributions to another project that provided the groundwork for this discussion.

REFERENCES

Anson, C. M., & Miller, H. (1988). Journals in composition: An update. *College Composition and Communication, 39,* 198–216.

Archer, J. W. (1955). Six-year history of the CCCC. *College Composition and Communication, 6,* 221–223.

Becher, T. (1989). *Academic tribes and territories: Intellectual enquiry and the cultures of disciplines.* Milton Keynes, England: Society for Research in Higher Education/Open University Press.

Berlin, J. A. (1982). Contemporary composition: The major pedagogical theories. *College English, 44,* 765–777.

Berlin, J. A. (1984). *Writing instruction in nineteenth century American colleges.* Carbondale: Southern Illinois University Press.

Berlin, J. A. (1987). *Rhetoric and reality: Writing instruction in American colleges, 1900–1985.* Carbondale: Southern Illinois University Press.

Blair, C. (1992). Contested histories of rhetoric: The politics of preservation, progress, and change. *Quarterly Journal of Speech, 78,* 403–428.

Booth, W. C. (1965). The revival of rhetoric. *Publications of the Modern Language Association of America, 80,* 8–12.

Brown, S. C., Meyer, P. R., & Enos, T. (1994). Doctoral programs in rhetoric and composition: A catalog of the profession. *Rhetoric Review, 12,* 240–389.

Burhans, C. S., Jr. (1983). The teaching of writing and the knowledge gap. *College English, 45,* 639–656.

Burke, K. (1966). *Language as symbolic action: Essays on life, literature, and method.* Berkeley: University of California Press.

---

[6]The arguments for why rhetoric has provided an attractive intellectual and pedagogical alternative to composition are far too complex to explicate in any satisfactory way here. For individual stories of why rhetoric, and specifically, classical rhetoric has provided a rich framework for some in our field, see Nelms and Goggin (1993). On a larger level, an epistemic shift that overturned modernity, moving us toward postmodernism is no doubt significantly responsible for permitting a more dynamic, complex, and rigorous understanding of rhetoric. See, for example, Foucault's (1972) discussion of epistemes.

Butts, R. F. (1978). *Public education in the United States: From revolution to reform.* New York: Holt.

Cahn, M. (1993). The rhetoric of rhetoric: Six tropes of disciplinary self-constitution. In R. H. Roberts & J. M. M. Good (Eds.), *The recovery of rhetoric: Persuasive discourse and disciplinarity in the human sciences* (pp. 61–84). Charlottesville: University Press of Virginia.

Combies, P. L. (1987). *The struggle to establish a profession: A historical survey of the status of composition teachers, 1900–1950.* Unpublished doctoral dissertation, Carnegie Mellon University, Pittsburgh, PA.

Conley, T. M. (1990). *Rhetoric in the European tradition.* New York: Longman.

Connors, R. J. (1993, October). *Learning from the past: What's new about the new abolitionism.* Paper presented at Composition in the 21st Century: Crisis and Change, Oxford, OH.

Corbett, E. P. J. (1965). *Classical rhetoric for the modern student.* New York: Oxford University Press.

Crowley, S. (1986). The perilous life and times of freshman English. *Freshman English News, 14,* 11–16.

Crowley, S. (1990). *The methodical memory: Invention in current-traditional rhetoric.* Carbondale: Southern Illinois University Press.

Douglas, W. (1985). Accidental institution: On the origin of modern language study. In G. Graff & R. Gibbons (Eds.), *Criticism in the university* (pp. 35–61). Evanston, IL: Northwestern University Press.

Elliott, A. M. (1889). Secretary's report. *Publications of the Modern Language Association of America, 6,* vi–viii.

Enos, R. L. (1993). *Greek rhetoric before Aristotle.* Prospect Heights, IL: Waveland Press.

Enos, T. (1990). Gender and publishing. *Pre/Text, 11,* 311–316.

Foucault, M. (1972). *The archaeology of knowledge* (A. M. Sheridan Smith, Trans.). New York: Colophon/Harper & Row.

Francis, W. N. (1953). Our responsibility to the English language. *College English, 14,* 328–332.

Franklin, P. (1978). English studies in America: Reflections on the development of a discipline. *American Quarterly, 30,* 21–38.

Franklin, P. (1984). English studies: The world of scholarship in 1883. *Publications of the Modern Language Association of America, 99,* 356–370.

Freidson, E. (1986). *Professional powers: A study of the institutionalization of formal knowledge.* Chicago: The University of Chicago Press.

Gerber, J. C. (1952). Three-year history of the CCCC. *College Composition and Communication, 3*(3) 17–18.

Gerber, J. C. (1956). CCCC facts—1956. *College Composition and Communication, 7,* 117–120.

Gerber, J. C. (1960). Committee on future directions. *College Composition and Communication, 11,* 3–7.

Goggin, M. D. (1994). *The shaping of a discipline: An historical study of the authorizing role of professional journals in rhetoric and composition, 1950–1990.* Unpublished doctoral dissertation, Carnegie Mellon University, Pittsburgh, PA.

Goggin, M. D., & Long, E. (1993). A tincture of philosophy, a tincture of hope: The portrayal of Isocrates in Plato's *Phaedrus. Rhetoric Review, 11,* 301–324.

Gorrell, R. M. (1961). Philosophy and structure. *College Composition and Communication, 12,* 14–18.

Greenbaum, L. (1969). The tradition of complaint. *College English, 31,* 174–187.

Hackett, H. (1955). A discipline of the communication skills. *College Composition and Communication, 6,* 10–15.

Hairston, M. (1985). Breaking our bonds and reaffirming our connections. *College Composition and Communication, 36,* 272–282.

Hamilton-Wieler, S. (1988). Empty echoes of Dartmouth: Dissonance between the rhetoric and the reality. *The Writing Instructor, 8,* 29–41.

Hartzog, C. P. (1986). *Composition and the academy: A study of writing program administration.* New York: Modern Language Association.

Hatfield, W. W. (1959). James Fleming Hosic: 11 October 1870–13 January 1959. *College English, 20,* 307–308.

Hook, J. N. (1955). The CCCC and the NCTE. *College Composition and Communication, 6,* 218–221.

Hook, J. N. (1979). *A long way together: A personal view of NCTE's first sixty-seven years.* Urbana, IL: National Council of Teachers of English.

Horner, W. B. (Ed.). (1983). *Composition and literature: Bridging the gap.* Chicago: University of Chicago Press.

Hoskin, K. (1993). Education and the genesis of disciplinarity: The unexpected reversal. In E. Messer-Davidow, D. R. Shumway, & D. J. Sylvan (Eds.), *Knowledges: Historical and critical studies in disciplinarity* (pp. 271–304). Charlottesville: University Press of Virginia.

Huber, B. J. (1992). The changing job market. *Profession, 92,* 59–73.

Hunt, T. W. (1884). The place of English in the college curriculum. *Publications of the Modern Language Association of America, 1,* 118–132.

Jarratt, S. C. (1991). *Rereading the sophists: Classical rhetoric refigured.* Carbondale: Southern Illinois University Press.

Jarratt, S. C. (1993). Afterword. In V. J. Vitanza (Ed.), *Pre/Text: The first decade* (pp. 282–285). Pittsburgh, PA: University of Pittsburgh Press.

Kaufer, D. S., & Carley, K. (1993). *Communication at a distance: The influence of print on sociocultural organization and change.* Hillsdale, NJ: Lawrence Erlbaum Associates.

Kennedy, G. A. (1980). *Classical rhetoric and its Christian and secular tradition from ancient to modern times.* Chapel Hill: University of North Carolina Press.

Kitzhaber, A. R. (1990). *Rhetoric in American colleges, 1850–1900.* Dallas, TX: Southern Methodist University Press. (Original work published 1953)

Knoblauch, C. H., & Brannon, L. (1984). *Rhetorical traditions and the teaching of writing.* Montclair, NJ: Boynton/Cook.

Kuhn, T. (1970). *The structure of scientific revolutions* (2nd ed.). Chicago: University of Chicago Press.

Kultgen, J. (1988). *Ethics and professionalism.* Philadelphia: University of Pennsylvania Press.

Larson, R. L. (1994). Enlarging the context: From teaching just writing, to teaching academic subjects *with* writing. In W. R. Winterowd & V. Gillespie (Eds.), *Composition in context: Essays in honor of Donald C. Stewart* (pp. 109–125). Carbondale: Southern Illinois University Press.

Lauer, J. (1984). Composition studies: Dappled discipline. *Rhetoric Review, 3,* 20–29.

Lloyd-Jones, R. (1978). A view from the center. *College Composition and Communication, 29,* 24–29.

Miller, S. (1991). *Textual carnivals: The politics of composition.* Carbondale: Southern Illinois University Press.

Moglen, H. (1988). Report on the commission on writing and literature. *Profession, 88,* 70–76

Murphy, J. J. (Ed.). (1990). *A short history of writing instruction from ancient Greece to twentieth century America.* Davis, CA: Hermagoras Press.

Nelms, G., & Goggin, M. D. (1993). The revival of rhetoric for modern composition studies: A survey. *Rhetoric Society Quarterly, 23,* 11–26.

North, S. M. (1987). *The making of knowledge in composition: Portrait of an emerging field.* Upper Montclair, NJ: Boynton/Cook.

Parker, W. R. (1953). The MLA, 1883–1953. *Publications of the Modern Language Association of America, 68,* 3–39.

Petraglia, J. (1995). Spinning like a kite: A closer look at the psuedotransactional function of writing. *Journal of Advanced Composition, 15*(1), 19–33.

Phelps, L. W. (1988). *Composition as a human science: Contributions to the self-understanding of a discipline.* New York: Oxford University Press.

Phelps, L. W. (1991). Practical wisdom and the geography of knowledge in composition. *College English, 53,* 863–885.

Raymond, J. C. (1987). *College English:* Whence and whither. *College English, 49,* 553–557.

Resnick, D. P., & Resnick, L. B. (1977). The nature of literacy: An historical exploration. *Harvard Education Review, 47,* 370–385.

Rice, W. G. (1960). A proposal for the abolition of freshman English, as it is now commonly taught, from the college curriculum. *College English, 21,* 361–367.

Roberts, C. W. (1950). Editorial comment. *College Composition and Communication, 1*(3), 22.

Roberts, C. W. (1955). A course for training rhetoric teachers at the University of Illinois. *College Composition and Communication, 6,* 190–194.

Robertson, L. R., Crowley, S., & Lentricchia, F. (1987). The Wyoming Conference Resolution opposing unfair salaries and working conditions for post-secondary teachers of writing. *College English, 49,* 274–280.

Robertson, L. R., & Slevin, J. F. (1987). The status of composition faculty: Resolving reforms. *Rhetoric Review, 5,* 190–194.

Rudolph, F. (1977). *Curriculum: A history of the American undergraduate curriculum since 1936.* San Francisco: Jossey-Bass.

Rudolph, F. (1990). *The American college and university: A history.* New York: Vintage. (Original work published 1962)

Russell, D. R. (1991). *Writing in the academic disciplines, 1870–1990: A curricular history.* Carbondale: Southern Illinois University Press.

Russell, D. R. (1993). Vygotsky, Dewey, and externalism: Beyond the student/discipline dichotomy. *Journal of Advanced Composition, 13,* 173–197.

Schilb, J. (1989). Composition and poststructuralism: A tale of two conferences. *College Composition and Communication, 40,* 422–443.

Schilb, J. (1991). What's at stake in the conflict between "theory" and "practice" in composition? *Rhetoric Review, 10,* 91–97.

Schilb, J. (1994). Getting disciplined? *Rhetoric Review, 12,* 398–405.

Shumway, D. R. (1985). A unified-field theory for English. *Reader, 14,* 54–67.

Smith, L. Z. (1993). Profession and vocation: Trends in publication. *Focuses, 6,* 75–86.

Stewart, D. C. (1978). Composition textbooks and the assault on tradition. *College Composition and Communication, 29,* 171–176.

Stewart, D. C. (1985). The status of composition and rhetoric in American colleges, 1880–1902: An MLA perspective. *College English, 47,* 734–746.

Stratton, R. E. (1985). The profession, 1984 (part one). *Rhetoric Review, 3,* 164–178.

Tate, G. (1972). From the editor. *Freshman English News, 1,* 1.

Tate, G. (1993). A place for literature in freshman composition. *College English, 55,* 317–321.

Toulmin, S. (1972). *Human understanding* (Vol. 1). Princeton, NJ: Princeton University Press.

Vandenberg, P. (1993) *The politics of knowledge dissemination: Academic journals in composition studies.* Unpublished doctoral dissertation, Texas Christian University, Fort Worth.

Varnum, R. (1986). From crisis to crisis: The evolution toward higher standards of literacy in the United States. *Rhetoric Society Quarterly, 16,* 145–166.

Veysey, L. R. (1965). *The emergence of the American university.* Chicago: University of Chicago Press.

Vitanza, V. J. (1987). Rhetoric's past and future: A conversation with Edward P. J. Corbett. *Pre/Text, 8,* 247–264.

Ward, W. S. (1960). A short history of the NCTE college section. *College English, 22,* 71–76.

Welch, K. E. (1987). Ideology and freshman textbook production: The place of theory in writing pedagogy. *College Composition and Communication, 38,* 269–282.

Welch, K. E. (1990). *The contemporary reception of classical rhetoric: Appropriations of ancient discourse.* Hillsdale, NJ: Lawrence Erlbaum Associates.

Wilson, G. (1967). CCCC in retrospect. *College Composition and Communication, 18,* 127–134.

Winterowd, W. R., & Gillespie, V. (1994). Editor's introduction. In W. R. Winterowd & V. Gillespie (Eds.), *Composition in context: Essays in honor of Donald C. Stewart* (pp. vii–xiii). Carbondale: Southern Illinois University Press.

Wyche-Smith, S., & Rose, S. K. (1990). One hundred ways to make the Wyoming Resolution a reality: A guide to personal and political action. *College Composition and Communication, 41,* 318–324.

Yoos, G. E. (1990). Ich gelobe meine treue dem banner. *Rhetoric Society Quarterly, 20,* 5–12.

Young, R. (1978). Paradigms and problems: Needed research in rhetorical invention. In C. R. Cooper & L. Odell (Eds.), *Research on composing: Points of departure* (pp. 29–47). Urbana, IL: National Council of Teachers of English.

Young, R. E., Becker, A. L., & Pike, K. L. (1970). *Rhetoric: Discovery and change.* San Diego: Harcourt Brace Jovanovich.

II

Classroom Writing Within Social and Cognitive Frameworks

3

Activity Theory and Its Implications for Writing Instruction

David Russell
Iowa State University

The United States is the only nation that requires of most students in higher education a course in what is known as *composition*. That is, a course in what Kaufer and Young (1993) called "writing with no particular content," or what many contributors to this anthology are calling general writing skills instruction (GWSI). Other nations teach what Kaufer and Young term "writing with specific content" as part of the regular learning of a discipline and allot virtually no curricular space in higher education for formal writing instruction per se.

The U.S. system has many benefits. It has the potential for making students more aware of the uses of written discourse in higher education and in society. It can and often does provide a curricular space for welcoming students to higher education and thus, potentially, for broadening rather than restricting access to those social roles colleges and universities prepare and credential students to enter. Since the 1960s, GWSI courses have provided a focus for an unprecedented research effort on writing in a range of social institutions.

However, there are trade-offs. The fundamental limitations of GWSI courses in higher education have been felt since the courses were begun over a century ago, and many have called for the abolition of this peculiar U.S. curricular institution. Seven years ago I published an article tracing the history of attempts to abolish first-year composition courses (Russell, 1988). I discussed Kitzhaber's (1960) famous article, "Death—Or Transfiguration," as an antiabolitionist argument, because it was written in response to Rice's (1960) "Proposal for the Abolition of Freshman English."

However, on rereading Kitzhaber's article in light of the last 7 years of growth in writing across the curriculum programs and research into writing in academic and nonacademic settings in the United States and abroad, I now see his article in a different light. It is at bottom another call for abolition of GWSI, and a very prescient one, as well as a call for a first-year course *about* writing.

Let me summarize four of Kitzhaber's points, points that seem to me to describe the current state of first-year composition as well as they described its state three decades ago when Kitzhaber (1963) conducted his major national research study of the course, *Themes, Theories, and Therapy*. First, he said, there is a "lack of general agreement about course content, so that depending on the prejudices of the teacher, departmental policy (or lack of it), or current fads, the course may center on" (p. 367). There follows a list of 1950s approaches, for which one could supply an equally long and varied list of 1990s approaches. Second, the course cannot "be said even by the most charitably disposed critic to be on the same level of intellectual rigor and maturity as textbooks and class work in other freshman courses such as chemistry or economics" (p. 367).

Third, Kitzhaber called the aims of the course "over-ambitious—to eradicate, in three hours a week for 30 or 35 weeks, habits of thought and expression that have been forming for at least 15 years and to which the student is as closely wedded as he is to his skin; and to fix indelibly a different set of habits from which the student will never afterwards deviate" (p. 367). Fourth, instead of going on to defend the course, as one might expect in a rebuttal to an attack on it, Kitzhaber admitted that those who have studied its effectiveness (and no one had studied this more than he) have "too seldom" been able to find "a comforting relationship between the degree of improvement and the quantity of labor expended" (p. 367). Such a relationship might exist, he said, but it is difficult to tease out of the complex of factors that make up the improvement of writing (p. 367).

Kitzhaber went on to argue that these problems are inherent in the course's institutional position in U.S. education. That is, he did not argue that the course merely needs firmer content, more intellectual rigor, more realistic expectations, and greater effectiveness. The problems of the course cannot be understood by looking at the course itself, but only by analyzing the relation of the course to the U.S. education system. Kitzhaber concluded by proposing, as I repropose, what he called a *transfiguration* of the first-year composition course, not another reform of it.

In this article I extend Kitzhaber's analysis of these longstanding problems of GWSI using the framework of activity theory. I first explain the theory and use it to analyze the problems. Second, I use the theory to analyze the institutional position of GWSI courses. Finally, I re-examine two reforms Kitzhaber suggested in the structure of secondary and higher education that, he argued, will permit the transfiguration of first-year composition courses as we know them. The first and most important is the expansion of writing across the curriculum. The second is the creation of a liberal arts course in the uses of writing in society, which would redeem the curricular space now occupied by GWSI for activities that may better accomplish the democratic goals of U.S. higher education. I conclude by suggesting that through these reforms we might preserve and extend the many benefits that composition studies have given and continue to give to U.S. higher education while overcoming the structural problems inherent in GWSI.

ACTIVITY THEORY

Activity theory is a tradition of psychological theory and research originating with the Soviet psychologist Vygotsky in the late 1920s and early 1930s. It was first developed by his colleagues Leont'ev, who coined the term, and Luria (Wertsch, 1981). Beginning in the 1970s, developmental psychologists and educational researchers in several other nations elaborated the theory and conducted empirical research, both quantitative and qualitative. In the United States, activity theory first influenced studies of literacy through the work of Scribner, Cole, and others at the Laboratory for Comparative Human Cognition. In the 1980s the theoretical tradition also became central to related lines of research into cognition in everyday life, particularly of adults engaged in labor and the acquisition of labor-specific practices through apprenticeship (Lave & Wenger, 1991; Rogoff, 1993). Although this tradition is by no means the dominant one in U.S. developmental psychology, activity theory is an increasingly important perspective.

Activity theory analyzes human behavior and consciousness in terms of *activity systems*: goal-directed, historically situated, cooperative human interactions, such as a child's attempt to reach an out-of-reach toy, a job interview, a "date," a social club, a classroom, a discipline, a profession, an institution, a political movement, and so on. The activity system is the basic unit of analysis for both cultures' and individuals' psychological and social processes. This unit is a functional system (see Fig. 3.1) consisting of a subject (a person or persons), an object(ive) (an objective or goal or common task), and tools (including signs) that mediate the interaction (Engestrom, 1987). I use the term *object(ive)* because it refers not only to persons or objects in a passive state (what is acted on) but also to the goal of an intentional activity, an *objective*, although the objective may be envisioned differently by different participants in the activity system.

In an activity system, the object(ive) remains the same and the mediational means, the tools, may vary. In a very simple activity system,

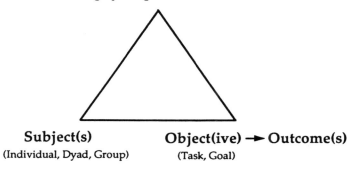

Mediational Means (Tools)

(Machines, Writing, Speaking, Gesture, Architecture, Music, etc.)

Subject(s)   **Object(ive)** → **Outcome(s)**

(Individual, Dyad, Group)   (Task, Goal)

FIG. 3.1. An activity system.

for example, a 2-year-old child (subject) wishes to reach a toy on a high shelf (object[ive]). She might drag a chair (one mediational means or tool) under the shelf and climb up to reach the toy, or in frustration she might cry out for her father (another mediational means or tool—a verbal sign) who might get a chair for her. Or her father might point to a chair (another—an indexical sign), describe what to do (another verbal sign), or even demonstrate its use in this activity (another—a gestural sign). An invariant function (reaching an object out of reach) may be performed by variable mechanisms, but the functional system, the activity, is the same.

Although activity theory is very much open and developing, most theorists in the tradition recognize five key constituents of activity systems. Activity systems are historically developed, mediated by tools, dialectically structured, analyzed as the relations of participants and tools, and changed through *zones of proximal development*.

First, activity systems have histories that are essential to their workings. For human beings, these histories are predominantly cultural (although phylogenic change may also play a role). New interactions with the present environment arise from a dialog with the cultural past, preserved in mediational means (artifacts, texts, etc.). Mediational means (tools) may consist not only of tools in the usual sense (hammers, computers) but also semiotic tools: speaking and writing, as well as gestures, music, architecture, physical position, naturally occurring objects, and so on (Engestrom, 1990; Smagorinsky & Coppock, 1994, in press). Texts are tools for carrying on some activity and they vary with the activity, just as hammers vary in their design and use depending on the work to be done using them. Variance in semiotic tools according to the activity might be called *genre*. The tools within each culture and each activity system within it have a history, and that history is reflected in their form and/or use, whether ordinary tools such as hammers, or tools such as the marks on a page called writing, or tools such as the moon when it is used, say, for navigation. For human beings (apart from the few instances of *enfants sauvages*), all mediational means are cultural, with meanings arising from the history of their use. For those tools that are in the form of texts, meanings almost always arise in relation to previous texts (intertextually) as well as in relation to nontextual phenomena. Every word, as Bakhtin (1986) put it, carries with it its history.

Second, as the example of the child suggests, changes in human behavior and consciousness, individual or collective, are mediated by other human beings through the use of tools (in the example: the chair, the child's cry, the father's pointing, etc.). No mind is self-sufficient. Activity systems are inherently social. Change occurs through the historically situated interactions of people and tools over time. As Leont'ev (1981) wrote, an activity system is not "an aggregate of reactions, but a system with its own structure, its own internal transformations, and its own development. . . . If we removed human activity from the system of social relationships and social life, it would not exist and would have no structure" (pp. 46–47). Human activities are complex systems in constant change, interaction, and self-reorganization as human beings collaboratively adapt to and transform their environments through their actions with tools (including writing). Thus, consciousness is not individual but intersubjective, networks of systems mediated by our tools of interaction. Indeed, to paraphrase Robert Frost, human activity is social whether we work together or alone, for even the writer alone in a study is formed by and (potentially) forming the actions of others through the tool of writing. The solitary writer is part of some activity systems that give meaning and motive to individual acts of composition.

Third, activity systems are dialectal. Change is not unidirectional. It is accomplished through joint activity, whether cooperative or conflictual, face-to-face or widely separated in space or time. The participants in an activity system *appropriate* (borrow and transform) the tools and object(ive)s and points of view of others, leading to changes in the means of pursuing the object(ive) of the activity system. For example, a discipline may appropriate some terminology (and thus concept) from another discipline and thus transform the way it goes about its work, just as it might appropriate a mechanical research instrument from another discipline. In the process, it may also transform the terminology it has appropriated, investing it with new meaning, just as it might redesign for its own object(ive) mechanical research instruments appropriated from another discipline.

Fourth, the unit of analysis in activity theory is not the workings of an individual mind but the relations among the participants and their shared cultural tools. Thus, activity systems can be analyzed from multiple perspectives (of the various participants) and at many levels (from the individual to the broadest cultural levels). An analyst can shift among multiple views to study an activity system, triangulating the various views (Engestrom, 1990). A central question for activity theory analysis is choosing the most useful "lenses" or perspectives for analysis among the many possible ones (Rogoff, 1993).

Fifth and finally, activity theory explains change in terms of the zone of proximal development (ZPD): the object(ive)-directed interactions among people, where one or more of the participants could not, by themselves, effectively work toward the objective (Newman, Griffin, & Cole, 1989). In these "construction zones," writing and learning take place as people, using their tools, mutually change themselves and their tools. All learning is situated within some activity system(s), and one learns by participating—directly or vicariously—in some activity system(s).

From this perspective, adolescents and adults do not "learn to write," period; nor do they improve their writing in a general way outside of all activity systems and then apply an autonomous skill to them. Rather, one acquires the genres (typified semiotic means) used by some activity field as one interacts with people involved in the activity field and the material objects and signs those people use (including those marks on a surface that we call writing). This activity theory formulation of the acquisition of writing resists what Street (1984) termed the *myth of autonomous literacy*. Literacy is not learned in and of itself and then applied to contexts (activity systems). It does not exist autonomously, divorced from some specific human activity. Literacy is always and everywhere bound up with the activity systems that it changes through its mediation of behavior—and that change it. Writing is an immensely protean tool that activity systems are always and everywhere changing to meet their needs.

ACTIVITY THEORY ANALYSIS OF GWSI AS WRITING WITH NO PARTICULAR CONTENT

What is the activity system of a first-year composition course? The subjects of the activity are clear: the students and the teachers, primarily. However, the object(ive) and the semiotic tools of the activity system are extremely ambiguous, and this ambiguity may help explain the four problems Kitzhaber noted. I examine two traditional formulations of the object(ive)s of the course: improving students writing in general and teaching students a general academic or public discourse.

GWSI as Teaching or Improving Writing in General

The object(ive) of GWSI is most often described as teaching students "to write" or to "improve their writing." If writing were an autonomous skill generalizable to all activity systems that use writing, improving writing in general would be a clear object(ive) of an activity system. However, writing does not exist apart from its uses, for it is a tool for accomplishing object(ive)s beyond itself. The tool is continually transformed by its use into myriad and always-changing genres. Every text is some genre, to paraphrase Bakhtin (1986), part of some activity system(s). Learning to write means learning to write in the ways (genres) those in an activity system write (although one must remember that this is complicated by the fact that activity systems and their tools—including genres—are always in dialectical change). From this theoretical perspective, the object(ive) of GWSI courses is extremely ambiguous because those involved in it are teaching and learning the use of a tool (writing) for no particular activity system, and the tool can be used for any number of object(ive)s (in myriad activity systems) and transformed into any number of forms (genres).

To illustrate the ambiguity inherent in GWSI courses, let me draw an analogy between games that require a particular kind of tool—a ball—and activity systems (disciplines, professions, businesses, etc.) that require a particular kind of tool—the marks that we call writing. Many different games are played with a ball. The originators of each game have appropriated this tool for the object(ive) of each, the "object of the game." The kind of game (activity system) changes the form of the ball (tool)—large, small, hard, soft, leather, rubber, round, oblong, and so on. The object(ive) and the history of each game also condition the uses of the ball. One could play volleyball by using the head, as in soccer, but it is much less effective in achieving the object of the game than using the wrists and hands.

Some people are very adept at some games and therefore at using some kinds of balls, whereas they may be completely lost using a ball in another game because they have never participated in it. (I play ping-pong pretty well, but my 9-year-old daughter laughs at my fumbling attempts to play another game with a ball of similar size—jacks.) However, ways of using a ball (ball handling, if you will) are "generalizable" to the extent that in two or more games the tool (ball) is used in similar ways for similar object(ive)s. A good croquet player might easily learn to putt, or a good tennis player learn squash. However, there is no autonomous, generalizable skill called ball using or ball handling that can be learned and then applied to all ball games.

As one becomes adept at more and more ball games (and thus learns more ways of using more kinds of balls), it is more likely—but by no means certain—that one will be able to learn a new ball game more quickly, because it is more likely that there will be some ways of ball using in the new game that resemble ways of ball using in a game one already knows. It may also be true that one may have "learned how to learn" ball games. That is, a person may have learned how to keep one's eye on the ball, how to monitor one's movements in relation to the ball, how to watch more experienced players for clues on ball handling, and so on. However, this does not mean that person's ball-using skill is autonomous and general in any meaningful sense. It is the accumulation of some specific ball-using skills (and not others) learned in some specific ball games that bear some similarities.

To try to teach students to improve their writing by taking a GWSI course is something like trying to teach people to improve their ping-pong, jacks, volleyball, basketball, field hockey, and so on by attending a course in general ball using. Such a course would of necessity have a problem of content. What kinds of games (and therefore ball-use skills) should one teach? How can one teach ball-using skills unless one also teaches students the games, because the skills have their motive and meaning only in terms of a particular game or games that use them? Such a course would have a problem of rigor because those who truly know how to play a particular game would look askance at the instruction such a course could provide (particularly if the instructor did not herself play all the games with some facility). It would also have a problem of unrealistic expectations, because it would be impossible to teach all—or even a few—ball games in one course. Finally, it would be extremely difficult to evaluate the effectiveness of a course in general ball using because one always evaluates the effectiveness of ball using within a particular game, not in general. Ways of using a ball that work well in one game (e.g., volleyball) would bring disaster in another (such as soccer).

Let us apply the analogy to GWSI. Many different kinds of activity systems are carried on with writing (to many of them, writing is as indispensable as balls are to ball games). The kind of activity—its object(ive) and its history—changes the way the tool, writing, is used. The activity also changes the tool itself: the grammar, lexicon, format, and so on. These differences, as I noted earlier, might be called genres—historically constituted ways of forming and using this tool called writing among the people who carry on an activity. Some people are very adept at writing certain genres because they have participated a great deal in the activity system that uses them, whereas they may be much less adept (or even incompetent, from the point of view of an adept) at writing a genre from an activity system in which they have not participated. A Nobel Laureate who wrote a world-changing scientific paper might fail miserably at writing a straight news account of the discovery for the front page of the local newspaper, although the scientist reads the newspaper every day. This is because scientists do not ordinarily participate in the activity system of journalism and have not learned its genres.

Like the handling of balls, the writing of genres is generalizable to the extent that written text is handled in similar ways for similar object(ive)s. A person who can write a footnote in a history paper may find it easier to learn to write a footnote in a chemistry paper than a person who has never written a footnote (although the differences in citation purposes and practices may actually make it more difficult—what second language teachers call *interference*; Swales, 1990). However, from the activity theory perspective I am developing here, there is no autonomous, generalizable skill or set of skills called "writing" that can be learned and then applied to all genres or activities.

As one becomes adept at more and more activities that require writing and hence at writing more genres, it is more likely (but by no means certain) that one will be able to master a new genre more quickly, because it is more likely that there will be some features of the new genre or activity that resemble features in a genre or activity one already knows. It may also be true that a person may have "learned how to learn" new genres. That is, one may have learned to be alert to the role language plays in an activity system, to take instruction from an adept in the genres one is trying to learn, to notice the differences in writing processes of various activity systems, and so on. Indeed, research in second language acquisition suggests strongly that it is easier for adults to learn a third language than a second, and perhaps the same is true for learning genres (Ellis, 1994).

However, to try to teach students to improve their writing in general by taking a GWSI course is to encounter the problems of our mythical ball-using course, the longstanding problems Kitzhaber noted with first-year composition courses.

1. Disagreements over content spring from the inevitability of linking writing to some activity system(s) and thus certain genres. One must always choose genres—and hence choose the activity systems that give those genres meaning and purpose. But which genres and activities, out of the myriad?

2. Problems of rigor arise from the distance between the activity of GWSI teaching and the activities that gave rise to (and thus meaning to) the genres that are taught. Those who know well the activity systems from which GWSI's genres are drawn must inevitably find the coverage in those courses shallow because the genres are taught under severe time constraints and by faculty largely unacquainted with the activity systems for which the genres exist. It is not surprising that writing is treated as detached techniques or skills, divorced from the object(ive)s that give the genres their meaning.

3. Unrealistic expectations are inevitable when the course has as its object the teaching or improvement of all writing, because one can only introduce a tiny fraction of the possible genres.

4. It is extremely difficult to evaluate the effectiveness of the course because outside the activity system of GWSI, one always evaluates the effectiveness of writing within a particular activity system and its object(ive), not in general.

GWSI as Teaching Academic or Public Discourse

A second frequently mentioned object(ive) for GWSI courses is that they teach students to write or to write better what is thought of as a universal educated discourse, a general kind of discourse that all educated (or truly educated) persons in a culture share. This hypothetical universal educated discourse (UED) is most often termed *academic discourse* or, even more broadly, *public discourse*. These formulations of the activity system of composition seem to narrow somewhat the genres (and thus the content) of GWSI, but like the myth of autonomous literacy, of which they are really a part, they also rest on a widely held myth about the nature of discourse, a myth of UED. From the activity theory perspective I am developing, there is no distinctive genre, set of genres, linguistic register, or set of conventions that is academic discourse or public discourse per se, because "academia" and the "public" are not activity systems in any useful sense for writing instruction. These categories create and preserve the false notion that there can exist "good writing" independent of an activity system that judges the success of a text by its results within that activity system, and that the teaching and learning of such writing can be divorced from any activity system beyond GWSI (Miller, 1991).

Academia in general has no object(ive) that those carrying on its immensely varied activities share. It exists to select and prepare people for a wide range of activity systems within and beyond institutions of higher education. From this perspective, academic discourse consists of the dynamic aggregate of all the many specialized discourses of all the activity systems (disciplines and departments) that make up academia. The protean tool called writing is appropriated and transformed by each activity system according to its object(ive)s and the material conditions of its work to evolve myriad genres within academia. The genres of various disciplines within academia are much more usefully characterized by their differences in discourse than by their similarities. Disciplinary discourses vary immensely, and even when activity systems appropriate identical discourse features, they do so for differing object(ive)s and thus often use the features differently. For example, pointing to the footnotes in a theoretical physics article and those in an article from *Publications of the*

Modern Language Association (PMLA) would not be very helpful to a novice learning to write in both genres, as compared with pointing out the very different object(ive)s of the two disciplines' activity systems, the very different material conditions of their work, and the vast differences in their histories—differences that explain the profound and crucial differences in their *uses* of citation and documentation (Bazerman, 1988).

Moreover, many of the genres written in institutions of higher education are not particular to academia, because many of the activity systems involved in academic institutions are also involved in other, nonacademic institutions, and with them their genres. Thus, any feature of academic writing that one might point to will also likely be found in a great deal of nonacademic writing, and it is those connections—not the connections among academic departments—that are most important to those who use writing. Many texts written by chemists, engineers, economists, creative writers, musicians, and so on outside of academia are virtually indistinguishable from many texts written by their counterparts within academia, and vice versa. An activity system with its object(ive) and tools—including the tools I have called genres—is not confined to one institution but can be shared among several. For example, the writing of an ecologist in a biology department will likely have far more in common with the writing of people of engaged in studying and preserving the environment in a government agency or nonprofit organization than with the writing of colleagues down the hall in history or engineering, because ecologists in various institutional settings share certain object(ive)s, a certain history passed on through their training, and certain tools of their activity (including genres) that have developed historically to meet those object(ive)s.

As in all institutions that bring together people from many activity systems, universities appropriate and evolve genres to carry on their common work: interdepartmental memos and proposals, course catalogs, policy and mission statements, forms, minutes of governing bodies, contracts, and so on. However, these are not characteristically "academic discourse" either, as they resemble similar genres evolved for similar bureaucratic purposes in large governmental, corporate, and nonprofit organizations.

In the same way that academic discourse consists of an aggregate of activity systems (and therefore discourses) that do not share an object(ive) or a discrete set of genres, public discourse consists of the all the dynamic, interacting, activity systems (and therefore genres) through which public life is negotiated: news stories; advertisements; position papers; trial testimony; transcripts of the deliberations of public bodies; government reports; press releases by unions, corporations, or consumer groups; brochures; and confidential documents leaked to the press. These activity systems do not share a single object(ive). Their interests vary, and so do their genres.

These activity systems and their genres are constantly interacting dialectically as they pursue their different object(ive)s and negotiate their different interests. An activity system sometimes appropriates features of the genres of other—usually more powerful—activity systems in order to pursue its object(ive)s (e.g., contesting a law that affects it, replying to accusations of misconduct in the press, etc.). A discipline or profession appropriates a term or some other feature of a genre from another discipline or profession in order to accomplish its work.

Indeed, whole activity systems have developed to facilitate the dialectical interactions (and thus appropriation of discourse features) among activity systems: journalists specializing in science, negotiators and arbitrators, congressional aides, lobbyists, and communications and public relations specialists. For example, the Modern Language Association (MLA) (an activity system specializing in the study of discourse) in 1993 hired a public relations firm to explain its actions—and its discourse—to the press, after the MLA had been unsuccessful in countering press reports that had been damaging to its reputation. Such specialists in turn develop their own genres to carry on their activity of facilitating the interaction of activity systems. Sometimes these specialists even evolve academic programs to select and prepare neophytes (e.g., public relations, science journalism, etc.).

However, in these dialectical processes there is no overarching academic or public discourse that exists beyond the interaction of specific activity systems, no metalanguage into which one could "translate" the "jargon" of an activity system. A text is never academic or public discourse per se. It is, to appropriate Bakhtin's (1986) phrase again, "always some genre"—part of some activity system(s). No single genre or subset of genres includes the whole of public discourse, for no activity that requires written discourse is shared by all citizens or even all educated citizens. Journalism perhaps comes closest, but it too has its own techniques, its own discourse features ("jargon"), its own genres that require participation in the activity system of journalism to learn—and it has its own academic discipline and department.

Although no autonomous genre or discrete set of genres exists that can meaningfully be called "academic" or "public" or "educated" discourse, people nevertheless interact (speak, write, use numbers, etc.) in ways that other people recognize as "educated" or "college educated" or "uneducated." That recognition depends on the history and activities of the group doing the recognizing. A person can participate (or have participated) in many activity systems. In modern or postmodern societies, some powerful activity systems in, for example, government and the media, interact with a wide range of other activity systems (and their genres) to carry on their work successfully.

These powerful activity systems tend to select participants who have had a liberal arts education, not in the sense that they learned a general "academic" or "public" discourse, but in the sense that have been exposed to certain activity systems (and thus their genres) that are useful in these powerful activity systems: for example, certain formulations of economics, U.S. history, psychology, literary criticism, science, government, music, and so on. To successfully work, for example, as an editor for the *New York Times* or as a top congressional aide, one must be able to appropriate tools from various "educated" activity systems, including aspects of their genres. People in these activity systems tend to be recruited from certain institutions of higher education that provide exposure to these activity systems. This analysis suggests that to learn to write public discourse is not to learn one kind of discourse but to learn many—those that are frequently appropriated by the most powerful activity systems in a society for the genres they use to do their work.

In sum, learning to write academic discourse means learning to write some more or less specialized genre or genres. Learning to write public discourse means learning to write some more or less specialized genre or genres, because all writing is specialized in the sense that there is no overarching discourse of which others are merely subsets. Nor is there a generalizable skill or attainment called academic discourse or public discourse transferable to any academic writing situation or any situation calling for writing about public issues (Smagorinsky & Smith, 1992). To teach students to write academic discourse one must engage them in a specific activity system—and therefore specific genres—where academic work goes on.

Similarly, to prepare students to write public discourse, one might involve them in those activity systems on which much public discourse draws: through liberal arts or introductory courses in the sciences, social sciences, and humanities. One might also involve them in those activity systems—and therefore specific genres—where issues of public policy are negotiated, through professional courses that specifically train students to enter these activity systems. For example, in journalism and mass communication programs, students are taught the genres through which one may address the public at large through mass media. They learn to write a straight news story, a press release, a feature story, an advertisement, a direct mail solicitation, and a sales or grant proposal. These, however, are not the genres of GWSI.

In U.S. English departments the myth of UED has been powerful. GWSI courses are often seen as teaching an overarching discourse, which other activity systems (disciplines or professions) ought to use instead of their own "jargon." Yet GWSI courses must select genres—and thus activity systems or "content"—to teach. Because of the history of GWSI courses, these genres tend to be literary analysis (or, more recently, cultural studies), from the dominant activity systems of English departments, or essays of the type published in upscale magazines (e.g., *New Yorker*), read by those in activity systems for which GWSI courses were originally designed to prepare students when the courses were first introduced at Harvard in the 1870s (Ohmann, 1976; Wall, 1994).

Of course some genres that are often taught in GWSI classes may bring students into contact with certain activity systems where issues of public policy are negotiated (writing a letter to the editor or to a legislator, for example). So also GWSI courses—particularly those with a writing across the curriculum emphasis—sometimes expose students to some genres of some disciplines. However, because the teaching and the writing are carried on separately from the activity systems, students are only peripherally involved in the intellectual, cultural, and political activity systems these genres help to mediate. By contrast, in courses designed to teach activities other than composition, students have more opportunity to learn who the participants in an activity system are, what they do, and how and why they do it—and thus what, how, and why they write the ways they do. In these "content" courses, students can learn to write in those ways eventually, or perhaps make an informed decision to resist those ways of writing and acting.

Before GWSI courses became thoroughly institutionalized in the United States, the assumption that one could teach writing per se, without being involved intimately with a discipline's activity, struck many educators as presumptuous if not foolhardy. Thurber (1915) wrote of composition courses:

> The department of English is straining to become a forum of discussion of all questions that have assailed human intelligence. . . . Those instructors of English [who teach composition] are asked to become actively conversant with science, politics, philosophy. Though still devotees of belles lettres, they are also striving to speak with authority on every other subject. . . . Frankly the assumption is startling. May not a cog have slipped somewhere? (p. 328)

The cog metaphor is apt. Writing in GWSI courses is not *engaged* with the activity systems that give writing meaning and motive. It is, in other words, divorced from content. The problem of content lies behind the other three problems that Kitzhaber and many others before and since have found: lack of intellectual rigor, unrealistic expectations, and difficulty in assessing effectiveness. Rigor is the result of a history of using tools in certain ways for common goals, a tradition of shared expectations. Rigor is a product of an activity system where goals are shared and behavior can be assessed in terms of those goals. If literacy is not autonomous and writing is not a skill that is automatically generalizable to other activities, then the expectations placed on GWSI courses are inevitably unrealistic. If expectations are inevitably unrealistic, then it is perfectly understandable that it is difficult to assess the effectiveness of the course.

INSTITUTIONAL ANALYSIS OF COMPOSITION AS AN ACTIVITY SYSTEM

As an activity system interacts with other systems in a complex dialectic, contradictions arise that drive changes within activity systems (Engestrom, 1987) and thus within the genres that mediate their activity. GWSI is also an activity system, and its interactions with other activity systems—particularly disciplines and institutions of higher education—create a fundamental contradiction in its object(ive). It must attempt to teach writing without teaching the activities that give writing meaning and motive, those of other activity systems.

Because of this contradiction at the heart of GWSI, the course is alienated in its institutional position. GWSI is not linked to an activity system that goes beyond the GWSI course itself in the way almost all other general introductory courses are linked to disciplines and professions. It is not part of a path that leads students further into an activity system, as, for example, general chemistry or psychology leads on to the activity systems of the disciplines and professions of chemistry or psychology, within and outside academia. Some institutions do have a series of writing courses in creative, scientific, business, or technical writing that lead to careers in those disciplines and professions. However, the GWSI course is not traditionally structured to introduce students to the activities of those disciplines and professions (Russell, 1991). In activity theory terms, the course's object(ive) is contradictory, because writing in GWSI courses must be an instrument of different object(ive)s for each of the different activity systems it "serves," with no activity system of its own beyond the course itself.

This fundamental contradiction, however, has been masked by the myth of autonomous literacy and its corollary, the myth of UED. These myths mask the contradictions in the relationships of composition with the other activity systems: with English, other disciplines, institutions of higher education, and the education system as a whole.

To the institutional structure that usually houses GWSI, English departments, the course has often been seen as introducing students to or preparing them to enter its own activity system, literary criticism, and has thus served the object(ive) of that activity system (Carson, Chase, Gibson, & Hargrove, 1992). That object(ive) has conflicted with the object(ive) of higher education at large for composition: to help students write better for all courses. However, the myth of universal educated discourse has masked this contradiction by positing an overarching discourse that all disciplines (or all educated persons) use or should use. English departments have not generally had to confront the contradiction because the myth of UED allowed them to teach primarily their own discourse (and thus values) in GWSI classes as if that discourse (and those values) were, or ought to be, universal.

The myth of UED reinforced the values of the activity system of English, values that justified its distance from scientific and social scientific activity systems (Graff, 1987; Russell, 1991). English was able to criticize other disciplines for their technical "jargon" without feeling an obligation to investigate or teach the genres of other disciplines. The myth of UED served to reinforce and reproduce the values (and genres) of the activity system of literary criticism. Given its departmental position, GWSI has rarely had to engage and confront the profound differences in disciplinary discourses, because its interactions with other disciplines have been minimal. Such engagement would have made the contradiction in GWSI evident, but it would have been a distraction from the object(ive) of the activity system of literary criticism and a challenge to its values (as it would have been to any other disciplinary activity system that housed the course).

Moreover, from the perspective of English departments with large graduate programs (in which most college English teachers are trained), a central object(ive) of GWSI is the financing and training of future college English teachers—the reproduction of the discipline. It is difficult enough to train graduate students in the discourse (and pedagogy) of one activity system (literary criticism, in this case); it is simply impossible to train them in the discourses of all activity systems. Thus, the myths of autonomous literacy and UED made it possible to teach the courses that financed the reproduction and expansion of the discipline.

Other departments have also rarely had to confront the contradiction at the heart of GWSI: teaching writing without teaching the activities that give writing meaning and motive. First, the "quality" of disciplines' own writing rarely became an issue of sufficient weight to prod them into action, because their writing was and is adequate to their object(ive)s. Their genres originally evolved to meet their object(ive)s, and thus their "jargon" served their purposes well. When their genres did not serve, those genres evolved again. Second, disciplines were able to reproduce themselves (select and prepare future participants) without offering formal instruction in writing, through the normal, tacit process of apprenticeship in writing that goes on in any activity system that requires writing to function (Sullivan, 1988).

Writing tends to remain transparent, part of the "natural" daily actions of participants in a discipline—until something breaks down. Disciplines and professions consciously act to change the ways students acquire the writing of their activity system when they find that the kinds of discourse they socialize students to use are no longer adequate (as when employers complain) or when significant numbers of students do not learn in the usual ways to write the genres required for the activity system's work (as when there is an influx of second language students or students from very different language backgrounds in the mother tongue).

GWSI helps to mask the role of writing in disciplines' work of reproduction: selecting and preparing students. The myth of UED makes it easier for a discipline to assume that when students from previously excluded language backgrounds fail to successfully write its genres, the discipline has nothing to do with that failure. The existence of separate and general writing courses encourages disciplines to mistakenly assume that they do not teach "writing" but only "content." When some students cannot "write" (by the discipline's standards), the fault must lie elsewhere: in the students who do not master the "content" or in the secondary school English or college composition teachers who did not properly teach (autonomous) literacy. Thus, the disciplines are absolved of responsibility for consciously adapting their organization of learning, their zones of proximal development, to the language and culture of students from nontraditional backgrounds.

Nor have universities, secondary schools, or the wider society had to confront the contradiction at the heart of GWSI, because GWSI courses mask the differences in disciplinary discourses, and, apart from WAC efforts, there are no other institutional structures to bring these to light, because disciplines largely carry on their activities (including writing) in departments (literally and figuratively).

Finally, GWSI helps to mask the whole system of social selection in the United States. The vast majority of education systems select students for higher education on the basis of their extended writing in the disciplines, either in essay examinations, as with the French *baccalaureate*, or in course work portfolios, as with the English system of *moderation* (Russell, 1992, 1995). This writing in the disciplines is assessed collaboratively, by teams of examiners in the disciplines. Writing is thus tied directly to the curriculum and is visibly central to social selection, the object of intense attention and, often, controversy. However, there are virtually no GWSI courses in higher education.

In the United States, the role writing plays in selection is much less visible because writing is not directly tied to the disciplines or curriculum but viewed as a general, autonomous skill. The fact that first-year composition courses are general is crucial to their role in selection. Students are not assessed on their writing of some activity system's discourse within the curriculum; they are assessed on what is presumed to be their writing in general. Thus, a student's failure—or the limited success GWSI's unrealistic expectations lead to—gives the impression that the student is a poor writer in general ("remedial," is the common term), not that a student has not yet had sufficient participation in a particular activity system(s) to learn its genres. In this sense, a required GWSI course that most students take just after admission is the written counterpart of machine-scored, multiple-choice "ability" tests that they take just before admission, and that form the core of the visible selection mechanisms in the United States. These tests claim to measure students' general academic ability, not their ability to do certain actions successfully in certain specific activity fields, and they claim no specific relation to any curriculum. These examinations, like GWSI courses, have spawned their own activity field and industry, which serve disciplines and curriculums as an aid to selection.

By contrast, the written assessment model used by most other nations ties writing to the curriculum (disciplinary activity systems) of both secondary school and higher education. The genres—which is to say the expectations for participation—are announced from the beginning. Students write and revise coursework, do practice examinations, and receive instruction on their writing in each discipline (although little of this instruction is explicitly conceived as writing instruction).

In the written assessment model, the standards for written performance are evolved and maintained by each discipline, and each must collaboratively arrive at both the discipline's standards and the score on each student's written performance. This is inherent in the written assessment model, where objectivity depends on multiple raters. Raters must negotiate and eventually agree on what makes writing good within their activity system at each educational level. With some exceptions, in the United States model standards for writing are arrived at individually by each instructor (Coles & Vopat, 1985). This individualism and consequent subjectivity often allows the GWSI and the education system as a whole to continue without confronting the differences in discourse among disciplines or even among instructors within the same composition program. GWSI is thus alienated from other activity systems and prevented from forming a coherent one itself.

This lack of collegial written assessment in the disciplines and in GWSI has profound implications for first-year writing courses and for the role of writing in U.S. education in general. The U.S. model separates writing from the curriculum. To attempt to teach students all written discourse or even a UED is to attempt to initiate them into no activity system beyond that of a specific GWSI course. The U.S. system encourages the notion that writing is peripheral to success in disciplinary activity systems, whereas in fact the writing of specific genres is crucial to successful functioning in academic and professional activity systems.

TWO APPROACHES TO IMPROVING THE USES OF WRITING IN SOCIETY

From the theoretical perspective I have been developing, the central goal of composition studies is not how to teach students to write better in general, nor is it how to write a general academic or public discourse, for these are unrealistic expectations given the nature of writing in modern societies. Instead the problem is how to improve, from some perspective(s), the particular uses of this immensely plastic tool called writing in specific activity system(s). From the perspective of a student, improving the uses of the tool of writing means using certain genres to choose, enter, become a full participant in, and eventually change for the better one's chosen activity system(s)—and in doing so empower one's self. From the perspective of a discipline or profession, improving the uses of the tool of writing means more effectively using and transforming its genres to accomplish (and at times critique) its object(ive), including selecting and socializing newcomers into its activity system(s). From the perspective of educational institutions, the education system, and the society as a whole, improving the uses of the tool of writing in activity systems should also be a means toward greater social equity—helping those individuals and groups who have not been able to enter certain powerful activity systems to enter them and change them for the better.

I want to suggest here two ways of working toward this goal, ways that seem to me to offer more potential than GWSI courses, ways that avoid the myth of autonomous literacy and its corollary, the myth of UED. These are not new ideas. Kitzhaber devoted the majority of his article to discussing them, and on each he followed in a long tradition. Nor are these untried ideas. Each has received unprecedented development in recent years. They are writing across the curriculum efforts and redeeming the curricular space now occupied by GWSI courses, which claim to teach students *to* write, in favor of a liberal arts course that, in a scholarly, principled way, teaches students *about* writing.

Facilitate Writing Across the Curriculum

The most important means of improving the uses of writing in the activity systems that make up higher education is what has been called writing across the curriculum (WAC, or sometimes writing in the disciplines [WID]): that is, efforts to systematically study, make conscious, and, where possible, improve the uses of writing in specific activity systems, especially those aspects of activity systems that select and socialize neophytes—primarily institutions of higher education. WAC programs operate where students learn the discourses of power, not in a separate activity system such as a GWSI course, but WAC's task is nevertheless daunting, for several reasons.

As we noted earlier, an activity system does not, under normal circumstances, go about teaching writing to neophytes in a conscious, formal way. Nor does it ordinarily need to, because it typically teaches neophytes to write certain genres as part of its normal functioning, although that teaching is often indirect, tacit, and embedded in the everyday actions of the participants in the zones of proximal development a discipline evolves for novices. A discipline uses writing as a tool for pursuing some object. Writing is not the object(ive) of its activity. Thus, writing tends to become transparent, automatic, and beneath the level of conscious activity for those who are thoroughly socialized into it. Activity theory, as developed by Leont'ev (1981) argues that using a certain genre of writing (a certain kind of semiotic tool) as part of an activity system is like using the gearshift of a car (a certain kind of mechanical tool) as part of the activity system of commuting to work. When first learning to drive (or write), one must devote much conscious effort to using the tool. After sufficient participation in the activity system over a period of time, these conscious actions become automatic and unconscious. They come to be thought of as "natural," although they only seem natural. As a result, experts may have great difficulty explaining these operations to neophytes. They may assume that neophytes can (or should be able to) do these things already, or that neophytes will "pick up" these things as a normal part of going about the activity—as indeed most neophytes do.

However, if neophytes have some skillful help from adepts in the activity system, through conscious—even systematic and explicit—teaching, they may learn to perform an action more quickly and more easily than if they simply "picked it up." Students might do better at learning to use the genres of writing in some activity system if they had specific, conscious coaching, mentoring, or formal instruction in those genres of writing. Activity theory research suggests that by consciously creating more effective zones of proximal development, activity systems may be able to improve a novice's acquisition of the systems' genres, although that research is far from conclusive (e.g., Freedman, 1993; Markova, 1979; Williams & Colomb, 1993).

But such pedagogical efforts, whether formal or informal, require conscious effort and an awareness of the role of writing in the activity system—the very things that the daily functioning of an activity system tends to obscure. The WAC movement has nevertheless helped to make many faculty and students aware of the importance of writing as a tool in their work, helping them better to use it for teaching and learning their activities. To borrow a term from another context, bilingual education, WAC programs facilitate *mainstreaming* of writing teaching. Students learn genres in the process of learning to participate in the activity system rather than being taught genres in separate "remedial" classrooms segregated from high-status teaching and learning. Like second language programs in mainstreaming schools, WAC programs are focused on students and teachers pursuing object(ive)s in specific activity systems using the tool of writing. Such expert consultants in language-in-use help both students and teachers examine and improve their interaction and the tools that mediate it—the genres of activity system. Thus the activity system(s) of WAC, unlike GWSI courses, has a clear object(ive): the study and improvement of the roles writing plays in teaching and learning in specific disciplines and professions. Research on writing in the disciplines is at last bringing to light the differences among disciplinary discourses—and exposing the myth of autonomous literacy. WAC programs are helping students choose, enter, become full participants in, and eventually transform for the better some activity system(s). WAC is helping disciplines more effectively use writing to accomplish (and at times critique) their object(ive)s, including selecting and socializing neophytes.

By raising the consciousness of participants in disciplinary activity systems, WAC may also improve social equity, in a way that GWSI courses cannot. Ultimately it is the disciplines and professions themselves—not higher education admissions officers—who select people for their activity systems and thus for the powerful social positions that go with them. It is ultimately a discipline or profession—not colleges and universities per se—that excludes students from powerful social positions, based in part on their use of written language in the genres the discipline or profession values. Thus, gains in social equity due to writing instruction will not come primarily from raising the general level of writing (defined by the activity system[s] of GWSI), but from improving the ways writing is used within and among the activity systems of the disciplines and professions as they select and prepare neophytes.

WAC programs can provide expertise to disciplines on the role of writing in learning, helping them use writing to facilitate rather than refuse entrance. WAC programs can work with faculty to evolve effective zones of proximal development between an activity system and neophytes from underrepresented backgrounds, in much the way second language experts in English for academic purposes (EAP) programs work with disciplines that mainstream students rather than segregating them into remedial courses. GWSI courses, by contrast, can only hope that they have helped to prepare individual students to weather the often difficult writing apprenticeship ahead.

Ultimately, disciplines (and the education system in which they participate) may make writing visibly central to that most crucial (and often most hidden) aspect of education: selection. Instead of selecting students through a combination of grades from individual teachers and from multiple-choice "general ability" examinations, disciplines might use writing as the basis of selection for higher education and employment. In the written assessment model, as I noted earlier, a discipline collaboratively negotiates standards for the work of students at various educational levels. Students produce work during the course of their learning that is then collaboratively assessed by those within the activity system: teachers and other related professionals. In this way, writing becomes visible, part of the negotiation of selection—not a separate general skill—and the curriculum is constructed accordingly. Students must write (and thus learn to write) the genres that are important to each discipline; teachers are more likely to be aware of and consciously teach those genres. Thus writing becomes integral to the curriculum of each discipline (L. B. Resnick & D. P. Resnick, 1992).

Selection based on collaboratively assessed writing requires disciplines to acknowledge responsibility for selection, including the role writing plays in it. When a student is not selected, it is because he or she has not been able to perform specific kinds of actions related to a specific activity system, not because he or she lacks some "general" ability or "general" composition skill. Writing is tied to the curriculum and to selection in a way that allows students to set clear goals (genres) for their writing, directly related to their interests. Writing is not segregated into "remedial" courses where students are presumed to be preparing for any writing situation in general and none in particular.

The movement toward collaboratively assessed writing is well under way in certain professions in the U.S., such as law and medicine, which have added discipline-specific writing to national entrance examinations for professional schools. Written assessment in the transition from secondary to higher education is also being developed. For example, in the New Standards Project (O'Neil, 1993) secondary teachers across the nation are developing discipline-specific written assessment tasks. Thousands of teachers are learning to collaboratively assess portfolios with high rates of reliability, as teachers in many other nations have done for years. This development is promising. For until the kinds of texts (and thus knowledge and work) that each discipline values are taught, assessed, and made the basis for selection, the myth that writing is autonomous will help to mask the inequities in the U.S. selection system. Disciplines will rarely feel the need to consciously re-examine they way writing works in teaching, learning, and selection.

Introduce Students to Rhetoric/Language

A second way to improve the uses of writing in education is to directly raise the awareness of students, teachers, and the public *about* writing, its uses and its power—for good or ill—in the cultures and activity systems that employ it. I have argued that people learn (and know and work) *with* writing, as an immensely flexible tool, in many activity systems; and that people learn to write most effectively by participating in activity systems that use writing; but writing is also an object(ive) of study itself. Unfortunately, the traditional curricular site for studying language in use and raising the awareness of students to language, the discipline of rhetoric, became marginalized in the late 19th century and was relegated to speech departments, where the focus was on oral rather than written communication. However, in the last 30 years, a number of activity systems have formed within academia to study writing in society. Groups of scholars and researchers in a range of disciplines—not only in the revived discipline of rhetoric, but also in applied linguistics, semiotics, education, communication, psychology, sociology of science, literary theory, and so on—specifically study the role of writing in human activities. It is thus now possible and, I believe, desirable to teach a general introductory course *about* writing.

Such a course would not have as its object teaching students to write or improving their writing per se, any more than an introductory psychology course claims to make students better adjusted or a course in music appreciation claims to make its students better singers (although that might be one effect of the course). Rather its object would be to teach students what has been learned about writing in those activity systems that make the role of writing in society the object of their study. Such a course would continue to provide many of the benefits of the GWSI course, but in a way that directly uses the unprecedented research of the last 30 years. By looking at the research on academic discourses—writing and learning in the disciplines—students may become more aware of the uses of written discourse in their institution and of ways they can use writing to further their own exploration of the "strange lands" of various disciplines and perhaps facilitate their entry into one or more of them (McCarthy, 1987). By looking at research on workplace writing, students would be introduced to the roles writing plays in professions that colleges and universities prepare and credential students to enter—and eventually transform. By looking at how researchers in cultural studies, critical discourse analysis, and the sociology of knowledge provide insight into the uses of texts, students would critically examine some ways writing shapes social processes and power relations, through corporate, media, and governmental uses of writing.

As with any good course, students should do a good deal of writing in it, writing of the kinds that the disciplines that study writing employ: genres such as discourse analyses, rhetorical analyses, ethnographic accounts, cultural criticism, and so on. However, a course about writing would not claim to or attempt to improve students' writing in general, although that may be an effect, as it might be for any course that uses writing. A liberal arts course about writing in society might be particularly useful in this regard, because it would give students insight into the ways discourses interact to create academic knowledges and public policies. Such a course may thus help students to enter (and even create new and better) sites for discourse—academic, public, and so on—when they are in a position to do so.

As with most other introductory liberal arts courses, a central goal of this course would be to raise the awareness of students—and, indirectly, of higher education and of the public—to the importance of its object of study (writing) in human life and work. In a course on writing in society, a few students might well become fascinated with the subject and choose to become full participants in one or more of the research traditions the course exposes students to. The great majority of students, however, will become aware of the role of writing in society and in their lives, to make more informed decisions about issues that involve it. This is another way of saying that the course would be a "liberal arts" course rather than "practical" or "professional" course. It would accomplish the goals of liberal education by introducing students to a wide range of activity systems from the point of view of writing—a point of view that is central to a critical understanding of their workings.

Moreover, by teaching what the research traditions that study writing have learned about it, the course may help remove the remedial stigma from writing and its teaching in academia. At the least, it would, as Kitzhaber pointed out, provide content, intellectual rigor, realistic expectations, and some means of judging its effectiveness. It may also, through making students more alert to the roles writing plays in their lives, achieve those purposes GWSI courses have always excelled in: introducing students to higher education and making them aware of the importance of writing. Finally, it may enhance the status of those who have devoted their professional lives to composition studies, by giving their introductory teaching the same status as that of other faculty.

Implementing this proposal will not be quick or easy. There is not even, at present, a textbook that introduces the range of research in the subject to beginning students, as introductory textbooks in other disciplines do. The myth of autonomous literacy (and of UED) is so entrenched—and so useful—in higher education that institutions may be loath to give up the convenient notion that writing is an autonomous and, for college students, remedial skill. However, many GWSI courses already introduce students to research on the roles of writing in society, and with the burgeoning of research and upper level teaching in rhetoric and composition, the transfiguration of first-year composition into a full-fledged liberal arts course may become an increasingly attractive option for many teachers and institutions.

CONCLUSION

I have tried to show that activity theory can clarify the problems Kitzhaber and many others have found with GWSI courses. Lack of content, lack of intellectual rigor, unrealistic expectations, difficulty in assessing effectiveness—all are inherent in the assumptions about the nature of writing that undergird the course and in the course's institutional position: the myth of autonomous literacy with its corollary the myth of UED.

I have also proposed that educational institutions continue to improve the uses of writing in society in two ways: extend writing across the curriculum efforts and raise the awareness of students, the university community, and the public to the role of writing in society by having those who study writing teach an introductory liberal arts course on it. Both are important steps toward removing the remedial stigma attached to writing and its teaching, and toward combating the myth of autonomous literacy that reinforces the remedial stigma.

The writing across the curriculum movement is now 25 years old and growing. The large effort of the last three decades to study writing in society continues to generate courses at all levels of higher education that teach the methods and results of that study to new generations of students. These efforts will, I believe, increasingly challenge the myth that literacy is autonomous and activity systems do not teach (or should not "have to" teach) writing. As the current movements toward writing across the curriculum and research and teaching about writing expand, composition studies and institutions of higher education may conclude that GWSI courses should be "transfigured," as Kitzhaber put it, to teach first-year students about writing without claiming to teach students to write in general.

Mainstreaming writing instruction by expanding WAC efforts and transfiguring GWSI courses into liberal arts courses about writing will be a difficult decision for composition studies and for institutions of higher education. In the 120 years GWSI courses have been in existence, hundreds of millions of students have been helped to write some genres better (although we must always remember that students have improved their writing of genres in many other courses across the curriculum that use writing as a tool of teaching and learning). The question is not whether GWSI courses improve students' writing of certain specific genres. They do. The questions is whether other means of organizing efforts to improve writing will do greater good and less harm to students and to the society those students live in and will recreate.

The tens of thousands of people now involved in writing instruction in higher education might well do more good and find greater rewards, in every sense, if they focused their efforts on conducting research in the ways writing works in human activities at every level, sharing that research in a practical way with disciplines and professions who need their expertise to improve their work (and widen access to disciplines and professions), and teaching what they have learned about writing, both in introductory liberal arts courses and through professional courses that prepare future generations to carry on the task of making writing more useful to students and to the society that they will recreate using this immensely flexible tool.

REFERENCES

Bakhtin, M. M. (1986). *Speech genres and other late essays.* Austin: University of Texas Press.

Bazerman, C. (1988). *Shaping written knowledge: The genre and activity of the experimental article in science.* Madison: University of Wisconsin Press.

Carson, G. C., Chase, N. D., Gibson, S. U., & Hargrove, M. F. (1992). Literacy demands of the undergraduate curriculum. *Reading Research and Instruction, 31,* 25–50.

Coles, W., & Vopat, J. (1985). *What makes writing good?* Lexington, MA: D. C. Heath.

Ellis, R. (1994). *The study of second language acquisition.* Oxford, UK: Oxford University Press.

Engestrom, Y. (1987). *Learning by expanding: An activity theoretical approach to developmental research.* Helsinki: Orienta-Konsultit Oy.

Engestrom, Y. (1990). *Learning, working, and imagining: Twelve studies in activity theory.* Helsinki: Orienta-Konsultit Oy.

Freedman, A. (1993). Show and tell? The role of explicit teaching in the learning of new genres. *Research in the Teaching of English, 27,* 222–251.

Graff, G. (1987). *Professing literature.* Chicago: University of Chicago Press.

Kaufer, D., & Young, R. (1993). Writing in the content areas: Some theoretical complexities. In L. Odell (Ed.), *Theory and practice in the teaching of writing: Rethinking the discipline* (pp. 71–104). Carbondale: Southern Illinois University Press.

Kitzhaber, A. R. (1960). Death—Or transfiguration? *College English, 21,* 367–373.

Kitzhaber, A. R. (1963). *Themes, theories, and therapy: The teaching of writing in college.* New York: McGraw.

Lave, J., & Wenger, E. (1991). *Situated learning: Legitimate peripheral participation.* Cambridge, UK: Cambridge University Press.

Leont'ev, A. N. (1981). *Problems of the development of mind.* Moscow: Progress.

McCarthy, L. P. (1987). A stranger in strange lands: A college student writing across the curriculum. *Research in the Teaching of English, 21,* 233–265.

Markova, A. K. (1979). *The teaching and mastery of language.* White Plains, NY: Sharpe.

Miller, S. (1991). *Textual carnivals: The politics of composition.* Carbondale: Southern Illinois University Press.

Newman, D., Griffin, P., & Cole, M. (1989) *The construction zone: Working for cognitive change in school.* Cambridge, UK: Cambridge University Press.

Ohmann, R. (1976). *English in America: A radical view of the profession.* New York: Oxford University Press.

O'Neil, J. (1993, February). On the New Standards Project: A conversation with Lauren Resnick and Warren Simmons. *Educational Leadership, 50,* 17–21.

Resnick, L. B., & Resnick, D. P. (1992). Assessing the thinking curriculum: New tools for educational reform. In B. R. Gifford & M. C. O'Connor (Eds.), *Changing assessments: Alternative views of aptitude, achievement and instruction* (pp. 37–75). Boston: Kluwer.

Rice, W. G. (1960). A proposal for the abolition of freshman English, as it is now commonly taught, from the college curriculum. *College English, 21,* 361–367.

Rogoff, B. (1993). Children's guided participation and participatory appropriation in sociocultural activity. In R. H. Wozniak & K. W. Fischer (Eds.), *Development in context: Acting and thinking in specific environments* (pp. 121–154). Hillsdale, NJ: Lawrence Erlbaum Associates.

Russell, D. R. (1988). Romantics on rhetoric: Liberal culture and the abolition of composition courses. *Rhetoric Review, 6,* 132–148.

Russell, D. R. (1991). *Writing in the academic disciplines, 1870–1990: A curricular history.* Carbondale: Southern Illinois University Press.

Russell, D. R. (1992, March). *How the French boy learns to write: An 80–year retrospective.* Paper presented at the annual meeting of the Conference of College Composition and Communication, Cincinnati, OH.

Russell, D. R. (1995). Collaborative portfolio assessment in the English secondary school system. *Clearing House, 68,* 244–247.

Smagorinsky, P., & Coppock, J. (1994). Cultural tools and the classroom context: An exploration of an artistic response to literature. *Written Communication, 11,* 283–310.

Smagorinsky, P., & Coppock, J. (in press). The reader, the text, the context: An exploration of choreographed response to literature. *Journal of Reading Behavior.*

Smagorinsky, P., & Smith, M. W. (1992). The nature of knowledge in composition and literary understanding: The question of specificity. *Review of Educational Research, 62,* 279–305.

Street, B. (1984). *Literacy in theory and practice.* Cambridge, UK: Cambridge University Press.

Sullivan, P. (1988). *From student to scholar: A contextual study of graduate student writing in English.* Unpublished doctoral dissertation, Ohio State University, Columbus.

Swales, J. (1990). *Genre analysis.* Cambridge, UK: Cambridge University Press.

Thurber, E. A. (1915). College composition. *Nation, 56,* 328–329.

Wall, B. (1994, June). The personal essay as unmarked genre. *A critique of things that go without saying in composition.* Symposium conducted at the Summer Rhetoric Conference, University of Rhode Island, Kingston.

Wertsch, J. V. (Ed.). (1981). *The concept of activity in Soviet psychology.* Armonk, NY: M. E. Sharpe.

Williams, J. M., & Colomb, G. G. (1993). The case for explicit teaching: Why what you don't know won't help you. *Research in the Teaching of English, 27,* 252–264.

Writing as an Unnatural Act

Joseph Petraglia
Georgia Institute of Technology

To many practioners in the writing field, *cognitivism* is closely associated with the pedagogical aim of teaching students heuristics that can be enlisted in the cause of producing better compositions. As such, a cognitivist perspective would appear to be quite conventional in the sense that composition instruction has traditionally been geared toward teaching students to develop and exercise writing skills: those identifiable and broadly applicable rules, routines, and strategies that proficient writers seem to possess. Although cognitivism brings with it the language of *heuristics, problem spaces* and *task representations* one could argue that earlier compositionists had their own techniques and vocabulary that corresponded quite closely to these constructs; even current traditionalism was not without its rules of thumb and earnest recommendations to student writers that they should seek to understand the audiences and assignments to which their writing was a response. In this regard, then, to the extent that cognitivism is thought to offer something "new" it is generally not because it invites a significant reconceptualization of writing instruction, but because a cognitivist framework has permitted the social scientification of a somewhat motley practice that had heretofore inhabited a gray area between romanticism and teacherly lore.

Although I argue in this chapter that the teaching of writing skills—and cognitivism's contribution to that aim—rests on questionable assumptions, I remain nonetheless committed to a cognitivist framework for understanding writing. For far from just reinventing another rationale and method for enabling decontextualized classroom practices, I believe a cognitivist perspective can offer critical insights into the nature of writing, the nature of schooling, and the nature of writing in school. It also illuminates the shortcomings of the pedagogical framework most closely associated with the composition field: what I labeled in the introduction to this anthology general writing skills instruction (GWSI). Within a GWSI framework, writing is viewed as a masterable body of skills that can be formed and practiced irrespective of the formal context of the writing classroom. As such, GWSI can be understood as not just coincidental to most explicit teaching of writing (i.e., composition instruction), but intrinsically linked to it. My thesis is that a cognitivist perspective not only helps us understand why GWSI is seriously flawed, but can, more positively, suggest how we might morely closely integrate the nature of writing with the purposes of schooling.

I begin this chapter with some defining truisms about the nature of writing that suggest why cognitivists would frame writing as a variety of what is termed *ill-structured problem solving*. In making this point I am consistent with the earliest proponents of cognitivism in writing in suggesting that writing tasks are, by their nature, open-ended tasks with indeterminate cognitive parameters. More "originally," perhaps, I will argue that the nature of GWSI reflects a fundamental and unavoidable conflict between the teaching of rhetorically sound (i.e., context-dependent) writing strategies and skills on one hand, and the highly particular context of formal instruction on the other. This leads me to the conclusion that our growing appreciation of both writing as a rhetorical act and schooling as a specialized kind of learning context might be used to formulate guidelines that can adapt the natural role of writing to the postsecondary educational context, guidelines that would result in abandonning the notion of GWSI and, thus, the composition classroom.

WRITING AS ILL-STRUCTURED PROBLEM SOLVING

Any discussion of the nature of writing has always been dependent on whether the term's user meant "writing" in the sense of basic literacy, in the sense of note taking, in the sense of poetic performance, and so on. With the professionalization of the writing field and an interest in issues such as business writing and writing for self-discovery have come more "senses" in which writing and its nature can be considered. For my present purposes, however, I wish to delimit the sense of writing under consideration to that with which most compositionists and cognitivists in writing concern themselves. To this end, a short list of delimiting descriptors would have to include the following, mutually reinforcing characteristics: writing is instrumental, transactional, and rhetorical.

Writing is instrumental. Of all the truisms and metaphors for writing, this is perhaps the most clichéd: Writing is a tool. Writing gets things done. By transmitting information, writing directly facilitates the accomplishment of other tasks. If it did not, we might wonder why the need for writing would ever arise. Many historians of the subject have noted that the primary function of writing was largely scribal—that it was linked to the need to keep records of crop yields, taxation, and the like (cf. Cole, 1990; Goody, 1986; Harris, 1986). With the development of more sophisticated systems of writing and the evolution of literacy from a poor substitute for orality to a complete and largely independent mode of communication, the ways in which writing can be thought of as instrumental have become correspondingly complex but in no way diminished.

Writing is transactional. When we speak of writing in a more compositional sense, we still refer to it as a tool, but a second dimension begins to take precedence: its inherent transactivity. Writing mediates between writers and their audiences. In a recent paper (Petraglia, 1995) I gave a brief overview of transactionality as an issue in writing and noted that, although the term itself is often traced to Rosenblatt (1978), the writing field's importation of the term may be most clearly attributed to Britton and his colleagues (Britton, Burgess, Martin, McLeod, & Rosen, 1975) at the University of London. In their book on the functions writing serves in British secondary schools, "transactional" writing was that which was used to "'get things done' or participate in the world's affairs: i.e., in our model, to inform, persuade, or instruct" (p. 218). Although the definition is notable more for its inclusivity rather than for its specificity, perhaps that is the point: The centrality of the act of transaction is basic to practically any symbolic exchange between or among different parties that we would call "writing." Certainly, for members of the writing field, the idea that writing's chief function is to facilitate transaction is, like writing's instrumentality, profoundly unremarkable.

Finally, *writing is rhetorical.* Relative to the 10,000-year history of writing systems, the idea that writing is a rhetorical act is a recent understanding (a mere 2,000 years old). Yet, in our field it might be safe to say that this third aspect of the written word is the one with which we are most consciously concerned, for it is the one on which the profession of writing instruction is based. If one were to quickly characterize the general thrust of new movements in composition, it might be done by suggesting that the rhetorical nature of the writing act lies at their core. Gebhardt (1983) made the point that "compartmentalization (broadly speaking) of attention to rhetorical concerns and attention to the writing process is now essentially over. . . . All agree that identifying the rhetorical problem is central to writing" (p. 295).

Gebhardt's point is reflected in many mundane ways: PhD programs in writing are almost always entitled "Rhetoric and Composition" programs, current students of the field are required to be familiar with rhetoricians from Aristotle to Burke, and practically every new wave in the field, from Freirian pedagogy to cognitivist research into writing processes, presumes that the profession of composition serves as handmaiden to the discipline of rhetoric (see Goggin, chap. 2, this volume). Thus, the practice of writing (and the ability to write) centers on rhetorical issues such as invention, audience, voice, and purpose—those elements one needs to consider whenever using language strategically. Writing is not merely the ability to form letters or follow grammatical rules and stylistic conventions (although this is certainly part of writing, and a dimension of writing to which many educators usefully devote their attention), but in its fullest sense it is a social behavior that we use as a tool to achieve social ends in cooperation with others.

The foundation for the cognitivist paradigm in writing was laid when the notion of problem solving, well-established in psychology, was applied to writing tasks. In a cognitivist framework, the production of a text is the result of an individual's interaction with both content and audience information. The mental arena in which writing is planned and revised is the writer's task environment. A cognitive perspective on writing has always acknowledged that writing is instrumental, transactional, and rhetorical.

This framework for writing was given clearest voice, perhaps, by Flower and Hayes' (1977) linking of writing to a cognitivist perspective on human information processing which "as the study of cognitive or thinking processes . . . explores the wide array of mental procedures people use to process information in order to achieve their goals" (p. 450). In subsequent work, Flower and Hayes (1981) set out the broad principles that continue to define a cognitive approach to writing:

> 1) The process of writing is best understood as a set of distinctive thinking processes which writers orchestrate or organize during the act of composing.
>
> 2) These processes have a hierarchical, highly embedded organization in which any given process can be embedded within any other.
>
> 3) The act of composing itself is a goal-directed thinking process, guided by the writer's own growing network of goals.
>
> 4) Writers create their own goals in two key ways: by generating both high-level goals and supporting sub-goals which embody developing sense of purpose, and then, at times, by changing major goals or even establishing entirely new ones based on what has been learned in the act of writing. (p. 366)

This fourth principle is especially important, for it sets out writing's strategic nature and, in doing so, suggests a distinction that is critical to understanding writing as a problem-solving activity: the difference between ill-structured and well-structured problem solving.[1]

---

[1] In making a distinction between these two ends of a spectrum, various writers have juxtaposed ill-defined, ill-structured, and fuzzy on one side to well-defined, well-structured, and sharp on the other (Newell & Simon, 1972). Solely for the sake of consistency, this chapter employs the well-structured/ill-structured terminology.

Minsky (1961) explained the distinction by stating that a well-structured problem is one in which we are given some systematic way to decide when a proposed solution is acceptable. Such well-structured problems were those confronted by cognitivists in the beginning stages of investigation into artificial intelligence and information processing. Classic examples of well-structured (although complex) problems include chess playing (de Groot, 1965) and solving math problems (Collins, Brown, & Newman, 1989; Silver & Marshall, 1990). Using Minsky's definition we can see that both types of problems are well-structured, for they culminate in an unequivocal result: arriving at checkmate or the mathematically correct answer.

Conversely, as Reitman (1965) and many others have suggested, most problems we confront on a daily basis are not well structured. They do not lend themselves to the sort of formalism acceptable in artificial intelligence. In ill-structured problem-solving, contingency permeates the task environment and solutions are always equivocal. The idea of "getting it right" gives way to "making it acceptable in the circumstances." In Reitman's words:

> To the extent that a problem situation evokes a high level of agreement over a specified community of problem solvers regarding the referents of the attributes in which it is given, the operations that are permitted, and the consequences of those operations, it may be termed . . . well-defined with respect to that community. On the other hand, to the extent that a problem evokes a highly variable set of responses concerning referents of attributes, permissible operations, and their consequences, it may be considered ill-defined. (p. 151)

When we think about the sorts of situations we find ourselves in, and the many (perhaps too many) choices left to us, we would have to concur that most "problems" we confront on a daily basis lie on the ill-structured end of the spectrum. Spiro, Feltovich, Jacobson, and Coulson (1992) elaborated on the nature of ill-structuredness by suggesting that such problem solving is distinguished, first, by the myriad and simultaneous interactions among a variety of general schemas, organizing principles, and perspectives and, second, the fact that "the pattern of conceptual incidence and interaction varies substantially across cases nominally of the same type" (p. 60). In other words, ill-structuredness means that problems that appear to share salient characteristics and might thus be categorized as similar "problem types" are, at root, fundamentally and unpredictably different.

As one might expect then, cognitivists interested in composing processes have been quick to enter writing tasks on the ill-structured side of the ledger. But to fully understand the nature of writing as a type of rhetorical problem solving, then, one must not only consider the context-dependent nature of the problem space within which the act transpires, but also the nature of the information required.

Whereas some information can be characterized as formal and finite—what Toulmin might call field-independent (e.g., knowledge of the alphabet, knowledge of formatting conventions)—other kinds of information, and especially the sort of input that dominates rhetorical cognition, are inseparable from their field-dependent nature (e.g., knowledge of how a given reader is likely to react to a given idea). Information about an interlocutor's response, the register and domain knowledge appropriate for the situation, even knowledge of one's own motives, are highly unstable, shifting with the accumulation of new information, further reflection, and a thinker's mood. Rhetorical problem solving, for reasons of both its task environment and the nature of the information on which it depends, resists all but the most general truisms in regard to its production and procedures.

Seen in this way, it is clear that a instrumental, transactional, rhetorical task (such as writing) may present the ill-structured problem par excellence. Conversely, I would argue that only if we consider writing ill structured does a cognitivist framework for discussing composition merit serious attention, at least when speaking of writing at the college level. If we limited our focus only to those elements of writing that are scribal and well structured we are no longer speaking of writing as a sophisticated rhetorical behavior, but of its most basic building blocks of orthography and writing conventions, something to which most writing professionals do not limit themselves.

THE NATURE OF SCHOOLING AND GENERAL WRITING SKILLS INSTRUCTION

Defending a conception of writing as a type of ill-structured problem solving is not this chapter's primary objective; as I have suggested, the point is fairly uncontroversial and perhaps needs no defenders. Instead, the larger thesis of this chapter argues that the ill-structured nature of writing (as I have already stipulated) and the nature of schooling do not combine effortlessly. It is, in fact, when one attempts to explicitly school a student in writing that we see how the very idea of writing is often distorted to fit the constraints of formal education. To support this claim, one can draw on an ever-growing body of research and theory into situated cognition—the ways in which educational contexts shape learning rather than merely furnish a site for it.

The interest in the effects of the educational context on problem solving is relatively new. This might be attributable to what Scribner and Cole

(1973) noted is the tacit and pervasive overestimation of the continuity between formal and informal education. They:

> Argue for the necessity of distinguishing school-based education from the broader category of formal education. [Their] thesis is that school represents a specialized set of educational experiences which are discontinuous from those encountered in everyday life and that it requires and promotes ways of learning and thinking which often run counter to those nurtured in practical daily activities. (p. 553)

The sense that there is a disjuncture between formal education and the world outside of school is echoed by Young (1994), who wrote that as learning occurs within a particular situation:

> Then part of the attributes of the situation for most traditional instruction is a classroom, where learning is competitive among individuals, the subject and nature of problems change on the hour in a predictable succession, and the major, if not only, source of information is one person: the teacher. This is not a context that transfers to many situations outside the educational system. (p. 45)

It would be impossible to exhaust a list of every contextual element that has been either shown to have an impact on learning or is suspected of having an impact.[2] Some of these aspects lie in the realm of the interpersonal. Cohen (1971), for instance, suggested that outside the formal classroom, individuals are socialized rather than taught. The consequences of this for learning are enormous. For one thing, the learner associates context with knowledge, and the value of information is closely related to the "instructor" who imparted it. This association of ethos with information is one example of how the affective and cognitive domains are fused to a greater extent in nonformal learning. According to Cohen, "One of the most outstanding characteristics of socialization . . . is the high affective charge that is associated with almost everything that is learned in context" (p. 11). Nix (1990) seconded the importance of affect in distinguishing in-school from out-of-school learning. He noted that "in normal life, as is well known, children learn through participation in activities and thoughts triggered by their lives as humans. There is often a feeling of ownership concerning what they know. In the abnormal world of a school setting, such self-directed learning is unusual for the majority of children" (p. xi).

---

[2]Research anthologies and treatises on situated cognition are proliferating rapidly and any recommendation to the reader will undoubtedly be superceded by newer research by the time this chapter gets to print. Three books that provide a representative sampling of work in situated cognition include Lave and Wenger's (1991) *Situated Learning: Legitimate Peripheral Participation* and two anthologies edited by Resnick: *Knowing, Learning, and Instruction: Essays in honor of Robert Glaser* (1989) and *Perspectives on Socially Shared Cognition* (1991).

Another salient difference between school and nonschool learning, according to Howard Becker (1972), lies in the necessary homogenization of the learner from the perspective of the teacher. He noted that:

> Schools . . . process students in batches, treating them as if each were the prototypical normal student for whom they have constructed the curriculum. Being part of such a batch naturally constrains the student to behave, as best he can, as though he were prototypical; it is the easiest way to fit into the collective activity he is part of. (p. 88)

Conversely, as Cohen claimed, learning situations outside of school are more commonly one-on-one with the "teacher" or role model adapting instruction to the learner's personal history, motivation, and particular strengths and weaknesses.

Empirical research on formal versus everyday cognition in humanities such as applied ethics also suggests major differences that may be of interest to the writing field. For instance, studies have shown that the ethical persona an individual projects when questioned about how he or she would act when placed in a hypothetical situation bears little resemblance to what that person does when put in a similar situation in real life (cf. Haan, 1975; Villeneuve-Cremer & Eckensberger, 1985). Other research suggests that hypothetical tasks in the humanities—even when the teacher or researcher explicitly acknowledges their value-ladenness and ill-structuredness—prompt students to reason formalistically rather than "real"istically (Haan, 1975; Potts, Elstein, & Cottrell, 1991). My own research (Petraglia, 1994) into real problem versus hypothetical problem solving confirms this and suggests that hypothetical tasks encourage a seeming objectivity when considering arguments. When reasoning hypothetically, one's emotional stake in the issue (if any such stake exists) is attenuated or sublimated in favor of "good reasons."

Resnick (1990) categorized the major differences in school vs. everyday context as the following four:

1. In school, cognition is individual rather than shared.
2. In school, students rely on pure mentation rather than reliance on external resources.
3. Thinking in school relies to a much greater extent on the manipulation of symbols rather than objects.
4. School promotes highly generalizable learning rather than situation-specific learning.

Resnick suggested that these fundamental differences make problem solving in school a very particular kind of problem solving. Because schools have to strip away interpersonal and situational contexts to get at the generalizable formulae students are expected to apply to a broad range of problems, it is not surprising that the problems considered most pedagogically sound are those with relatively unambiguous solutions and whose accurate method of solution can be taught in advance and evaluated objectively. Thus, research suggests that school is best suited to the algorithmic procedures associated with learning well-structured information. For the same reason teachers are compelled to treat students as prototypical, school tasks have to be effectively decontextualized for accuracy of assessment—today's students are often quasi-strangers to teachers who are confronted with an enormous range of student aptitudes and attitudes and who intervene in the students' educational process for the merest fraction of the time a student spends in school. Given the logistics of modern education, which have to take into account high student–teacher ratios, the mobility of families, and teacher specialization, it is clear that well-structured problems are used in formal schooling, not in spite of their limitations, but because of them.

The necessarily artificial (i.e., decontextualized) nature of the problems presented to learners in formal settings have led some psychologists interested in the interaction of context and thinking to write that "many of the activities students undertake are simply not the activities of practitioners and would not make sense or be endorsed by the cultures to which they are attributed. What students do tends to be ersatz activity" (Brown, Collins, & Duguid, 1989, p. 34). Such statements have been read by some as a blanket indictment of the institution of formal education. It has been suggested that situated cognitivists see school learning as a corruption of naturalistic learning and as such, view schooling with suspicion and even contempt.

Whether or not this jaundiced view of school is one actually taken by many situated cognitivists (and there is evidence to suggest that this is not the case), it is not the perspective taken here. Rather, it might suffice to say that school provides a highly particular context within which certain skills can be optimally developed and in which certain information transfer is best facilitated. Also, just as clearly, even informal learning is riddled with episodes of teacher–learner interaction that contain "formal" elements such as practice drills, explicit teaching, and disincentives for error. So the question is not whether school learning is "bad," but rather, what kind of information types are best taught formally and directly and how they can be distinguished from information types that lend themselves to other forms of transfer. Work in situated cognition would seem to suggest that, in cognitivist terms, tasks in which situational variables are containable and solutions are predeterminable (i.e., as in well-structured problems) are the sorts of task that formal schooling is best able to accommodate. With this in mind, then, I would like to return to the subject of writing, and consider more specifically the paradigmatic way in which writing is generally taught at the postsecondary level.

General Writing Skills Instruction

Attention to the context of formal schooling has rightly served as a catalyst for rethinking in many disciplines. Although one might consider "school history" a sort of history manqué or "school physics" as a simplified study with little correspondence to physics done in laboratories, I believe the issue of school-boundedness is nowhere so problematic as it is for the field of composition, which purports to be, after all, the study of appropriately addressing contexts.[3] The difficulty is apparent in the fact that the writing truisms I presented earlier are routinely confounded by the texts with which most writing teachers and researchers are familiar: those compositions students produce as a result of general writing skills instruction (GWSI). GWSI is meant as shorthand for a number of curricula that have at their root the tenet that writing is a body of practical, practiceable skills. Such curricula, in short, reflect the belief that writing can be taught. In a recent essay, Kaufer and Young (1993) noted that (in what I am calling GWSI), "it is assumed that pretty much the same skills of writing will develop no matter what content is chosen . . . language skills taught and learned are generic" (p. 78)[4] As such, GWSI is the embodiment of contemporary writing instruction, as it has been for several decades.

If one accepts the twin premises that writing is a variety of ill-structured problem solving and that formal instruction is best suited to teaching students to solve well-structured problems, one might well wonder what it is that students in GWSI classes are doing when they make marks on a paper. One well-known answer is Macrorie's (1988) suggestion that they are "Engfish"-ing: They are engaging in the "say-nothing, feel-nothing, word-wasting, pretentious language of the schools" (p. 22). Whereas I would suggest that Engfish is a perfectly natural response to the context of GWSI, most in the writing field regard such writing as a symptom requiring treatment. Applebee (1982) wrote that:

> In English classes where the "content" is writing skill itself, a . . . kind of distortion is introduced. Here when the teacher acts in the role of examiner, what the tudent writes about becomes (within certain limits) irrelevant: The task becomes one of demonstrating language skills rather than extending a shared knowledge base. (p. 377)

To redress this, Applebee invited us to work to "broaden the range of rhetorical situations, to ask student to share information that they possess with others who need to be persuaded of its interest and importance" (p. 380).

---

[3]It can be argued that other disciplinelike areas such as critical thinking and speech, which share composition's roots in rhetoric, are equally undermined by research into formal versus informal learning as they are equally implicated in the teaching of context sensitivity.

[4]The term used by Kaufer and Young is *writing-WNCP* (with no content in particular).

Applebee, like many other writing professionals, seemed to suggest that the context of GWSI is easily adjusted to create the rhetorical dynamics that bring about rhetorical response. A good example of how this attitude plays out in the GWSI classroom (and of the status the field accords GWSI composition) is illustrated in Anson's (1985) *Exploring the Dimensions of Purpose in College Writing.* Anson's research suggests that some students' "models of writing" more easily accommodate the rhetorical situation of the classroom writing context than do other students' models. This first group he characterized as "rhetorically flexible." They are able to role play and produce texts that he suspected would be created outside the classroom—that is, in an authentic situation. For these writers, Anson suggested that "the classroom seems to drop away from the thinking of writers . . . they enjoy a kind of rhetorical gaming, using different styles for different purposes" (p. 11). Conversely, the rhetorically *in*flexible students show much less ability to move away from the narrow constraints imposed by the assignment. For Anson, then, the willingness to suspend disbelief is, in fact, critical to rhetorically interesting classroom writing.

Anson's report of his study raises some interesting points and reveals what I think are telling assumptions underlying GWSI. First, it is positively judged that students pretend to "be rhetorical" using generic features although both students and teachers know that the writing's stated rhetorical exigence is not the real exigence (i.e., the performance is at the behest of an instructor). A corollary of this first assumption is that "good" classroom writing looks like writing as we would expect to see it outside of the classroom—that is, that classroom writing skills transfer to extracurricular contexts—even though our understanding of writing outside the academy is far too inadequate to make such a claim (cf. Heath, 1993). Finally, although Anson articulated a clear understanding of the way in which a classroom might encourage inauthentic conceptions of purpose and audience, he (and I suppose many GWSI instructors) located the source of the problem in a student's "unproductive" model of writing rather than in the nature of rhetorical training itself. The valuing of rhetorical flexibility in this sense seems somewhat ironic.

My argument to this point has been that GWSI has more to do with "doing school" than it does with teaching students to perform rhetorical tasks. But rather than fault GWSI on this account, we might wonder if the problem with GWSI is not that it could be doing something better, but whether it is attempting to do something that needs to be done at all. Freedman (1993) asked:

If the textual features are secondary to the prior communicative purpose, is there any value in explicating the textual features out of context as a way of learning the genre? Or, if genres are responses to contexts, can they be learned out of context by explicating features and specifying rules of either form or context? (p. 225)

Research of linguists such as Freedman (1990, 1993, chap. 6, this volume) suggests that students acquire rather than learn the critical aspects of writing. This is echoed in Berkenkotter and Huckin's (1993) position that "learning the genres of disciplinary or professional discourse would therefore be similar to second language acquisition, requiring immersion into the culture, and a lengthy period of apprenticeship and enculturation" (p. 488). The object of this acquisition process includes not only specialized vocabulary and syntactic features, but also micro- and macro-level rhetorical patterns. Freedman's research suggests that discipline-specific features can be acquired without reference to models or formal instruction in the target genres. In her study of law students and legal writing, she reported that students did not seem to need rules, nor did they formulate rules for themselves. Her results suggested that "clearly, explicit teaching may not be necessary for the acquisition of even very sophisticated school genres" (1993, p. 230). One might go a step further and suggest that not only is the explicit teaching of the rhetorical elements of writing unnecessary, but it may be counterproductive, as it promotes the mistaken belief that rhetorical behavior can be rule governed and independent of the context in which it is used. As Brown et al. (1989) have cautioned, "School cultures and school problems usually do not reflect cultures or problems elsewhere in the world, and they often subvert students' understanding of those cultures and problems" (p. 34). Several other contributors to this volume come to this same conclusion in regards to writing.

Again, it is clear that school provides a very particular context for the learning of practically all subject matters. Some disciplines (applied ethics comes readily to mind) have determined that formal education's particularity must be part of the discipline and have taken steps to identify ways in which their applied subject differs from the subject when unconstrained by pedagogical imperatives (Covey, 1990; Rest, 1984). The composition profession, conversely, has largely resisted making the in-school/out-of-school distinction.[5] I have elsewhere identified (Petraglia, 1995) two critical features of "school life" that I claim are intrinsic aspects of formal education that the writing field has largely ignored: It is formative in that school presumes that students are developing rather than merely exhibiting knowledge and skills, and it is evaluative in that students are not the arbiters of their success; others are. In this situation, for most students, school does not provide an opportunity to engage in just any rhetorical practice. Demanding genuine rhetorical sensitivity from students who may

---

[5]A welcome departure from this rule is Chin's (1994) recent ethnographic study of journalism students in which both the in-class/out-of-class distinction and the issue of authenticity are raised.

have little or no intrinsic motivation to act as rhetors, who often lack the domain knowledge critical to playing the role of rhetor very convincingly, and who are supplied with an audience less intent on learning than on evaluating writing performance seems unrealistic and perhaps even unethical.

Returning to the problem-solving framework, the classroom context within which composition generally takes place is a limited one, one in which the pedagogical goals of formation and evaluation strongly encourage, if not dictate, fairly well-structured problem solving. A key element that permits GWSI assignments to be pedagogically "workable" is the fact that their parameters are often fictive; that is, in much classroom writing the "rhetorical" goals of the writing are often identified (or legitimated) for the writer beforehand even if the specifics are left "open." Consequently, one of the teacher's principal functions is to guide the writer toward reaching those goals in an acceptable manner, again, an evaluation determined by someone other than the writer. This, of course, requires a teacher as audience to show as much consistency and predictability as possible—qualities that "real" audiences rarely demonstrate. Other problem-structuring "rules" of GWSI writing that have no analog in the world of genuinely rhetorical writing include the following: a piece of writing's thesis and topics should be easily identifiable and unambiguous, information should not be esoteric (at least not in the teacher's opinion), the writer should not presume an emotional stake in the issues, and he or she should presume a homogeneous, "universal" audience—preferably one that fully appreciates the writing skills the teacher believes deserve appreciation.

Of course, one could argue that students do not view GWSI writing as formulaic as they themselves might like—in fact, students often fail to see any method to the madness and are eager for someone to impose a little well-structuredness (the "just tell me what you want" syndrome). However, I would caution that this confusion on the part of a student should not be mistaken for a writer's response to rhetoric's natural ill-structuredness. When students complain of not knowing what the assignment really requires they are not so much suggesting that they are bewildered by the complexity of the rhetorical problem placed before them as much as signaling their anxiety and frustration vis à vis the curious task environment in which GWSI places them.

Paradoxically, then, the artificiality and hypotheticality that permits composition skills to be taught in the first place is in direct conflict with assumptions of ill-structuredness on which a cognitivist understanding of writing must be based. Early cognitivist research in writing, and indeed, most subsequent writing research, has never made a meaningful distinction between a writer's "rhetorical situation" and a writing assignment (e.g., Flower & Hayes, 1981). However, the cognition entailed in producing

GWSI compositions is fundamentally different from that of writers who address out-of-school exigencies. As Smith (1994) remarked "In the real world, writing's motives are clear . . . [writers] already feel the force of an issue and sense ignorance or error in their would-be audience" (p. 206). If we extrapolate from work in situated cognition it is easy to suppose that the problem solving entailed in writing for real audience, with real purposes, using situationally appropriate information differs significantly from cognition devoted to *appearing* to address an audience, *looking like* you have a purpose, and *pretending* to be knowledgeable.[6]

Thus, although from its inception the cognitivist framework for writing has been based on the premise that all writing is ill-structured problem solving, in reality, the sort of pseudotransactional tasks students often encounter as a result of GWSI lie closer to the well-structured end of the spectrum. As writing teachers, we know our students, once out in the real world, will be faced with rhetorically complex and messy situations, but part of our instructional mission is to make the mess seem manageable if not orderly. This has had the effect, in Nystrand's (1982) words, of treating "writing as a series of discrete forms to master rather than situations to manage" (p. 4).

ACCOMMODATING THE NATURE OF WRITING IN SCHOOL

Nystrand's (1982) sense that "writing in the absence of a rhetorical context is not really discourse; it is the bloodless, academic exercise of essay-making" (p. 5) is one shared by many dedicated compositionists who have argued for students to be given more authentic opportunities for writing in which students can "naturally" develop rhetorical skills. Traditionally, the writing field has presumed that authenticity could be manufactured without rearranging much institutional furniture. That is, if we "let students write what they want to write" (cf. Stewart, 1992) or "make students submit their writing to a real reader" (cf. Applebee, 1982) or "have students write about real-world issues" (cf. practically any textbook author you can think of) GWSI is workable. I disagree. I believe that such efforts to authenticate students' writing—within the confines of a course intended to teach writing—underestimates the intransigence of schooling as a context and is rooted in what I would consider to be a reductive view of a rhetorical situation. An example from outside the writing field may prove instructive.

---

[6]In fairness, I should note here that in a study I am currently undertaking I have found students who claim to suspend disbelief entirely and insist that classroom requirements have no effect on their writing behavior (Anson might identify these as rhetorically flexible writers). If this is indeed the case, there may in fact be little difference between these individuals' in-class and out-of-class writing. Their accuracy in representing their own writing aside, thus far these students do not appear to be representative, however.

The Cognition and Technology Group at Vanderbilt (CTGV; 1990) wrote on how the interactive video materials they produce serve to create more natural learning environments. Specifically, the "Jasper" materials as they are currently developed are intended to support mathematical problem formulation and problem solving. The videodisc follows the adventures of one Jasper Woodbury as he encounters a variety of situations that invite the disc user to assist him in applying problem-solving skills. The CTGV believes the videodisc "anchors" instruction, that is, creates an authentic learning environment that provides the sort of contextualization of problems that situated cognitivists have called for. They suggest that the Jasper materials are "authentic" for two reasons: first, and perhaps most obviously, because the videodisc uses actual facts and data; second, they propose that the materials are more natural and authentic because the tasks that individuals are asked to perform are those that they could legitimately be expected to perform if they found themselves in the actual situation. Then, however, they pose a question that, at first blush, looks as if it complicates this objectivist notion of authenticity: "for whom are these tasks authentic?" (p. 7). Further reading, however, reveals that they are not asking "who is perceiving these tasks as authentic?" but rather "who can make best use of the authenticity with which he or she is presented?" In other words, for the CTGV's purposes, authenticity is objective—the programmer *made* the software authentic.

Although I would not argue with the CTGV's central premise—that authenticity brings with it cognitive resources that are otherwise "inert" (to borrow Whitehead's term for prior knowledge that goes untapped when dealing with a new task)—it seems that their conception of authenticity only accounts for what is known about a situation, not what is felt about it. Similarly, writing theorists and teachers who present "anatomically correct" rhetorical situations to students in the belief that they are providing "real" writing experiences are wrongly assuming that accuracy equals authenticity. A task is not authentic unless its would-be performer appropriates it as such.

To summarize this point, the job of making writing real is complicated by learners who stubbornly refuse to bow in the face of our good intentions. In the call for creating more authentic writing situations in the GWSI classroom there lies an assumption that we can bend reality to fit our writing assignments rather than adapt writing assignments to the learning context we find ourselves in. Although ultimately the writer–reader relationship is what embues a texts with authenticity, in the final section of this chapter I suggest how writing assignments might reflect an acquiescence to the context of formal education to accommodate and encourage this relationship.

Back to Rhetorical Basics

Scholarly research in situated cognition, experiential learning, or apprenticeship notwithstanding, I think common sense tells us that school is not the sort of rhetorical context in which just any rhetorical purpose can be set and achieved. This is a difficult idea for the writing field to accept, for I believe it means abandoning GWSI, the pedagogical vehicle on which the field has pinned its identity since its inception and perhaps the only profession many of us have known. Nevertheless, I think we must confront, first, the inevitable logic that the richness of rhetorical response cannot be taught using a general writing skills approach, and second, the uncomfortable fact that the composition classroom—no matter how thoroughly it is fiddled with—is rooted in some variation of just such an approach.

If one agrees with the contention that writing, in its fullest sense, cannot really be taught, we might then turn our attention to how we could at least provide the environments in which it naturally occurs. Framed in another way, the question becomes: What does the "natural habitat" of the academic writer look like? In applying the lessons of recent research in nonacademic writing, genre, and situated cognition, I have compiled the following suggestions in the form of guidelines. In providing these guidelines, I do not mean to suggest any particular restructuring of the writing field, although I think it is clear that they bear a strong resemblance to certain de facto elements of writing across the curriculum.

The Natural Audience for Academic Writing Is an Evaluator. As I have already suggested, the nature of the audience is one that is especially problematic in the GWSI classroom. As Resnick (1990) put it:

> The typical audience for student writing is only the teacher, who knows (or is thought to know) all the information conveyed. For the large majority of students, then, no place—neither home nor school—provides an extended opportunity to engage in high levels of authentic informational literacy practice. (p. 180)

Although Resnick was speaking of teachers generally, I argue that most instructors outside the framework of GWSI do, in fact, have something they want to know: Did the student "learn" the assigned information?[7] My first suggestion, then, is that we make clear to students that the audience for their writing in school is the teacher-evaluator. Although play-acting rhetorical

---

[7]The issue of what is a legitimate purpose for a teacher to read a student's writing is an important and complex one, but one that is beyond the scope of this chapter. I am merely suggesting that one way teachers may play the role schooling has carved out for them is by assuming the mantle of "expert evaluator" to the student's "disciplinary novice."

response has a pedigree dating back to Greek declamation, genuinely rhetorical responses cannot be divorced from genuine audiences. In the case of formal education, it is no secret to student-writers that the audience for their writing—assignment notwithstanding—is a teacher who is paid to evaluate how well they have understood information delivered in class.

The Purpose of an Academic Writing Assignment Is for the Student to Demonstrate Mastery Over Content. In accordance with the first guideline suggesting that teachers read as evaluators, a second argument I advance is that it should be made clear in any formal schooling context that the legitimate function of writing is to demonstrate mastery over a disciplinary content rather than to demonstrate a mastery of rhetorical skills. In terms of current GWSI pedagogy, I am suggesting that instructors should not require students to "invent" a purpose for writing, but assign one. The natural sort of writing in the academy is done in response to a disciplinary content rather than as a self-conscious exercise in invention for invention's sake (see Royer, chap. 8, this volume).

Implied here is the idea that there is a content—a body of knowledge about which a student can legitimately be held accountable. Although, again, my purpose in writing this chapter is not to explore the implications for the field's future of eliminating GWSI, on this point it is clear that adapting writing to the function of schooling will entail forsaking the teaching of writing as a productive art—a study devoted to the proposition of rhetoric on demand. This does not suggest that writing does not need its professionals, it only suggests that these professionals have to consider teaching a content (e.g., rhetorical theory, theories of literacy, media and argument, grammar, etc.) on which they may legitimately require students to write and that such writing should be evaluated in light of its adequacy vis à vis content rather than "writing skill" or rhetorical acumen. Only if their writing is unencumbered by fictive purposes can students gain an appreciation for how rhetorical exigence shapes their choices as writers.

The Natural Writing Assignment Derives Much of its Rhetorical Nature From Reading. A third guideline, or perhaps an elaboration derived from the first two guidelines, is that those of us seeking to instill rhetorical abilities through writing should not ignore the possibilities presented by teaching rhetoric as a *sensibility* rather than as a productive skill. By this I mean educators should focus less on making our students "produce" rhetorical responses and more on helping students gain an appreciation of the rhetoricality of the responses of others.[8] This idea is

---

[8]The construct of rhetorical sensitivity as a pedagogical objective has received some careful attention in the speech communications field; I would refer readers to Hart and Burks' (1972) article on the subject.

hardly revolutionary, in fact, the notion that one learns to write best when responding to readings tacitly underlies most of the content courses found in English departments. Second language expert Krashen (1984) also suggested that writing abilities are not so much the result of conscious learning and exercises in production as they are of reading. What is new in this suggestion, however, is that reading (broadly construed) should be acknowledged as lying at the very core of developing rhetorical abilities rather than as a peripheral activity merely intended to prompt the writing in which we are "really" interested.

The Natural Writing Assignment Permits, but Does Not Require, Overt Persuasion. My final suggestion is one that runs counter to what many have seen as the trend in writing instruction: We should not demand that students write persuasively. There is something almost oxymoronic about the idea of "assigning persuasion." As the lack of domain knowledge and the rhetorical constraints imposed by the audience-evaluator can only lead to what Brown et al. (189) called "ersatz activity," requiring students to produce arguments in an informational vacuum would seem to do little to further genuine appreciation of the complexity of rhetorical behavior. As with the other guidelines, the gist of my criticism is familiar to writing professionals who have experimented with ways to circumvent it. Traditionally, GSWI teachers have sought to fill this informational vacuum by assigning readings before taking a stand, but I would suggest that giving students a nodding acquaintance with a topic (and realistically, this is all that can be done in the few days or weeks writing teachers have to prepare their students to write a persuasive essay) is not a plausible substitute for the knowledge the effective rhetor typically possesses (see Jolliffe, chap. 10, this volume). Of course, this is not to foreclose on the possiblity that a given student writer may be comfortable, indeed desirous of, writing to persuade the instructor of his or her viewpoint. In such instances, but only in such instances, it seems entirely legitimate to evaluate the writing's informational soundness as well as its persuasive strengths.

The guidelines for creating "authentic" academic writing contexts as I have presented them here are clearly in need of more careful refinement. Terms like *mastery*, *content*, and *persuasion* demand further qualification, and may even point to latent GWSI assumptions of my own. For instance, does the idea of a disciplinary content include conventions commonly found in the field's discourse (and if so, why couldn't these be identified and taught)? When I speak of demanding mastery of a content to what extent can traditional GWSI issues of invention and style be left out, for are these not part of what it means to master information in a discipline? And depending on one's epistemological assumptions, one might wonder if it is possible to have a student write any way other than persuasively.

Although I find all of these interesting issues (and may call into question my own model of what promotes authenticity), I do not believe they obscure the basic critique of GWSI instruction I have presented.

To the extent that rhetorical writing can be learned, it will only be so by students building individual models of how to be rhetorically effective and adapting those models to everday situations where writing is called for or can serve a strategic purpose. Whereas formal instruction in rhetorical theory and the nature of textuality may usefully stimulate students' thinking about what it is they are doing when they sit with pen in hand or at a keyboard (and personally, I think the future of writing studies might lie in this direction), student writers are their own best writing teachers—by limiting their classroom writing experiences to more easily authenticated writing experiences, I believe educators can perform a great service without explicitly dictating how good rhetors write.

CONCLUSION

Baldly stated, the position I have taken here is that general writing skills instruction—perhaps the very notion of the composition classroom—is an idea whose time has gone. It is a curriculum shaped by the needs of English departments and universities (Goggin, chap. 2, this volume; Miller, 1991), and is not one that can be supported by a consideration of either rhetorical theory or contemporary educational psychology. Fictive rhetorical exigencies create a relatively well-structured problem space that certainly has its pedagogical charms, but ultimately does little to teach students about the instrumental, transactive and, above all, rhetorical nature of writing. Although the goal of instilling rhetorical abilities is a laudable one, I am suggesting that there is something intrinsic to the nature of rhetoric that defies its production on command. Although there are some legitimate rhetorical demands we can place on writing performed as a classroom activity, I would argue that we should, for ethical as well as logical reasons, relieve students of the burden of pretending to be effective rhetors in contexts in which writing has no rhetorical "effect" other than the teacher's appraisal of the text.

Of course, the degree to which training in writing can be characterized as unnatural or inauthentic depends on one's curricular objectives. For instance, if courses in speech are intended to prepare young people for debate club activities and instruction in writing is largely intended to teach mechanical accuracy and conventions of organization and structure (again, scribal literacy), general skills classrooms can provide the ideal setting for the acquisition of such knowledge. Nothing I have suggested is intended to deny the importance of teaching the building blocks of literacy. If, as I suspect, however, most writing professionals define their job as one that encourages an appreciation for the context-sensitive and strategic nature of language use, formal instruction in the production of rhetoric seems both counterintuitive and counterproductive. If we genuinely accept the premise that writing is ill-structured problem solving, we will be dissuaded from insisting that rhetorical skills can be taught as a generative set of axioms or procedures that can be induced within the confines of the writing classroom. More positively stated, the fact that writing is, by its very nature, rhetorical, would seem to suggest that writing's production at the behest of an instructor can (and should) avail itself of the rhetorical situation inherent in formal education.

If any elements of this argument sound like a reprise of the art/knack debate presented in Plato's *Gorgias*, that may not be entirely coincidental. GWSI, and perhaps the writing profession at large, owes its institutional status to the sophistic triumph of *techne* over the less manageable notion of rhetoric as naturally embedded in understanding and experience. However, in this chapter I have argued that the field may have won a hollow victory. Given our increasingly sophisticated understanding of what it means to write as a rhetor, the confines of the general writing skills classroom seem more restrictive and less relevant than ever. Yet I do not believe that the rejection of GWSI and some theorists' talk of "abolitionism" spells disaster for the rhetoric and writing field. Rather, it provides an occasion for us to consider what we would do if *techne* had not won out. What sort of profession would we be—can we be—if we treated rhetorical behavior as the highly complex, and situated phenomenon we know it is? I know I join many others in my eagerness to put GWSI behind us in order to begin addressing this question.

REFERENCES

Anson, C. (1985). *Exploring the Dimensions of Purpose in College Writing*. ERIC Document Service ED 274 964.

Applebee, A. (1982). Writing and learning in school settings. In M. Nystrand (Ed.), *What writers know* (pp. 365–381). New York: Academic Press.

Becker, H. S. (1972). A school is a lousy place to learn anything in. *American Behavioral Scientist, 16*, 85–105.

Berkenkotter, C., & Huckin, T. (1993). Rethinking genre from a sociocognitive perspective. *Written Communication, 10*(4), 475–509.

Britton, J., Burgess, T., Martin, N., McLeod, A., & Rosen, H. (1975). *The development of writing abilities* (pp. 11–18). London: Macmillan.

Brown, J. S., Collins, A., & Duguid, P. (1989). Situated cognition and the culture of learning. *Educational Researcher, 18*(1), 32–42.

Chin, E. (1994). Redefining "context" in research on writing. *Written Communication, 11*(4), 445–482.

Cognition and Technology Group at Vanderbilt. (1990). Anchored instruction and its relationship to situated cognition. *Educational Researcher, 19*(6), 2–10.

Cohen, Y. A. (1971). The shaping of men's minds: Adaptations to imperatives of culture. In M. Wax, S. Diamond, & F. Gearing (Eds.), *Anthropological perspectives on education* (pp. 19–50). New York: Basic.

Cole, M. (1990). Cognitive development and formal schooling: The evidence from cross-cultural research. In L. Moll (Ed.), *Vygotsky and education* (pp. 89–110). Cambridge, UK: Cambridge University Press.

Collins, A., Brown, J. S., & Newman, S. (1989). Cognitive apprenticeship: Teaching the crafts of reading, writing and mathematics. In L. Resnick (Ed.), *Knowing, learning, and instruction* (pp. 453–494). Hillsdale, NJ: Lawrence Erlbaum Associates.

Covey, P. K. (1990). Integrating emotion in moral reasoning and learning. In R. Kozma & J. Johnston (Eds.) *Educational computing in the humanities.* Hillsdale, NJ: Lawrence Erlbaum Associates.

Flower, L. S., & Hayes, J. R. (1977). Problem-solving strategies and the writing process. *College English, 39*(4), 449–461.

Flower, L. S., & Hayes, J. R. (1981). A cognitive process theory of writing. *College Composition and Communication, 32,* 365–387.

Freedman, A. (1990). Reconceiving genre. *Texte, 8/9,* 279–292.

Freedman, A. (1993). Show and tell? The role of explicit teaching in learning new genres. *Research in the Teaching of English, 27,* 222–251.

Gebhardt, R. (1983). Writing processes, revision and rhetorical problems. *College Composition and Communication, 34,* 294–296.

Goody, J. (1986). *The logic of writing and the organization of society.* Cambridge, UK: Cambridge University Press.

de Groot, A. D. (1965). *Thought and choice in chess.* The Hague: Mouton.

Haan, N. (1975). Hypothetical and actual moral reasoning in a situation of civil disobedience. *Journal of Personality and Social Psychology, 32,* 255–270.

Harris, R. (1986). *The origin of writing.* London: Duckworth.

Hart, R., & Burks, D. (1972). Rhetorical sensitivity and social interaction. *Speech Monographs, 39*(2), 76–91.

Heath, S. B. (1993). Rethinking the sense of the past: The essay as legacy of the epigram. In L. Odell (Ed.), *Theory and practice in the teaching of writing: Rethinking the discipline* (pp. 89–110). Carbondale: Southern Illinois University Press.

Kaufer, D., & Young, R. E. (1993). Writing in the content areas: Some theoretical complexities. In L. Odell (Ed.), *Theory and practice in the teaching of writing: Rethinking the discipline* (pp. 71–104). Carbondale: Southern Illinois University Press.

Krashen, S. (1984). *Writing: Research, theory, and applications.* Oxford, UK: Pergamon.

Lave, J., & Wenger, E. (1991). *Situated learning: Legitimate peripheral participation.* Cambridge, UK: Cambridge University Press.

Macrorie, K. (1988). *The I-search paper.* Portsmouth, NH: Boynton Cook.

Miller, S. (1991). *Textual carnivals: The politics of composition.* Carbondale: Southern Illinois University Press.

Minsky, M. (1961). Steps toward artificial intelligence. *Proceedings of the IRE, 49,* 8–29.

Newell, A., & Simon, H. A. (1972). *Human problem solving.* Englewood Cliffs, NJ: Prentice-Hall.

Nix, D. (1990). Introduction. In D. Nix & R. Spiro (Eds.), *Cognition, education, and multimedia: Exploring ideas in high technology* (pp. ix–xiii). Hillsdale, NJ: Lawrence Erlbaum Associates.

Nystrand, M. (1982). Rhetoric's audience and linguistic's speech community: Implications for understanding writing, reading, and text. In M. Nystrand (Ed.), *What writers know* (pp. ix–xiii). New York: Academic Press.

Petraglia, J. (1994). Mediated realism and the representation of a health care controversy. *Journal of Biocommunications, 21*(3) 10–17.

Petraglia, J. (1995). Spinning like a kite: A closer look at the pseudotransactional function of writing. *Journal of Advanced Composition, 15*(1), 19–33.

Potts, D. L., Elstein, A. S., & Cottrell, J. J. (1991, April). *Expert/novice differences in reasoning about a medical ethical dilemma: The "escape" dilemma.* Paper presented at the annual meeting of the American Educational Research Association, Chicago.

Reitman, W. R. (1965). *Cognition and thought: An information processing approach.* New York: Wiley.

Resnick, L. (Ed.). (1989). *Knowing, learning, and instruction.* Hillsdale, NJ: Lawrence Erlbaum Associates.

Resnick, L. (1990, Spring). Literacy in school and out. *Daedalus,* pp. 169–185.

Resnick, L. (1991). Shared cognition: Thinking as social practice. In L. Resnick, J. Levine & S. Teasley (Eds.), *Perspectives on socially shared cognition* (pp. 1–20). Washington, DC: American Psychological Association.

Rest, J. R. (1984). The major components of morality. In W. Kurtines & J. Getwirtz (Eds.), *Morality, moral behavior, and moral development* (pp. 24–38). New York: Wiley.

Rosenblatt, L. (1978). *The reader, the text, the poem.* Carbondale: Southern Illinois University Press.

Scribner, S., & Cole, M. (1973). Cognitive consequences of formal and informal education. *Science, 182,* 553–559.

Silver, E. A., & Marshall, S. P. (1990). Mathematical and scientific problem solving: Findings, issues, and instruction implications. In B. F. Jones & L. Idol (Eds.), *Dimensions of thinking and cognitive instruction* (pp. 265–290). Hillsdale, NJ: Lawrence Erlbaum Associates.

Smith, J. (1994). Against "illegeracy": Toward a pedagogy civic understanding. *College Composition and Communication, 45*(2), 200–219.

Spiro, R., Feltovich, P. J., Jacobson, M. J., & Coulson, R. L. (1992). Cognitive flexibility, constructivism, and hypertext: Random access instruction for advanced knowledge acquistion in ill-structured domains. In T. Duffy & D. Jonassen (Eds.), *Constructivism and the technology of instruction* (pp. 57–75). Hillsdale, NJ: Lawrence Erlbaum Associates.

Stewart, D. (1992). Cognitive psychologists, social constructionists, and three nineteeth-century advocates of authentic voice. *Journal of Advanced Composition, 12,* 279–290.

Villeneuve-Cremer, S., & Eckensberger, L. H. (1985). The role of affective processes in moral judgment performance. In M. Berkowitz & F. Oser (Eds.), *Moral education: Theory and application* (pp. 175–194). Hillsdale, NJ: Lawrence Erlbaum Associates.

Young, M. F. (1994). Instructional design for situated learning. *Educational Technology Research and Development, 41*(1), 43–58.

5

Writing and Learning at Cross Purposes in the Academy

Cheryl Geisler
Rensselaer Polytechnic Institute

A few years ago, our literature was replete with descriptions of writing as a way of learning.[1] Just putting words together on the page, it was argued, would encourage thinking (Emig, 1977), foster learning (McGinley and Tierney, 1989), and engender critical reflection (Fulwiler, 1986). As Knoblauch and Brannon put it, "Writing enables new knowledge because it involves precisely that active effort to state relationships which is at the heart of learning. Composing always entails the search for connections: its nature is to compel the writer to undertake that search" (pp. 467–468).

These claims about writing and learning have been important in rhetoric and composition because they have supported both the upgrade of what contributors to this collection are calling general writing skills instruction (or GWSI) and the development of Writing Across the Curriculum programs (see Knoblauch & Brannon, 1983; Russell, 1991). And, as we shall see, these arguments are correct insofar as they acknowledge that the core issue at stake in the writing practices of the academy is knowledge rather than mechanics.

What these arguments fail to acknowledge, however, is that learning already extant knowledge and making new knowledge are quite distinct activities. Learning already extant knowledge requires the acquisition of a web of *facts* and underlying *values*. Learning, for example, that "writing facilitates learning" requires acquiring a web of facts and values that might be something like:

---

[1]Many of the arguments contained in this chapter are drawn from chapter 2 of the author's monograph, *Academic Writing and the Nature of Expertise: Reading, Writing, and Knowing in Academic Philosophy* (1994), also from Lawrence Erlbaum Associates.

Fact: The main business of the university is learning.

Fact: Writing is the best way to facilitate that learning.

Therefore

Value: Writing ought to have a important place in a university education.

Value: Writing instructors ought to be given a greater role to play in that education.

Making new knowledge, on the other hand, requires the creation of new *counterfacts* placed in opposition to current facts, and the exploration of new *countervalues* at odds with current values:

Current fact: Many have argued that writing facilitates learning.

But

Counterfact: Research suggests that this is not the case.

This result requires us

Countervalue: to rethink the basic purpose of a university education.

Countervalue: to construct an alternative role for ourselves in the university.

Although, as this analysis suggests, both learning extant knowledge and making new knowledge share a common orientation toward facts and values, they are currently assigned to two quite distinct groups in the academy. Learning extant knowledge is the job of students. Making new knowledge is the job of academic professionals. These two groups, even though they inhabit the same institutions and organize their activities around interactions with texts, are actually worlds apart with respect to knowledge, separated across what I have called the Great Divide between expert and layperson (Geisler, 1994). As we shall see, students in the academy do not use writing for the making of new knowledge in the sense already described. Instead, they use writing primarily for the "lay" purpose of learning extant knowledge made by others more "expert" than they. And, as the research reviewed in this chapter indicates, writing is a fairly poor tool for this purpose.

For this reason, teachers and researchers who believe that writing and learning go hand in hand are making the mistake of assuming that what students do with writing in the academy is naturally what they themselves do. Such a simplistic assumption is problematic, for it seriously mischaracterizes the task we undertake when we endeavor to teach writing as epistemic. It is only by understanding the complicated relationship between writing and learning, I argue, that we can better design writing instruction for the purposes we intend or, perhaps more importantly, better design the purposes for which we intend our writing instruction.

WRITING IN THE ACADEMY

Two decades of research on student writing suggest that the actual writing practices of students in the academy are far from the epistemic practices that motivate those of us in the academic professions. Instead, students write most often to demonstrate that they have read and understood texts written by others. This patterns shows up when we examine the why, the what, and the how of student writing in academic settings.

Why Students Write in Academic Settings

Why do students write in academic settings? Two major studies, one conducted in England in the late 1960s and one conducted in the United States in the late 1970s, suggest that, by and large, students usually write for the purpose of demonstrating knowledge for a teacher as examiner. The first study, carried out by Britton, Burgess, Martin, McLeod, and Rosen (1975), solicited writing samples from students enrolled in a range of British schools in their first, third, fifth, and seventh years in a range of content areas. Over 2,000 texts were finally selected, the work of 500 boys and girls. The second study, carried out by Applebee and his colleagues (Applebee, 1981), surveyed 754 teachers nominated for their teaching excellence in their content areas in a stratified sample of U.S. schools in Grades 9 and 11. These teachers answered a questionnaire about the writing they had assigned to a recent class and supplied sample papers from that class. In both studies, the researchers analyzed the results using similar categories for audience and function, Applebee using a modification of the categories developed earlier by Britton.

The results for both studies point to the limited nature of the writing students are asked to do in academic settings. In both cases, the predominate audience for students' writing was the teacher. The predominate function was informative. By and large, students' texts appeared to function either in a teacher–student dialogue as a means for students to acquire academic knowledge or in a pupil–examiner relationship as a means of demonstrating that knowledge had been acquired. In Britton's (Britton et al., 1975) study, for example, nearly 90% of all students' work was written for the teacher in one of these two roles: In the early years, the teacher usually functioned in a teacher–learner dialogue; by the seventh year, however, the teacher usually functioned as a examiner. Most of this writing was transactional (64%) with nearly 37% given to classification.

Because Applebee's (1981) criteria for what counted as writing was broader than Britton's (Britton et al., 1975), his results allow us to examine the place of this extended writing in the secondary schools he surveyed. His results show that although students were often asked to put words on paper in school, they did not frequently do so to develop their ideas in any extended way. In fact, Applebee found that only 26% of his 9th-grade teachers and 36% of his 11th-grade teachers frequently assigned writing of a paragraph or more. Most reported assigning shorter pieces—multiple-choice, fill-in-the-blank, copying, and short answers—that did not require extensive thinking. Again, as in Britton's study, most of this writing was for informative purposes.

Two follow-up studies by Applebee (1984) confirm the limited nature of the writing students do in academic settings. In the first study, Applebee surveyed the kinds of writing assigned in the three most popular textbooks used in seven content areas. He found that most of these textbooks recommended writing activities of less than a paragraph with the teacher as examiner in mind as audience. Second, in a case study of 15 students enrolled in a good school in the San Francisco Bay area, Applebee found that even these students in a good school produced most of their writing for teacher-as-examiner for informative purposes.

What Students Write in Academic Settings

When students write to demonstrate knowledge for the teacher as examiner, they typically produce what is known as the "school essay" (Hounsell, 1984; van Peer, 1989, 1990)—a text that introduces a thesis in its opening paragraph, provides support for this thesis in succeeding paragraphs, and restates and occasionally comments on this thesis in the closing paragraph. In Applebee's (1984) longitudinal study of 15 students mentioned earlier, for example, fully 66% of students' texts used this essay form, which he called analytic, often to compare alternatives or to analyze cause and effect relationships. Another 22% of the students' texts used a more simple narrative structure, often simply to restate an idea provided by a teacher's question and then provide elaboration with a time-ordered sequence of information. Occasionally, these students' texts exhibited a mixed structure with more easily managed narrative structures embedded in a more global thesis-support analytic framework.

Interestingly, almost all of these student texts are based on other writers' texts. Applebee (1984) found, for example, that 72% of student writing relied on either the teacher or school texts as its source of information, and only 27% used personal experience. This reliance on texts as sources appears to characterize not only the school essay studied by Applebee, but also a range of more specialized texts that students write in school. Perhaps the least complex of these texts is the summary, but the synthesis and the research paper are also found at more advanced levels as well. In all three of these genres, students appear to use writing to reproduce rather than extend what they have read and, in doing so, often frustrate the expectations of teachers operating under more epistemic assumptions.

A summary is the simplest text that attempts to represent in some form what another text says. According to Brown and Day (1983), summary strategies span a range from those that simply delete information from the source text, through those that combine information, and finally to those that call for inventing whole new topic sentences. In an early study, Brown, Day, and Jones (1983) found that students as young as fifth grade could use simple deletion strategies to summarize, whereas students in the 11th grade and first year of college were more likely to use strategies that combined and reordered information. A later study by Garner, Belcher, Winfield, and Smith (1985) suggests that fifth graders could recognize the benefits of these more complex strategies even when they did not use them.

Nevertheless, students seemed to prefer to write summaries by selecting what they consider to be important information from other writers' texts and deleting extraneous information. Few students at any level actually reordered this information and even fewer invented new topic sentences. The 10 undergraduates studied by Sherrard (1986), for example, used the following set of strategies, rank ordered for frequency, for moving information from source to summary text: (a) omitting a sentence from the source text, (b) including a sentence from the source text "as is," (c) combining two consecutive sentences in a source text, (d) combining three consecutive sentences in a source text, and (e) combining four consecutive sentences in a source text. In the taxonomy originally developed by Brown and Day, this represents the lower end of possible summary strategies.

On the face of it, other texts written from sources appear not to allow for such a simple set of reproductive strategies. Synthesis, for example, requires students to combine information from more than one text, a sophisticated skill usually reserved for the later years of undergraduate and graduate school. The results of several studies seem to indicate, however, that even students at these upper levels preferred the same kind of copy and delete strategies we observed for simple summary. In a study comparing college juniors and seniors who were more or less able in reading comprehension, for example, Spivey (1984) found that more able comprehenders invented thematic chunks as a way of organizing information from the source texts. The less able comprehenders, by contrast, organized their texts in a flat structure reminiscent of a simple list of facts with little invented structure. In a later study in which the same level of student was asked to write a comparison of sources, Spivey (1991) found similar results: Students with greater verbal ability as measured by a prescreening reading test were more likely to invent their own macrostructures to organize information from sources. Significantly, however, less than half of these upper division college writers used this inventional strategy. Nevertheless, teachers seem to prefer this more rhetorical strategy: In Spivey's second study, syntheses that contained invented higher level organization were rated more highly than those that did not.

A study by Ackerman (1991) of students in graduate school suggests that students' propensity for engaging in more rhetorical strategies depends on the students' relative status in the text's domain. In a study of 40 graduate students, 20 in psychology and 20 in management, Ackerman found that when students were asked to synthesize information from texts outside of their specialization, they tended to reproduce the text they read: They made few elaborations while reading and included less original information when writing. When they were asked to synthesize information from source texts in their own fields, however, they adopted a more rhetorical stance: They read to construct an image of the rhetorical context in which the texts were written and attempted to respond to those texts by saying something new based on their own personal knowledge.

The research paper, the last genre of "writing from sources" that we examine, shows a similar duality of strategic approaches, one simply reproductive, one more rhetorical. College students surveyed by Schwegler and Shamoon (1982), for example, believed that research papers were supposed to help them learn about a topic and demonstrate that learning to a teacher. Faculty, on the other hand, believed the research paper should be an exploration of the state of an issue at a particular time. Nelson (1990), following 13 students through six different courses at Carnegie Mellon University, also found students' interpretations diverging from faculty expectations: Her students often interpreted teachers' assignments as simple requests for the demonstration of course content. The course faculty, however, often had the construction of independent argument in mind.

How Students Write in Academic Settings

When students write in academic settings, they appear to be using what Bereiter and Scardamalia (1987) called a knowledge-telling strategy: Students begin by retrieving ideas from long-term memories in response to cues in either the assignment topic or the discourse's genre conventions. Once they remember an idea, they test it for appropriateness to the composition. If it passes, they add it to the text. Students continue content generation in this fashion until they can retrieve no more ideas. At this point, composing stops. This knowledge-telling strategy apparently results in a highly cursory writing process for students: As studies have repeatedly

Avoid the template

shown, students tend to write quickly, attend to low-level details, edit to clean things up, and then turn the essay in to a reader who evaluates it against a mental "template" for what is expected.

Emig (1971) first observed students' cursory writing process in the late 1960s with a study of eight high school students—two average and six above-average writers—from Chicago area schools. Despite their writing success, only one of these eight students regularly engaged in any kind of planning in advance of composing. Lynn, for example, spent just 3 minutes planning the essay she wrote in her first session with Emig, and a similar amount of time planning the second essay even though she was told to think about it in advance. According to Emig, the interview comment from one of these students was typical of almost all these students' attitude toward planning: "'I start to write and just wherever I end up, I end up'" (p. 82).

A similar pattern emerged in Pianko's (1979) study of 10 remedial and 7 traditional writers enrolled in a freshman composition course in a community college in the fall of 1976. On five separate occasions, Pianko asked these students to take as much time as they needed to compose a 400-word essay under what she described as "fairly usual classroom conditions" (p. 7). These students remained remarkably disengaged from their writing: Their average prewriting time was 1.26 minutes; the average total writing time was just 38 minutes. Fourteen of these 17 students did no planning on paper and most reported mental planning during rather than before writing.

In two articles published in 1980, Flower and Hayes (1980a, 1980b) reported similar observations on students' cursory planning. Using think-aloud protocols, Flower and Hayes found that the one more experienced writer for whom they gave specific data engaged in far more rhetorical planning than the novice with whom she or he was contrasted (Flower & Hayes, 1980a). They also reported the results of an unpublished study in which they found that student writers generated 60% of their ideas in response to the topic and 30% in response to the rhetorical problem. Experienced writers reversed these proportions, spending 60% of their time thinking about the rhetorical problem and only 30% of their time thinking about the topic.

Unpublished data from Zbrodoff (1984) also suggest that students engage in a highly cursory process. In this study, students in Grades 5 and 10 spent less than 10 seconds planning before starting to write a simple assigned story even when given unlimited composing time. Adults spent considerably more time planning—although their time was still generally under 1 minute (Bereiter & Scardamalia, 1987). In their own studies, Bereiter and Scardamalia similarly found that students spent on average less than 1 minute planning before beginning to write.

Although we do not have time to review the extensive literature on student revising (Emig, 1971; Faigley & Witte, 1981; Fitzgerald, 1987; Flower, Hayes, Carey, Schriver, & Stratman, 1986; Hayes, Flower, Schriver, Stratman, & Carey, 1987; Perl, 1979; Selfe, 1984) and teacher response (Brannon & Knoblauch, 1982; Horvath, 1984; Onore, 1989; Siegel, 1982; Sommers, 1982; Sperling & Freedman, 1987; Ziv, 1984), it is important to note that patterns in both of these practices reinforce what we have seen for student planning: Students for the most part believe that revising means editing and seldom make changes to text that affect meaning. Teachers routinely respond to students' texts by evaluating them against a mental template for what they expect to see. Overall, then, students appear to be remarkably unengaged in the process of reproducing knowledge.

WRITING AND LEARNING IN THE ACADEMY

The pattern that emerges from this research suggests, then, that in the academy, students do not actually do very much extended writing and the writing they do is for the purpose of demonstrating knowledge to the teacher as examiner. As we noted in our introduction, however, the underlying assumption of much recent research and teaching has been that writing can do something more. In particular, writing has often been assumed to lead to a deeper level of processing and therefore to better learning. Much effort has been expended trying to test this hypotheses since it was first articulated by Emig in 1977, but, as two recent reviews suggested, the results have been both contradictory and confusing (Penrose, 1992; Schumacher & Nash, 1991). In what follows, however, we see that these results can be understood once we distinguish between the literacy practices required of students in the academy and those used by academic professionals.

Early Studies of Writing and Learning

Early studies seem to confirm the hypothesized benefits for writing on learning. For example, Copeland (1985) reported the results of a study in which she asked 120 sixth-grade students in central Texas to read passages about an unfamiliar game, engage in postreading activities, and then take two kinds of comprehension tests, one on applying the information to another task and the other on simple factual recall. The results showed that students did significantly better on both tests after writing than after answering multiple-choice questions or doing directed rereading. Follow-up analyses indicated, furthermore, that both the nature of the writing and the nature of the test were important to producing these positive results. Students who wrote texts that attempted to explain the game to a friend as required by the directions did better on the application test than did those who wrote simply to describe. They also did better if they included ideas related to the ones on the later test. Only the inclusion of test-related ideas seemed to make a difference on the comprehension test for factual recall however. Whether or not the students had undertaken the task of explaining the game to a friend did not affect their ability to remember what they had read.

At roughly the same time but a half continent away, Langer and Applebee were undertaking a line of research that initially yielded similar positive results for writing on learning (Langer, 1986; Langer & Applebee, 1987). Langer asked six high school students to read two passages from an American history textbook, thinking aloud as they worked. Sometimes students were asked to take notes in their usual manner; sometimes they were asked to answer study questions; sometimes they were asked to write an analytic essay. The results showed that students took about twice as long to complete their task when writing than when taking notes or answering study questions. Furthermore, they apparently used this extra processing to engage in activities that were relatively rare in the other two conditions: hypothesizing, making metacomments, using evidence and validation, and evaluating. Finally, this extra processing seemed to pay off: Langer found that students improved the quantity and organization of their broad topic knowledge to a greater extent when writing than in the other two conditions.

One of Applebee and Langer's graduate students, Durst (1987), completed the final study usually taken to suggest positive effects for writing on learning. In this study, rather than comparing essay writing to other kinds of postreading activities, Durst compared the effects of analytic essay writing with summary essay writing. He asked 20 high school juniors from the San Francisco Bay area to read passages taken from American history textbooks. Like Langer (1986; Langer & Applebee, 1987), his prompt for the analytic essay asked students to develop a personal opinion about the material from this reading. The prompt for the summary essay simply asked, "In your own words, summarize the events discussed in the reading passage." Also like Langer, Durst asked these students to compose aloud as they worked. To measure the effects of writing, Durst analyzed the essays the students wrote as well as the cognitive activities in which they engaged.

Like Langer (1986; Langer & Applebee, 1987), Durst (1987) found that students writing the analytic essay took the longest time to complete their work. And, like Langer, he found that students who wrote analytic essays spent proportionately more of their time in higher order thinking than did the writers of summary. Thus Durst's analysis appears to bear out Langer's finding that analytic essay produces a distinct pattern of higher level cognitive operations. Students' cognitive activities while writing analytic essays do appear to be more complex than when they take notes, answer study questions, or write simple summaries.

Subsequent Studies

Presumably, the results of these studies, when combined with Copeland's (1985) earlier results, seem to offer support to teachers who want to change current school practices by assigning more extended analytic writing in their courses as a way of helping students to learn. Such a conclusion, however, would be premature. In fact, a second set of studies that actually measured the effects of writing on students' learning of passage-specific knowledge suggest that writing, particularly analytic writing, may be a poor way to acquire school knowledge.

The first of these studies was published by another of Applebee and Langer's graduate students, Newell (1984). Newell asked eight high school juniors from the San Francisco Bay area, all recommended by their teachers as good readers and writers, to read and write about passages taken from social science and science textbooks. The writing tasks were the same as those used by Langer—study questions, note taking, and analytic writing—but this time, the students did all three tasks twice, once on passages about which they had poorly organized knowledge and once on passages about which they had highly organized knowledge. Before reading and writing, students were told they were going to be tested on the passages, and afterward, they were tested for the depth and organization of their broad topic knowledge related to the passage as well as for their recall of passage-specific information.

The results of this comparison confirm, first of all, that analytic essay writing does take a long time. Newell's (1984) students took an average of twice as long to finish the analytic essay as they did to take notes or answer study questions. This increase in processing time apparently benefited the students who had poorly organized topic knowledge to begin with: They gained an average of 1.42 more on their knowledge score measuring the depth and organization of their topic knowledge after writing. Study questions also brought about significant increases however: Students with poor topic knowledge gained an average of .83 on their knowledge score after answering study questions. For students with highly organized knowledge, the results were not dramatic or significant. High-knowledge students gained an average increase of only .54 on their knowledge score after writing and a gain of only .25 after answering study questions.

In measuring changes in the depth and organization of students' topic knowledge, Newell (1984) was duplicating Langer's (1986; Langer & Applebee, 1987) design. In measuring recall, he was going beyond it to ask how well the writing tasks affected students' ability to learn specific pieces of information present in the passage. His study, then, was the first to look for specific learning effects for analytic writing comparable to those Copeland (1985) found for writing an explanation to a friend. Here the results showed no benefit for analytic writing. That is, students recalled just about as much when they took notes and answered study questions as they did when they wrote analytic essays. This result, clearly not what Newell expected, suggested that even though students spent twice as long on the task of writing analytic essays, they did not improve their memory for specific pieces of information in the original text. In fact, Newell's students turned out to have the best memory for text-specific information when they were allowed to take notes in their normal fashion.

A study by Penrose (1992) also suggests that students may be the best judge of how to study texts when the goal is to acquire specific knowledge for tests. Penrose asked 40 college freshmen to read one of two texts on which they had low topic knowledge. One of these texts was a popular science article on hurricanes originally published in the *Smithsonian* magazine. The other was a more analytic discussion of the nature of paternalism written by an academic for his students. After reading, half the students were asked to "study for a test"; the other half were asked to "write a report." The overall results showed, in Penrose's words, that "students were more likely to remember individual facts from their reading if they had directly studied the text than if they had written an essay about it" (p. 476). That is, the nature of the study task had a significant effect on students' ability to take the comprehension test. Specifically, students who studied in their normal fashion did significantly better in answering the questions requiring simple recall and application.

A third study using a comprehension test similar to that used by Penrose (1992), this one reported by Langer and Applebee (1987), showed similar negative results for writing. After reading passages selected from high school social studies texts, 208 students, half from ninth-grade English classes in the San Francisco Bay area, the other half from the 11th grade, engaged in one of four study conditions: normal studying, note taking, answering study questions, and analytic writing. Four weeks later, students took a 20-item multiple-choice comprehension test as well as a recall test similar to that used earlier by Newell (1984). These results also showed a significant negative effect for analytic writing. At both the ninth and 11th grades, students asked to write analytically after reading did worse on both the comprehension test and the recall test than they did in the other three conditions.

As Schumacher and Nash (1991) noted in a recent review of this literature, the results of these studies suggest that analytic writing is not a good way for students to acquire the kinds of information routinely tested in school. A final study conducted by Langer and Applebee (1987) suggests why: When the students in this study wrote analytic essays, they focused on a narrow range of information relevant to the thesis they were developing. That is, if they were trying to identify "the two or three most important reasons for industrial growth in the late nineteenth and twentieth centuries"—the typical prompt used by Langer and Applebee in all of their studies—they simply reviewed the text to pick out their "two or three most important reasons" and ignored the reasons they judged less important. On just this subset of content to which they paid attention, they did seem to have an advantage over those who answered study questions or wrote simple summaries. However, when content was looked at more broadly, their performance suffered compared to those who had used other postreading activities.

Factors Affecting the Relationship Between Writing and Learning

In general, then, students and teachers in academic settings appear to be justified in not using very much extended analytic writing. In fact, this kind of writing seems to distract students from learning the broad range of content required by the tests they take. The more common types of school writing, note taking and answering study questions, appear to be better suited to preparing students for kinds of knowledge displays routinely required in academic settings.

When students are asked to do something other than read standard textbook prose or demonstrate factual content on tests, the story changes dramatically however. To begin with, if students are required to make significant selections and transformations of knowledge, extended writing may be of benefit. Copeland (1985), for instance, asked students to read about a game, write to explain it to a friend, and take a test predicting the next move. These are all very different tasks from those normally encountered in school, and in this situation, writing did seem to offer students an advantage. In fact, it directed them to exactly the kinds of information that formed the basis of the test and helped them to process it in a way the test required.

Durst (1987), likewise, departed from the standard school tasks in significant ways. Both he and Langer (1986; Langer & Applebee, 1987) asked students to develop a position on an issue using evidence from the textbook reading. Unlike Langer, however, Durst did not specify the content on which the students were to focus, only the general area of concern, economic lessons. Furthermore, Durst's students had a much bigger job to accomplish in developing their theses. Whereas Langer's students simply had to make a selection among points already made in the analysis provided in the source text, Durst's students had to construct their own points out of source texts deliberately chosen to be narratives rather than analyses. Durst had thus forced students to create a text structure different than the one they had read. To do so, they appear to have engaged in higher level cognitive activities than normal. Both Durst and Copeland's positive effects for writing on thinking occurred, then, in the contexts of tasks that made significant departures from the standard knowledge-transmission purposes of the schools.

The kind of text assigned seems to make a difference to learning as well. When Penrose (1992) asked her students to read the popular science article on hurricanes, she found the differences between studying and "writing a report" to be significant although complex: Those who wrote a report used more complex thinking strategies; those who studied reread the source text more and did better on the application questions; and those who studied by writing generative notes took longer but did better than those who simply copied down factual information.

On the paternalism passage, however, all these effects disappeared. It did not seem to matter much how the students approached this text: After both studying and writing, students could apply concepts equally well; they took the same amount of time to read and did about the same on the comprehension passage; and they engaged in the same level of cognitive activity. In fact, students appear to have used more constructive effort to process the paternalism text than did those students who read about hurricanes, even though they actually spent less time with the text and, in the end, scored lower on its content when tested. Overall, then, the paternalism text itself seemed to have determined the way it would be processed, whereas the hurricane text afforded two distinct patterns of processing.

Penrose (1992) noted several differences between the hurricane text and the paternalism text that may account for these differences. First, they were at different levels of difficulty: The hurricane text measured at a 12th-grade reading level; the paternalism text at 17+. Second, they were from different disciplines: The hurricane text was scientific; the paternalism text was from the humanities. Third, they had different organizational structures: The hurricane text was a narrative of scientific change; the paternalism text was an analysis of paternalistic practices.

From the perspective of this review of the writing practices, we can note one additional difference between these texts: The hurricane text more closely resembled the kind of textbook prose that students are accustomed to reading in schools; the paternalism text was more closely related to texts written by academic professionals. In particular, the two texts used different styles of metadiscourse (Crismore, 1989) to invite readers to enter into different kinds of relationships with the knowledge they presented.

The hurricane text, for instance, referred to the reader exactly twice, both in the same sentence, as part of a "we" who now know a great deal about hurricanes thanks to the efforts of scientists: "Today *we* know a great deal about these storms, but *we* knew very little only a century and a half ago" (Penrose, 1992, p. 493, italics added). The text that preceded and followed this statement was a mixture of statements about events leading to scientific discoveries made by other people in the past ("early weather observers were puzzled by what appeared to be sudden shifts in wind direction") and statements about what hurricanes actually do now in an eternal present ("Around the fringes of the enormous whirlwind, gale-force winds spin out like sparks from a pinwheel."). Thus at no time in the text was knowledge about hurricanes presented as something that readers could construct as agents. In this sense, then, it was closely related to standard decontextualized textbook prose.

The paternalism passage, by contrast, referred to its readers on 10 separate occasions, and the metadiscourse did not keep the readers outside of the construction of knowledge about its topic. Instead, it invited readers to join the author in offering a critique of mistaken beliefs held by historians and sociologists: "Historians and sociologists have described such relationships as 'paternalistic.' . . . Too often, however, the term misleads. Describing such systems as paternalistic causes *us* to overlook important characteristics of these relationships" (Penrose, 1992, p. 495). The text then went on to provide a timeless description of the parent–child relationship ("Parents are caring protectors") and an analysis of that description as a critique of the commonplace beliefs ("We now need to ask what features of the original parent/child relationship transfer to the notion of social or economic paternalism."). In sum, then, this text was an academic argument with all the typical moves identified by Swales and Najjar (1987) for establishing the significance of a topic, summarizing the previous knowledge on that topic, and moving to fill a gap in that knowledge.

Once we see the two texts in Penrose's (1992) study as typifying the two distinct groups that make up the academy, we can better understand her complex results. When students were asked to study the kind of material they were used to reading in academic settings (the hurricane text), they spent some time on the task and did well on the comprehension task, but they did not seem to become overly engaged in the process. When they were asked to write about this same text, however, they spent more time and became more engaged, but with a consequent decline in their test performance. These results, then, echo the earlier findings of Newell (1984) and Langer and Applebee (1987).

On the academic argument, however, it did not seem to matter whether students were asked to study or write. In neither case did they spend much time on the text, perhaps because they could not find the kinds of factual information they were accustomed to looking for, and they did not do well on the comprehension tests afterward. However, they did seem to engage in some higher level processing, perhaps in the effort to make sense of the unfamiliar genre of academic argument. These results seem to echo the results of Durst's (1987) earlier study when students were asked to create original analyses.

WRITING AND LEARNING AT CROSS PURPOSES IN THE ACADEMY

Researchers of writing have been particularly reticent about drawing out the negative impact of writing on learning just described. After finding negative effects for writing on comprehension, for example, Newell (1984) concluded that "essay writing may aid the learning of concepts found in prose passages excerpted from science and social science textbooks" (p. 281) even though his own results did not support this conclusion. In their book-length monograph, Langer and Applebee (1987) similarly concluded that writing helps learning, although they acknowledged that different kinds of writing seem to produce different kinds of learning. In a comprehensive review of this literature published in the *Handbook of Reading Research*, Tierney and Shanahan (1990) concluded that "the previous research studies provide consistent support for viewing writing as a powerful tool for the enhancement of thinking and learning" (p. 272).

Reviews, however, have begun to acknowledge more openly the inappropriateness of using extended writing for the kind of learning typically required in academic settings. As we have seen, Schumacher and Nash (1991) suggested there is a mismatch between writing and the goal of acquiring knowledge. Furthermore, Penrose (1992) was fairly plain that her results "remind us . . . that students can 'engage in' writing without much thought, without the active involvement or critical reflection we associate with participating or generating knowledge in a discipline" (p. 491). Copeland (1985) warned of the limitations of using writing to learn:

> [I]n using writing to help students to learn, one should structure writing activities so that they help students incorporate in their writing those particular ideas they are expected to learn. If students write about a topic but are not asked to do so in a way that helps them to focus upon the targeted information, writing may not help students achieve the learning goals set forth. (p. 25)

But although these warnings are well taken and indicate that, like all instruction, writing instruction will achieve only what it sets out to teach, they still do not directly address the issue of what is actually entailed when we decide to teach writing as epistemic. As I have attempted to indicate throughout this review, most of us assume without thought that writing is a way of thinking and learning and we are repeatedly distressed to see our students doing something less. What we need to recognize, however, is that the relationship between writing and learning is far trickier than is generally acknowledged.

Writing does, indeed, require some learning—when learning is characterized as an *acquaintance* with a set of cultural facts and values. Without this kind of learning, writing fails, for it is only over the bridge of common facts and values that rhetorical action can be taken. However, writing also is at odds with learning—when learning is characterized as the *acceptance* of a web of cultural knowledge. With this second kind of learning, writing inevitably fails, for passive acceptance of cultural facts and values precludes the rhetorical agency that motivates us to pick up the pen (or turn on the computer) in the first place. We write, in other words, both to contribute to and to counter the current trajectory of our culture.

For many in the academic professions, this love–hate relationship with learning is embedded in our scholarly activities: We routinely set aside time to read what others have said and, just as routinely, turn away from reading them when we want to be alone with our thoughts and work things out for ourselves (Geisler, 1994). We rarely extend this privilege to our students, however. We fear that, given license to pick and choose among the knowledge they acquire and to rearrange and reconstruct that knowledge as they see fit, students will get it wrong; they will misunderstand. Perhaps not incidentally, we often worry that they will fail to develop proper respect for knowledge, accepting as equally valid claims based on sound disciplinary methods and anyone's half-baked opinion.

We need to recognize that such fears derive directly from current knowledge-making arrangements in the academy. Since the late 19th century, rights to knowledge production in the United States have been gradually taken out of the sphere of the lay public, where they used to be part of general education (Halloran, 1982), and redistributed to the professions as part of their disciplinary practices (Russell, 1991). The move to professionalize can, in fact, be defined as a move to remove knowledge from the public sphere.

This professionalization has had its most direct impact on our teaching practices through its effect on the general education in which writing instruction is usually embedded. Almost universally, theories of general education, which were formulated in the postwar era to cope with an influx of GIs, begin with the assumption that general education is archival in purpose. For instance, according to a faculty committee at the University of Iowa reporting in 1948, general education was to acquaint students with "the origins and meaning of the customs and political traditions which govern the life of their time" (McGrath et al., 1948, p. 9). A similar committee working at Harvard in 1945 contrasted this archival purpose with the productive purposes of specialized learning:

> [T]wo complementary forces are at the root of our culture: on the one hand, an ideal of man and society distilled from the past but at the same time transcending the past as a standard of judgment valid in itself, and, on the other hand, the belief that no existent expressions of this ideal are final but that all alike call for perpetual scrutiny and change in the light of new knowledge. Specialism is usually the vehicle of this second force. It fosters the open-mindedness and love of investigation which are the well-spring of change, and it devotes itself to the means by which this change is brought about. (Buck et al., 1945, p. 55)

Both of these influential committees of academic professionals assumed, in other words, that general education is an education for social stability. Only specialized education effects social change.

Placed in the context of general education, then, the patterns of writing practice that I have described in this chapter become less surprising. Writing does not have universal or intrinsic functionality that will push it, in all contexts, toward an association with knowledge making. Contrary to what Knoblauch and Brannon and a host of others have claimed, composing does not always entail "the search for connections." Its nature is not always "to compel the writer to undertake that search" (Knoblauch & Brannon, 1983, p. 468). Instead, writing, like a variety of other cultural practices, takes on the values and functions of the culture in which it is embedded (see also Scribner & Cole, 1981). In the case of student writing in the late 20th century, that culture is a lay culture, a culture of knowledge consumption—not the culture of knowledge production inhabited by members of the academic professions.

Teaching students to use writing for epistemic purposes is, then, a teaching task fraught with a variety of cultural complications we should not fail to recognize. If we attempt this task in the traditional manner, in the context of the general education curriculum, we take on a bizarre task: We ask students to make knowledge without tools. With writing assignments like the personal essay, we force them back on the resources of lay culture, with the attendant danger of solipsism ("everyone has the right to his or her own opinion on this and here's mine"). Or with assignments like the research paper, we force them forward onto the resources of professional culture, with the attendant danger of absolutism ("experts say this, so it must be so"). In neither instance, however, do we engage them in the balancing act between consumption and production necessary for making new knowledge (Kaufer & Geisler, 1989).

If we decide to forego our traditional context and undertake the task of teaching writing in the context of specialized professions, we will be taking on a conceptually simpler task: We will be helping students to do what they already want to do. We need only support their acquisition of the professional practices they are already eager to acquire. And we will confirm their assumption that knowledge-making activities go hand and hand with professional status.

Unfortunately, we will also be putting ourselves in the position of claiming to teach the practices of professions of which we are not members. The problem is that these professions, although they may be willing to let our students in, are certainly not willing to let us in. Thus claims to teach practices that we ourselves are not allowed to learn will not sustain us for long.

The third alternative is by far the most difficult: We can attempt to reinvent general education. Only in the context of an education that is more than consumption can writing be taught as epistemic. And only in the context of an education that is more than professional can we as writing teachers have something worth teaching. For this reason, we must attempt the construction of a third kind of education in the university, an education not for lay consumption or expert production, but an education for lay production.

This alternative, unlike the other two, does not ask us to take the cross purposes of writing and learning in the academy as fixed. Instead, it encourages us to work for a new relationship between experts and the general public, to find ways in which dialogue can be fostered and mutual dependency acknowledged. Only in this way will we be able to remake the writing practices of the U.S. academy into something other than a tool for the creation and recreation of the Great Divide between expert and layperson.

REFERENCES

Ackerman, J. (1991). Reading, writing, and knowing: The role of disciplinary knowledge in comprehending and composing. *Research in the Teaching of English, 25*, 133–178.

Applebee, A. N. (1981). *Writing in the secondary school: English and the content areas.* Urbana, IL: National Council of Teachers of English.

Applebee, A. N. (1984). *Contexts for learning to write: Studies of secondary school instruction.* Norwood, NJ: Ablex.

Bereiter, C., & Scardamalia, M. (1987). *The psychology of written composition.* Hillsdale, NJ: Lawrence Erlbaum Associates.

Brannon, L., & Knoblauch, C. H. (1982). On students' rights to their own texts: A model of teacher response. *College Composition and Communication, 33*, 157–166.

Britton, J., Burgess, T., Martin, N., McLeod, A., & Rosen, H. (1975). *The development of writing abilities* (pp. 11–18). London: Macmillan.

Brown, A. L., & Day, J. D. (1983). Macrorules for summarizing texts: The development of expertise. *Journal of Verbal Learning and Verbal Behavior, 22*, 1–14.

Brown, A. L., Day, J. D., & Jones, R. S. (1983). The development of plans for summarizing texts. *Child Development, 51*, 968–979.

Buck, P. H., Finley, J. H., Demos, R., Hoadley, L., Hollinshead, B. S., Jordan, W. K., Richards, I. A., Rulon, P. J., Schlesinger, A. M., Ulich, R., Wald, G., & Wright, B. F. (1945). General education in a free society: Report of the Harvard Committee. Cambridge, MA: Harvard University Press.

Copeland, K. A. (1985, November). *The effect of writing upon good and poor writers' learning from prose*. Paper presented at the annual meeting of the National Council of Teachers of English, Philadelphia. (Reproduced as ERIC Document Reproduction Service No. ED 276 993).

Crismore, A. (1989). *Talking with readers: Metadiscourse as a rhetorical act*. New York: Lang.

Durst, R. K. (1987). Cognitive and linguistic demands of analytic writing. *Research in the Teaching of English, 21*, 347–376.

Emig, J. (1971). *The composing process of twelfth graders*. Urbana, IL: National Council of Teachers of English.

Emig, J. (1977). Writing as a mode of learning. *College Composition and Communication, 28*, 122–127.

Faigley, L., & Witte, S. (1981). Analyzing revision. *College Composition and Communication, 32*, 400–414.

Fitzgerald, J. (1987). Research on revision in writing. *Review of Educational Research, 57*, 481–506.

Flower, L., & Hayes, J. R. (1980a). The cognition of discovery: Defining a rhetorical problem. *College Composition and Communication, 31*, 21–32.

Flower, L., & Hayes, J. R. (1980b). The dynamics of composing: Making plans and juggling constraints. In L. Gregg & E. Steinberg (Eds.), *Cognitive processes in writing* (pp. 31–50). Hillsdale, NJ: Lawrence Erlbaum Associates.

Flower, L., Hayes, J. R., Carey, L., Schriver, K., & Stratman, J. (1986). Detection, diagnosis, and strategies of revision. *College Composition and Communication, 37*, 16–55.

Fulwiler, T. (1986). The argument for writing across the curriculum. In A. Young & T. Fulwiler (Eds.), *Writing across the disciplines: Research into practice*. (pp. 21–32). Upper Montclair, NJ: Boynton/Cook.

Garner, R., Belcher, V., Winfield, E., & Smith T. (1985). Multiple measures of text proficiency: What can fifth-grade students do? *Research in the Teaching of English, 19*, 140–153.

Geisler, C. (1994). *Academic literacy and the nature of expertise: Reading, writing, and knowing in academic philosophy*. Hillsdale, NJ: Lawrence Erlbaum Associates.

Halloran, S. M. (1982). Rhetoric in the American college curriculum: The decline of public discourse. *Pre/Text, 3*, 245–269.

Hayes, J. R. Flower, L., Schriver, K. A., Stratman, J., & Carey, L. (1987). Cognitive processes in revision. In S. Rosenberg (Ed.), *Advances in psycholinguistics, Vol II: Reading, writing, and language processing* (pp. 176–240). Cambridge, UK: Cambridge University Press.

Horvath, B. K. (1984). The components of written response: A practical synthesis of current views. *Rhetoric Review, 2*, 136–156.

Hounsell, D. (1984). Learning and essay-writing. In F. Marton, D. Hounsell, & N. Entwistle (Eds.), *The experience of learning* (pp. 103–123). Edinburgh: Scottish Academic.

Kaufer, D. S., & Geisler, C. (1989). Novelty in academic writing. *Written Communication, 8*, 286–311.

Knoblauch, C. H., & Brannon, L. (1983). Writing as learning through the curriculum, *College English, 45*, 465–474.

Langer, J. A. (1986). Learning through writing: Study skills in the content areas. *Journal of Reading, 29*, 400–406.

Langer, J. A., & Applebee, A. N. (1987). *How writing shapes thinking: A study of teaching and learning*. Urbana, IL: National Council of Teachers of English.

McGinley, W., & Tierney, R. J. (1989). Traversing the topical landscape: Reading and writing as ways of knowing. *Written Communication, 6*, 243–269.

McGrath, E. J., Bloomers, P. J., Gerber, J. C., Goetsch, W. R., Jacobs, J. A., Longman, L. D., Olson, P. R., Smith, G., Stroud, J. B., & Van, Dyke, L. A. (1948). Toward general education. New York: Macmillan.

Nelson, J. (1990). This was an easy assignment: Examining how students interpret academic writing tasks. *Research in the Teaching of English, 24,* 362–396.

Newell, G. (1984). Learning from writing in two content areas: A case study/protocol analysis. *Research in the Teaching of English, 18,* 265–287.

Onore, C. (1989). The student, the teacher, and the text: Negotiating meanings through response and revision. In C. M. Anson (Ed.), *Writing and response: Theory, practice, and research* (pp. 231–260). Urbana, IL: National Council of Teachers of English.

Penrose, A. M. (1992). To write or not to write: Effects of task and task interpretation on learning through writing. *Written Communication, 9,* 465–500.

Perl, S. (1979). The composing process of unskilled writers. *Research in the Teaching of English, 13,* 317–336.

Pianko, S. (1979). A description of the composing processes of college freshmen writers. *Research in the Teaching of English, 13,* 5–22.

Russell, D. R. (1991). *Writing in the academic disciplines, 1870–1990: A curricular history.* Carbondale: Southern Illinois University Press.

Schumacher, G. M., & Nash, J. G. (1991). Conceptualizing and measuring knowledge change due to writing. *Research in the Teaching of English, 25,* 67–96.

Schwegler, R. A., & Shamoon, L. (1982). The aims and process of the research paper. *College English, 44,* 85–93.

Scribner, S., & Cole, M. (1981). The psychology of literacy. Cambridge, MA: Harvard University Press.

Selfe, C. L. (1984). The predrafting processes of four high- and four low-apprehensive writers. *Research in the Teaching of English, 18,* 45–64.

Sherrard, C. (1986). Summary-writing: A topographical study. *Written Communication, 3,* 324–343.

Siegel, M. E. A. (1982). Response to student writing from new composition faculty. *College Composition and Communication, 33,* 302–309.

Sommers, N. (1982). Responding to student writing. *College Composition and Communication, 33,* 148–156.

Sperling, M., & Freedman, S. W. (1987). A good girl writes like a good girl: Written response and clues to the teaching/learning process. *Written Communication, 3,* 343–363.

Spivey, N. (1984). *Discourse synthesis: Constructing texts in reading and writing.* Newark, DE: International Reading Association.

Spivey, N. N. (1991). The shaping of meaning: Options in writing the comparison. *Research in the Teaching of English, 25,* 390–418.

Swales, J., & Najjar, H. (1987). The writing of research article introductions. *Written Communication, 4,* 175–191.

Tierney, R. J., Shanahan, J. (1990). Research on the reading–writing relationship: Interactions, transactions, and outcomes. In R. Barr, P. B. Mosenthal, & P. D. Pearson (Eds.), *Handbook of reading research* (Vol. 2, pp. 246–280). New York: Longman.

van Peer, W. (1989). The invisible textbook: Writing as a cultural practice. In S. de Castell, A. Luke, & C. Luke (Eds.), *Language, authority and criticism: Readings on the school textbook* (pp. 123–132). London: Falmer.

van Peer, W. (1990). Writing as institutional practice. In W. Nash (Ed.), *The writing scholar: Studies in academic discourse* (pp. 192–204). Newbury Park, CA: Sage.

Zbrodoff, N. J. (1984). *Writing stories under time and length constraints.* Unpublished doctoral dissertation, University of Toronto, Toronto.

Ziv, N. D. (1984). The effects of teacher comments on the writing of four college freshmen. In R. Beach & L. S. Bridwell (Eds.), *New directions in composition research* (pp. 362–380). New York: Guilford.

The What, Where, When, Why, and How of Classroom Genres

Aviva Freedman
Carleton University

In *Writing Without Teachers*, Elbow (1973) recommended that, after periods of intense inquiry, writers prepare "little summings-up" (p. 35) as a way of moving toward a center of gravity amid the seeming chaos of their thinking and writing. This chapter is one such attempt, on my part, to stand back and sum up: to find an emerging center of gravity or to make some provisional overall sense of what research, theory, and experience have been so far suggesting about how students learn to write, and consequently about how we might best serve them as teachers. My qualms about the presumptuousness of this task are somewhat mollified when I recognize the degree to which any of the insights I present here are not so much mine as Bakhtinian (1986) "dialogic" responses to, modifications of, and often "ventriloquations" (Wertsch, 1991) of utterances made by colleagues, adversaries, and fellow questers after some firm ground on which to base a theory of writing.

Let me begin by describing the major theoretical perspectives that have shaped and currently shape my thinking about learning to write. Then within this framework, I attempt an overview of themes or motifs emerging from the research studies in which my colleagues and I have been engaged over the last 15 years, buttressed by our reading of the research findings and theoretical speculations of other scholars in this and related fields. Although my work's focus has been on learning to write, I want to extrapolate here to some provisional conclusions about the teaching of writing and especially about that specialized kind of teaching, which many contributors to this volume are calling general writing skills instruction (GWSI), and which is found specifically in those arenas designated as composition classrooms.

I would like to preface my remarks (hoping in part to add to my ethos as rhetor) by laying claim to the particular advantage afforded to me by my institutional location. Although my teaching experience has included the teaching of composition at the college and university levels, and although much of my research has focused on writing produced in elementary and secondary schools for the composition class, I teach currently in a department of linguistics and applied language studies, at a Canadian university where freshman composition is not even offered, let alone mandated. I believe—perhaps naïvely—that this situation gives me a relatively disinterested vantage point: On the one hand, my job is in no way dependent on the institution of university composition teaching; on the other, should such teaching become mandated in our university curriculum, it is unlikely that I, or anyone in my department, would be required to teach such a course (although we might be expected to train the teachers).

The reader may have inferred by now that my inclination is to question the value of GWSI. You are right; my position in the end is remarkably similar to that of most contributors to this anthology. However, the particular theoretical frame in which my argument is situated, and the research I draw on, are distinctly different from, although complementary to, the work that, for instance, Goggin, Russell, and Brannon draw on in their arguments. The consonance of our various positions, arrived at independently and through different routes, should strengthen each.

My plan in the chapter is this: First, I lay out my current understanding of the nature of writing and especially of learning to write, recognizing that such an understanding has evolved and will continue to do so—in response to my own research and that of others, and in response to new disciplinary insights. Then, I pause briefly to sketch out the implications of the theory itself for classroom instruction of writing. I go on in the second part of this chapter to point to some particularly relevant findings about learning to write that are based on my research (as it has been shaped by theory, of course) in order to extrapolate further and more specifically to conclusions for the composition classroom.

THE THEORETICAL PERSPECTIVE

Insofar as I can unearth and articulate all my assumptions, my provisional frame for understanding the process of learning to write draws on four relatively independent bodies of scholarship—all of which mesh powerfully as a way of illuminating what happens when we learn to write.

The first is the social paradigm that shapes much current theory and research in rhetoric. Writing is conceived as a social act, one that is best understood as an individual adaptation of conventionalized responses to recurring situations—or, more precisely, to situations that are socioculturally constructed as recurrent.

To understand something about how we learn to perform the social actions implicit in learning to write, I have had to turn to two other fields of scholarship: the psychological literature on situated learning or cognition and linguistic work on language acquisition. The relevance of each field for learning to write is developed in a separate section later.

None of the work already cited, however, provided enough insight into the perspective of the learner: how it feels to the individual who is engaged in this social action. In order to flesh out this theory with a complementary phenomenological framework, I turned to a further body of scholarship developed within the literature on the composing process—the work of Britton (1980), Perl and Egendorf (1979), and more recently, Brand (1989) and Petraglia (1995a).

Writing as Social Action and Genre Studies

Increasingly, since the early 1980s, theorists and researchers have been stressing the social dimensions of writing. Writing is seen as social, however, not just because most writing is addressed to a reader, nor because much writing is collaborative; more significantly, each act of writing is seen to be shaped profoundly by its sociocultural context; and further, the social is seen to play a major role even in the most seemingly private or "internal" aspects of the composing processes (cf. Bakhtin, 1986; Lefevre, 1987; Reither & Vipond, 1989).

One particularly productive strand of this scholarship has resulted in the flourishing field of genre studies. (For overviews of recent work in this field, see Berkenkotter & Huckin, 1993; Devitt, 1993; Freedman & Medway, 1994a, 1994b; Schryer, 1993; Swales, 1990.) Much of this work, at least in North America,[1] grows out of key notions developed in the New Rhetoric: for example, Burke's (1941, 1966) thesis that texts are best understood as "symbolic actions"—actions that are only interpretable in terms of motive and situation; and Bitzer's (1960) recognition that texts respond to rhetorical situations and exigencies. The genre theorists add to these rhetorical notions insights about recurrence, typification, and conventionalization—both in language and in our common construal of the world. Genres are defined as conventionally typified responses to situation types, or to situations that are culturally or socially construed as recurrent. Thus Miller (1984) reinterpreted Bitzer (1960) and argued that exigence is socially constructed, relying on Schutz's notion of situation types. Genres reflect both the social

---

[1]For distinctions between North American and Australian discussions of genre, see Freedman and Medway (1994b).

dimensions of language use and the socially constructed character of human experience.

It is this same emphasis on the social, on recurrence, and on conventionalization that characterizes the confluent theoretic work of Bakhtin (1986): "We speak only in definite speech genres, that is, all our utterances have definite and relatively stable typical *forms of construction of the whole*" (p. 78). This is not to ignore the role of the unique and the individual: In fact, Bakhtin highlighted the tension between, and the yoking of the individual with and through the social:

> This is why the unique speech experience of each individual is shaped and developed in continuous and constant interaction with others' individual utterances. . . . Our speech, that is, all our utterances . . . is filled with others' words, varying degrees of otherness or varying degrees of "our-own-ness" . . . . These words of others carry with them their own expression, their own evaluative tone, which we assimilate, reword, and re-accentuate. (p. 89)

Underlying all the work on genre, there is also the sense of a strong current of interactive energy. Bakhtin's concept of "dialogism" is based on the notion that all that we say is a response to, an amplification of, or an anticipation of something that has been or may be said or thought. There is a state of alertness to and energy directed toward the complex unfolding conversation of mankind. The same sense of energy, force, and engagement pervades Miller's rhetorical notions of exigence or social motive; both imply interaction, engagement, and the active enlisting of human energy. Freadman (1987) drew on the analogy of a tennis game to illuminate the nature of genre, insisting that the game does not reside in the balls, nor the rules, but rather in the playing. Genre is an activity that can be reified for analysis and inspection, but not for performance or acquisition.

As to genre acquisition, implicit in all this work is the view that individuals are first introduced into a context in which they are immersed in the ambient social languages and speech genres; they then respond, ventriloquating (to use Wertsch's [1991] term) and reaccentuating the generic forms thus made available, in the context of their own intention or "speech plan" (Bakhtin, 1986).

Situated Learning

Berkenkotter and Huckin (1993) grounded their sociocognitive theory of genre on notions taken from the literature on situated learning, pointing thus to the consonance between these two theories of human performance. Both emphasize the role of context, richly textured and highly specific local context, in shaping human action. For both, the focus is on the social; in fact, in the field of situated learning, a primary concern is to understand the effect of the interpersonal on the intrapersonal, to the extent that in some work (e.g., research on distributed cognition), the distinction between the two is dissolved. Implicit in both theories as well is the recognition that we learn through intricate processes of social interaction and collaboration, as mediated by cultural semiotic tools, such as language.

The literature on situated learning adds to genre studies a more detailed frame for understanding how we learn to write. Psychologists such as Rogoff (1990), Lave and Wenger (1991), and Resnick (1991) described processes of coparticipation between experts or guides and learners or novices in which novices learn through doing, and learn through guided collaborative performance. What is entailed for the "teacher" in each setting, as Hanks (1991) insisted, is not the transmission of "conceptual representations" but rather, the "ability to manage effectively a division of participation that provides for growth on the part of the learner" (p. 21). That is, newcomers' engagement in the process is carefully orchestrated and facilitated by their mentors so that there is a match between the learners' abilities to perform and the nature of the specific portions of the task that they are assigned to perform. Over time, more and more of the task is given over until newcomers become full participants. ·

Language Acquisition

Further elaboration and enhancement of this conception of learning to write can be found in the literature on language acquisition, especially second language acquisition. (This latter can offer particularly useful insights to college teachers because of the shared focus on the learning of adults or near-adults.) Although theories of language acquisition have tended to focus on syntax, there are grounds for at least considering extrapolations to large discourse structures.

Detailed applications of these models to learning to write can be found in Krashen (1984), Hornung (1987), and Freedman (1993). Here, it is enough to point to the following. What seems necessary for both processes, the acquisition of a second language and of written discourse, is, first and foremost, sufficient exposure to what Krashen called "comprehensible input"—a contextualized target language that can be, more or less, understood. Second, the focal attention (to use Polanyi's [1964] term) of the learner is not on language learning itself: Language learning takes place at a subsidiary level, with focal attention directed toward intention or meaning.

To learn to perform, novices need occasions to mean whereby they can draw on the rules they have inferred tacitly or "acquired" (as Krashen would say), from attending to comprehensible input. It may also be possible to enhance this learning through what Swain (1985) called "forced output"—that is, a kind of eliciting and shaping of learner output that resembles the guidance offered by mentors in situated learning.

In fact, there is a strong resonance between the psychological literature on situated learning and the models for learning suggested in the field of second language acquisition. Both involve initial extensive exposure to, or observation of, linguistic or other performance. For both, there needs to be collaborative engagement, between novices and experts, in authentic, meaningful tasks. Finally, common to both is a recognition of the complexity of what is learned, and the degree to which what is learned is learned through processes that are tacit where focal attention is fixed firmly elsewhere (Polanyi, 1964), and where the players all know far more than they can say. Similarly, Giddens (1984) pointed to the difference between discursive and practical consciousness—recognizing the degree to which some kinds of consciousness must remain beyond the realms of discursive formulation. It is not just metaphysics, but other areas of human experience that remain beyond the realm of explication, and ironically one of these areas seems to be verbal proficiency.

The Learner's Perspective

Finally, one can also try to understand performance from the perspective of the learner, and in order to do so, I would like to introduce a phenomenological model—relying on research and theory presented by Perl and Egendorf (1979), Britton (1980), Gendlin (1962), and Petraglia (1995a).

Young, Becker, and Pike (1970) pointed out that, in most creative endeavors such as learning to write, one begins with a "known unknown." When one first begins to write, as Britton (1980) explained, "we push the boat out and trust it will come to shore somewhere—not *anywhere*, which would be tantamount to losing our way—but somewhere that constitutes a stage on a purposeful journey" (p. 60). In other words, there is a direction, or what Perl and Egendorf (1979) called a "felt sense" of where to go in the writing.[2] I would extend the model suggested by Perl and Egendorf (and Britton) here, so that the "felt sense" is not only of the specific meaning but also of the genre, insofar as these can be separated; that is, current reconceptions understand genres to be meaningful in themselves.

This phenomenological framework provides another perspective on the conception of learning to write that has been presented so far in this chapter.

---

[2]For example, one of the students whom we observed in the process of learning to write for an undergraduate law course, was able to distinguish precisely between those situations in which she wrote without really knowing what she was supposed to be doing (without a felt sense) and those in which she had such a sense—but also knew that the task would be very difficult.

Presumably, the felt sense is itself based on exposure to the target language and immersion in speech genres, and is elicited dialogically by the rhetorical exigency to respond to some question or some issue within the local context. For Britton (1980), drawing on Perl and Egendorf (1979), and Gendlin (1962), the "shaping" that occurs "at the point of utterance" is among other things, a further reshaping of previously interpreted layers of patterning that have been constructed at nontacit, less accessible psychic levels. (Interpretations are continuously being constructed, based both on semiotic signs present within the discursive context as well as on a range of others cues and signals that we have yet to develop a language to describe.) Britton described the process thus: "Experiencing, or pre-representational experience, 'consists of continuously unfolding orders rather than finished products' (Perl & Egendorf, p. 122, as quoted in Britton). . . . It is fluid, global, charged with implicit meanings—which we *alter when by expressing them we make them explicit*" (italics added, p. 63). A little later, quoting from Harding, he wrote: "A great deal of speaking and writing involves the effort to be a little more faithful to the non-verbal background of language than an over-ready acceptance of ready-made terms and phrases will permit" (p. 63): This latter notion is vividly illustrated in the tension described in the following.

There is intention, there is tacit meaning, there is something that must be said—and in the course of trying to say it, with conscious attention fully focused on the intended meaning, the relevant features of various speech genres are brought into play. Especially significant is the phenomenon that Perl and Egendorf pointed to of a dynamic interplay between the intended sense and the unfolding words, so that each modifies the other in the course of the composing. Here we see something of the complexity of Bakhtin's dialogism: As we speak, we ventriloquate social languages and genres—and, in the process, find new ways to mean and say things that we might not have said; yet in the course of saying these things, our own intention or "speech plan" can reshape, reaccentuate, and refine what is being written or said so that the utterance becomes the site of tension between the personal and the social. Through re-"shaping at the point of utterance" (Britton, 1980), we enact our genres and yet reshape them at the moment of enactment.

This understanding of the phenomenological dimensions may be further enriched by what appears to be a growing interest in the role of affect in rhetorical understanding and production (cf. Brand & Graves 1994; McLeod, in press; Petraglia, 1994)—or rather, a renewed interest in affect for, as Petraglia (1995a) pointed out, rhetoricians have traditionally acknowledged the centrality of emotional experience to all rhetorical processes. In this same piece, Petraglia wrote of "the affective-cognitive fugue" and specifies several of the ways in which affect works to "situate rhetorical cognition." The degree to which one's ego is threatened or enhanced affects one's interpretation of incoming data, and mood, degree of anxiety, and attitude are all imbricated in the experience and processes of composing.

Such enlargement of our perspective to include the phenomenological also makes the emerging theory more consonant with the facts of conscious resistance and deliberate subversion (as described, e.g., in the literature on the role of gender: cf. Gilbert, 1994: Green & Lee, 1994). At the same time, it also allows for the more subtle reshaping that takes place when one simply wants to refine his or her thinking in the context of the language, the cultural motifs, and the speech genres that are available.

To sum up, any piece of writing is understood to be an utterance produced in response to a rhetorical exigence, within a situation marked by certain sociocultural dimensions to which the successful writer is attuned. Furthermore, the very exigencies themselves are socially constructed—that is, they are communally interpreted. Our pattern-making propensity as human beings encourages us to perceive the world and sets of circumstances as belonging to common stocks or types—types that are themselves socially constructed as similar. Writers, in their rhetorical formulations, respond both directly to some provocative preceding utterance (e.g., a conversational turn or, for university writing, an assignment) and to the larger sociocultural, discursive, political, ideological context (echoing and responding dialogically to the ambient social languages), at the same time anticipating potential future responses to their formulation. The interaction is profoundly "inter"-"active"—that is, it is profoundly dialogic and active in responding to what has been said and understood and predicting what may be said or understood.

Theory and the Teacher

What does all this suggest for the teaching of writing? The teacher's role is to provide the appropriate context, a context where the learner will have the requisite exposure, and then to engage the learner actively, prompting, guiding, and sometimes redirecting. As the literature on situated learning points out, this enables learning to take place through active engagement in a process—rather than through the passive reception of already formulated information (Hanks, 1991). As Polanyi's (1964) speculations and second language acquisition theory suggest, both the act and its learning rely on an immense amount of tacit understanding and knowledge.

Furthermore, the phenomenological literature suggests that the successful performer must begin with a felt sense (derived presumably from sufficient exposure) and that this felt sense itself often draws on levels of understanding that are preverbal and that become linguistically formulated only in the actual process of expression. And, as the word "felt" suggests, more than mentation or affectless cognition is entailed. Typically, some kind of affect informs the process—at the very least in terms of sharpening engagement and lessening resistance.

The power of this theory is that it can begin to explain failure as well as success. Students who have not been sufficiently immersed in a context, who have not been sufficiently exposed to its speech genres, will not be able to ventriloquate, to respond dialogically. Of course, sufficiency of exposure will vary from person to person: Threshold levels may differ according both to individual needs as well as to the degree to which the social languages or contexts to which learners were exposed earlier resemble new ones. This raises the question of "discourse transfer," in Popken's (1992) terms. I owe to my colleagues Yalden and Jones the analogy of fish scales to suggest successive stages of approximation, or overlap, in terms of social languages, genres, and learning contexts. However, as Popken (1992) illustrated, arguing on the basis of the literature on interlanguage in second language transfer, both positive and negative transfer can occur, and how students learn to select appropriately remains to be investigated. More specific and concrete implications for the teacher of writing will become apparent in the discussion of research findings that follow.

RESEARCH

In this second section, I draw on findings from a range of research studies in which I have been involved over the last 15 years. My goal is not to provide an overall meta-analysis, but rather to home in on those findings that have particular implications for GWSI.

Briefly, the research that grounds the argument to follow includes the following: several large-scale research and evaluation projects involving analyses of compositions produced by the whole population of students for the following grade levels, within several Ontario boards: Grade 5, Grade 8, Grade 12G(eneral), and Grade 12A(dvanced—i.e., university-bound; Freedman, 1987a; Freedman & Pringle, 1979, 1980a, 1984, 1989; Pringle & Freedman, 1985); analyses and comparisons by level of a range of discipline-specific texts written as part of students' academic work for four disciplines—with a view to contrasting performance in the final year of secondary school (Grade 13) and the third year of university (Freedman & Pringle, 1980b); analyses of texts accompanied by close observation of students participating in class and composing texts outside class for several undergraduate courses, including introductory law (Freedman, 1987b, 1990, in press), financial analysis (Freedman, Adam, & Smart, 1994), and business (Freedman & Adam, 1994); and, in order to highlight salient differences between school and workplace writing, analyses of texts accompanied by close observations of writers and readers in workplaces where the substance and format of the writing was believed to be much like that of the university (Freedman et al., 1994).

My goal in the pages that follow is to summarize some of our earlier findings concerning the social, cultural, and institutional realities that shape school writing and then to focus on how writing in the composition classroom is a specialized instance of such writing. In the end, I argue not only that writing in the composition class is atypical, but also that students in such classes receive, ironically, less useful guidance than in disciplinary courses and that their performance consequently is more likely to be influenced by their sociocultural backgrounds.

These are strong claims, and I lead up to them by pointing to a series of generalizations emerging from the research, beginning with those that are least problematic.

1. School Genres Are Complex, Sophisticated, Rhetorical Transactions

Despite a general feeling in the popular press that anyone should be able to write an essay, school genres are highly complex and sophisticated transactions, involving subtle, variable, pragmatic, and rhetorical rules. Herrington (1985) and Freedman (1990, in press) showed how specific courses elicit specialized genres that involve highly nuanced and sophisticated epistemological stances to new material. Giltrow and Valiquette (1994) demonstrated how different rules apply with respect to what can be assumed as shared knowledge in different university disciplines. Further, other research has suggested that subtlety and complexity are characteristic of writing for the composition class as well: For example, Kaufer and Geisler (1989) pointed to the complexity of what is considered to be appropriate "novelty" in student compositions.

This finding in itself poses questions about the viability of GWSI. Is there anything that can be deemed "general" besides scribal and mechanical skill? Second, isn't the GWSI class context, by definition, different from those of other courses—in its substance (or paucity thereof), in its epistemological assumptions, and in its ideological context? If so, what skills can we reasonably expect to be transferable to other settings?

2. The Complex Rules Underlying School Writing.Are Tacitly Acquired

A second finding is that, as with much linguistic performance, the accomplishment of school genres is achieved without either the writers or those eliciting the writing being able to articulate the sophisticated rules that underlie them. These rules are complex, nuanced, variable, context-specific, and as yet unamenable to complete reconstruction even by skilled researchers. Together these two findings underpin the argument that I have made elsewhere about the limited role in genre acquisition of decontextualized explication of rules—often a staple of GWSI (see Freedman, 1993).

3. One Inescapable Purpose of School Writing Is for Inspection and Evaluation

A pervasive institutional goal of schooling, however naturalized and thus invisible, is the Foucaudian (1977) one of inspecting and ranking students (see Foucault's 1977 discussion of the "normalizing gaze.") Hence, the recurrent extra- and intrauniversity concern about grade inflation. Our research (Freedman, 1987b; Freedman et al., 1994) has shown us the degree to which students appreciate this reality: They treat a writing episode as complete only once they have received the grade (whether they actually pick up the piece of writing from the teacher or not) and when asked about teachers' comments on their pieces, students often remember only the grade (Freedman, 1987b).

For their part, the reading practices of instructors (Adam, 1994; Freedman et al., 1994) are governed primarily by a need to grade and their comments are influenced by the need to justify the grade. This contrasts with the responses of workplace readers whose concerns, as supervisors, are to improve the draft documents, and whose comments are mostly directed to that end. As instructors, we are uncomfortable with the power assigned by our institutions—or at least we are uncomfortable acknowledging them. As Hubbuch (1989–1990) noted: "Power makes many academics uneasy. It smells of coercion, manipulation, exploitation—control" (p. 35). Petraglia (1995b) extended Hubbuch's argument thus: "Given the opportunity to decline authority over our students' writing in the classroom, no doubt many of us would . . . nevertheless, everyday reality continually reminds us that teachers do not, perhaps cannot, abdicate their authority" (p. 28).

4. School Writing Is Writer Oriented and Epistemic

Unlike much writing outside school, school genres are writer oriented in the specialized sense used by Freedman et al. (1994). That is, their goal is to reveal to the reader the degree to which the writer knows how to perform in ways consistent with the reader's goals for the course. Some might refer to this function as one of display, but that ignores the fact that disciplinary genres are not only demonstrations but also occasions for the performance of specific kinds of knowing or learning that are achieved through the writing. (See, however, the discussion of writing in the composition class later.) In other words, it is only through the activity of writing that the required mastery or insight is achieved.

The contrast with out-of-school writing was particularly salient in a study (Freedman et al., 1994) in which we compared workplace writing with university-based case study writing, where each case report was expected to conclude with a recommendation for action. The degree to which the social motive for the writing was distinct in the two sites soon became evident. The difference was that, despite the instructions on the assignment, the goal in the school writing was not to produce action, but rather to provide students with the occasion for developing and demonstrating knowledge of the kinds of arguments (warrants, trains of reasoning) that would be counted as persuasive in recommending action within the relevant discourse community. Different criteria, for that reason, were at play. Far more had to be specified for the reader (the teacher), far less could be assumed as shared (even though much of what was explicated was known to be shared knowledge), and only those warrants that coincided with the course's content could be drawn on. (The warrants appropriate in any workplace are more varied than those taught in any specific course; cf. Freedman et al., 1994.) The real social motive was not in fact action oriented but rather epistemic (see Willard's 1982 distinction)—to show that the students knew how to make recommendations for action that would be persuasive in the relevant community.

It is here that we begin to see a difference between disciplinary writing and writing for the composition class. Certainly writing for the composition class is teacher oriented, evaluation oriented, and intended for display, but display of what? That question continues to plague curriculum planners.

In those curricula favoring personal development, the display required is of a particular stance toward personal experience; in the liberationist composition classroom, the display is of a privileged stance to sociopolitical issues. But the nature of the relationship of these stances to the goals of a composition class still need to be theorized (see the discussion in the conclusion).

5. There Is Less Teacherly Support and Guidance in the Composition Classroom Than in the Disciplinary Class—A Phenomenon That Privileges Mainstream Students

Perhaps the most significant finding of our research for GWSI is this: Writing for the disciplines is more elaborately supported and facilitated than writing for the composition class; consequently, the evaluation of writing in the composition class is more likely to privilege students whose socioeconomic and literate backgrounds are more consistent with those of the instructor and the institution.

In order to clarify this difference, let me begin by describing some research that involved observation of writing in the disciplinary classroom in first and upper years of undergraduate schooling. This will stand in contrast to observations concerning writing elicited in the composition classroom.

Disciplinary Classes. Our analysis of discipline-specific writing at various secondary and postsecondary levels revealed that the writing in each class was remarkably homogenous according to a variety of rhetorical and discoursal criteria, and that the disciplinary writing was very different from the writing of arguments in the composition classes in this homogeneity.

Even though we looked at samples of writing representing the range of grades in a class, each class seemed to produce its own genre—in the light of traditional definitions relating to textual regularities. For the most part, these pieces were arguments, in which a thesis was stated and supported (sometimes with some digression, but significantly with different degrees of tolerance for digression by discipline so that digressions, for example, were more likely to occur in English papers than in biology or law). The lexicon for each course was, not surprisingly, distinctive, but there was variation at the macro-and microrhetorical levels as well, and even at the level of syntax, so that we found that the syntax for an undergraduate law class was significantly more complex (more T-units per sentence, more clauses per T-unit) than the writing of the same students for other academic classes (Freedman, 1990, in press).

Our first hypothesis was that students were being given models for their writing—in their textbooks, or by their professors as guides. In fact, however, in the classes we observed, students were given no such models and—significantly—never sought these out (Freedman, 1987b, 1993).

Something else was happening that was enabling or constraining students to write pieces within each class that were more uniform, more typified, and more like a genre. Current theories of genre, buttressed by work on situated learning and language acquisition, provided us with explanations for what transpired in these disciplinary classes, and how this differed from what went on in the composition class. Using contemporary genre theory, student texts can be seen not simply as sets of textual regularities but also as typified rhetorical responses to recurring situations. If the recurrence is understood to be synchronic rather than diachronic, in each class the students responded to the same rhetorical exigence—one that they had learned to interpret in the same way. In Bakhtin's (1986) terms, the students respond dialogically to what was experienced in the class, ventriloquating the social languages therein heard and read, as they each developed their own answers to the questions set in the assignment by the teacher.

From the perspective of situated learning, the disciplinary classes provided the same kind of "guided participation" that Rogoff (1990) described in *Apprenticeship in Thinking*. The guide or teacher shapes the context in such a way that the learner learns through doing (partly in collaboration). Rogoff cited the functions of the tutor in scaffolding a child's performance, as presented in Wood, Bruner, and Ross (1976). These include "demonstrating an idealized version of the act to be performed" and "marking critical features of discrepancies between what a child has produced and the ideal solution" (Rogoff, 1990, p. 94). In both the first-year undergraduate law and the upper-year finance classes, for example, we saw the professors select cases and model the way in which relevant warrants and grounds might be applied: for example, how certain statues might be interpreted in a court of law, or certain economic principles applied in solving a financial problem. Similarly, in a literature class, the professor modeled the focus of attention of a particular hermeneutic tradition, and the kinds of warrants and arguments considered appropriate.

Note, however, that the modeling is not of the discovery procedures. The professor is not Archimedes sitting in the bath and attempting to replicate the mental events preceding the sudden "*eureka*" as the water overflowed. Instead, he is Archimedes later arguing for his hypothesis on the basis of the warrants and grounds considered persuasive within his scientific community. This is an important distinction—one that Toulmin, Rieke, and Janik (1979) stressed. Discovery procedures are ill understood and mysterious; insights come to us in the shower or in the middle of the night, in ways that we cannot explicate or replicate. Further, according to recent psychological work on experts and novices (Sternberg, 1994), such discovery procedures differ for experts and novices, so that even if we could model our own processes, it is not clear that it would benefit our students. What are modeled then are not the creative moments of insights but rather the lines of reasoning—the ways of connecting grounds to claims through warrants and backing, modified by modalities that specific communities have agreed conventionally to regard as persuasive when claims are presented.

To sum up, our research revealed that through being immersed in the extraordinarily rich discursive contexts provided in disciplinary classrooms—where teachers lectured to students for 3 hours a week, with these lectures often accompanied by a seminar of 1 or 2 hours, and certainly accompanied by relevant readings—students began to be able to ventriloquate the social language, to respond dialogically to the appropriate cues from this context. Their learning was mediated through extraordinarily elaborated semiotic signs that shaped, constrained, and enabled their responses to the questions that were set.

Writing in the Composition Class. In our research, the writing elicited in the composition classes offers a striking contrast and provides an enriched understanding of the power of the shaping context of the disciplinary class. Our research focused on two kinds of writing: stories and arguments. Both were written in composition classes, in response to typical composition class prompts. The most relevant findings for this discussion were these. Students' performance varied according to the genre: The stories were far more homogeneous and sounded more like what our culture recognizes as "narrative" than the arguments resembled what our profession recognizes and values as "argument."

To determine the degree of control of structure, we looked at the compositions using traditional textual notions of genre and schema theory. We analyzed the stories, using the kind of story grammar developed in the field of discourse analysis—first by Stein and Glenn (1979) and then by Peterson and McCabe (1983). That is, we determined the degree to which stories contained at least some setting information and one complete episode as specified in the Stein and Glenn story grammar. For the arguments, we developed a much looser model, based on the kind of criteria presented in all rhetoric and composition handbooks and the work of Toulmin et al. (1979). An argument was a piece of writing animated by a single thesis (implicit or explicit), whose thesis was supported either by illustrative examples or a train of reasoning or both. Refutation of counterarguments was optional.

Our analyses according to these models showed that, although there was an increased degree of mastery of the conventional structure for both narratives and arguments over the grade levels, at each level, there was far greater mastery for the stories (both personal and invented) so that by Grade 12, all the stories conformed to the conventional schema, whereas only 60% of the arguments did—and that only for the university-bound students.

Our initial explanation (Freedman & Pringle, 1984) for this phenomenon had to do with the difference in cognitive complexity of the two tasks. Later analyses of this and similar data, however, began to point to other factors and other explanations. Thus, when we looked closely at the typology and incidence of "failed" arguments, we noticed the increased incidence with age of those that Kinneavy would label "persuasive" as opposed to "argumentative." For example, many more students wrote hortatory pieces: "Come on kids, you can help to fight pollution!" Part of the difficulty appeared to lie in the fact that the students were turning to the broader culture outside the classroom for models of persuasion and selected advertising or school homiletics, rather than the privileged academic argument. In other words, the students were invoking a different context; they were ventriloquating the social language of advertising.

This discovery was augmented by another more suggestive one. One subset of students wrote pieces that were uniformly rated highly in terms of structure: These were students who selected to write on subjects that they had clearly studied elsewhere in the curriculum—on acid rain or pollution, for example, or some historical issue. These students were evoking the richly elaborated discursive context of their disciplinary classes, and in the course of doing so, succeeding much better at the composition class task than their classmates who were floundering.

The point is that the composition classroom rarely has any of the richly elaborated discursive context of the disciplinary classroom described earlier. Sometimes, there may be some generalized discussion or a 10-minute stimulus to which students are encouraged to respond, but the paucity of this discursive context is dramatic in comparison to that of the disciplinary class.

What students do then, in the face of this, is invent or invoke the context to which they will respond dialogically, or whose social language they will ventriloquate. They select from their larger cultural experience. Turning to their out-of-school experience for narratives allows for success and leads to uniformity—at least for the students we observed (see Heath, 1994, for a discussion of the very different patterns of narratives found in the personal stories of inner-city students). For the students in our studies, the stories selected (even the personal stories) seemed to share the same future-oriented, melioristic, hero-inspired story grammar that has been specified in the grammars of Stein and Glenn (1979) and Peterson and McCabe (1983), and enshrined in mainstream narratives.

For the arguments, however, there was no such universally accessible ideal. Some students turned to advertising, sloganeering, or school homiletics relating to drug use and drinking. Their writing was amusingly inappropriate (although embarrassing in its apt imitation of the school homiletic form), as painfully inadequate data were trotted out and highly emotive appeals were brought to bear.

There are other factors that complicate students' attempts to write arguments. Oral arguments differ from written arguments in a way that is untrue of oral and written narratives. This is true on a number of levels. The point–counterpoint structure of an oral argument is not the form that is valued in written discourse. Secondly, as Bereiter and Scardamalia (1987) noted, an oral argument is necessarily collaboratively generated: It is accomplished by two or more people each taking different sides, with each one's memory or generating capacity prompted by the other's statements. Finally, Toulmin et al. (1979) pointed to the very different nature of warrants and grounds that are taken as persuasive is much everyday discourse. For all these reasons, the oral discursive context is less able to serve as an appropriate enabling cultural context for arguments than it is for narratives.

As suggested earlier, phenomenologically, writers need to begin with a felt sense of the genre and of what they want to say (insofar as these can be separated). Evidently, students writing narratives in a culture as uniform as was that of Ontario in the 1980s were able to tap into out-of-school experiences, both oral and written, for their narratives. In content-area classes, this felt sense was carefully constructed by the teacher. For the general discourse arguments, however, out-of-class models were diverse and students consequently invoked a range of contexts—some of them deemed highly inappropriate by the teachers.

To sum up, the teacher's role in eliciting writing is first and foremost to establish the discursive or semiotic context—to frame its bounds. One does so by delivering lectures, by both designating reading and modeling interpretive strategies for that reading, by enabling discussion in seminars and small groups, and by indicating through a range of cues what from the outside culture is relevant to a particular class, what should be imported, and what needs to be excluded. (The hortatory rhetoric of persuasion was not what was wanted for the argument essays; the prose of some newspaper op-ed pieces might have been more appropriate.)

It is here that the disciplinary teacher has an immense advantage over the composition teacher. The discursive context for each piece of writing is necessarily so rich—coming as it does after so many lecture hours, so much common reading, and often so many carefully orchestrated seminar groups.

The composition class seems bare and sparse by contrast. There is simply nothing of the same shaping and enabling from the environment. The context is barren, and consequently must be invented by the student, or rather, must be imported from the larger cultural context. This involves a process of trial and error, where students whose sociocultural background is more akin to that of the teacher are more likely to succeed. To put the issue another way, students must begin with a felt sense or a "known unknown." In the composition class, too frequently that felt sense is missing. All this may be another way of saying you cannot write writing: You have to write something to somebody. Neither the something nor the somebody are sufficiently actualized in a composition classroom, except that everyone knows (although most teachers prefer to ignore this fact) that the someone is a teacher in the role of evaluator.

Moral for the Composition Class

In the end, the point is this: The what, where, when, how, and even why of writing cannot be separated. What you write is determined by the entire discursive and sociorhetorical context. Form, at one level, Miller (1984) argued, is substance at another, and this fusion responds to and is shaped by the rhetorical exigence (which is itself socially constructed within a complex sociopolitical context). The what in the GWSI class is problematic, and consequently so are the where, when, how, and why—except insofar as the where and when are limited by their location within a university class.

The solution in some composition classes has been to encourage students to "look in your heart and write." But the wise student has known from the beginning that not just any heart, nor just any writing would do; that, in fact, a contemporary version of the Sidneian sincerity and sonnet form was called for, whether that took the form of "plain language" personal stories of victimization or adolescent angst or highly literary and allusive critiques of contemporary institutions.

Another option for the GWSI class has been to turn the lens of the class' scrutiny on the very discourses and institution of schooling, to get at their ideological foundations. Composition studies have become a locale for the teaching of critical theory. Often the rich discursive framework of a disciplinary class has been so approximated, and to that extent, such teaching has provided an appropriate site for eliciting writing. I would warn its proponents, however, that they forget at their peril the inevitability of the institutional mandate to inspect and rank. Whether the criteria the teacher uses are the same as those used elsewhere or not, the students must be ranked and graded. Although the instructors may choose a state of "denial" (see Petraglia, 1995b), no student will be so foolhardy as to ignore this reality. Schoolwise students know how to respond to the rhetorical exigence of such classes, just as they do to other disciplinary classes. In their words, they have learned how to "psych out" or "suck up to" the teacher in their writing—a phenomenon made more intellectually respectable in this time of postmodern insouciance about the donning and doffing of different personae.

Writing courses may indeed have other goals, such as raising consciousness about the power of, and ideology behind certain genres (e.g., school genres and the genres of political bureaucracy). Critical pedagogy is usefully brought to bear on these, and there is much to be said in favor of such pedagogy, as long as we do not identify the goal of such courses—to raise questions and to promote reflection—as synonymous with the goal of learning to write, which is achieved by other means.

Another possibility in terms of content is the following. As experts in rhetoric, we might reasonably choose to make this subject matter the focus of instruction in our class and to elicit writing in response: In other words, we could teach rhetoric as a disciplinary subject and students would probably learn to write, in the same way as they learn to write for other disciplinary courses. If the discursive context is rich enough—through lectures, readings, and seminars—the writing would be appropriately shaped. If we chose to add to this the opportunity for the kind of intervention during work in progress that is typically omitted in disciplinary classes (and that is described later in this section), we would indeed have a powerful combination. However, we might need to justify to ourselves at least, if not to the administration, why this particular subject matter deserved such privileging; in other words, why all students needed to study "rhetorical theory" as opposed, say, to history, or philosophy.

What Is to Be Done?   I do not intend to suggest here that the disciplinary class is a kind of shangri-la, where all learn to write naturally and effortlessly. Students do not all learn to write in those classes, and many of those who do not could be helped by those of us who have been thinking, in a more focused way, about the issue of writing and its teaching. Here I would like to draw on yet more research: research that has demonstrated how, in the workplace, strategies for teaching writing (although hardly defined in those terms by their teachers) are in place that are reminiscent of some of what we do and do well in the composition class. Specifically, research conducted at Carleton University and McGill University, comparing the composing of university disciplinary writing with the composing of workplace writing, has demonstrated the degree to which there is collaborative shaping and reshaping of initial drafts by old-timers in the workplace. The mode is very much that of the apprentice and the old-timer working together over work in progress. It is precisely this kind of intervention during the process that we, as writing teachers, do so well, and that there seems to be so little time for in the disciplinary class.

    In the workplace, there is constant revising of texts in response to feedback from peers and superiors; this kind of document cycling is very like the suggestions for revisions and the carefully worded prompts for rethinking and revising presented in many workshop-based classes, writing centers, and sheltered classes. (Sheltered classes are small workshoplike seminars attached to disciplinary courses to help students with specialized needs, such as ESL students.) I am thinking of all those kinds of intervention that take place once the writing has already been undertaken. Many writers need to be shown the basic techniques for revision, like cutting and pasting and its word-processing equivalents; more significantly, others need to experience a guiding, steadying collaborative hand as they are going through successive drafts in order to find that satisfying match between the unfolding words on the page and the felt sense created by the rhetorical exigence.

    This brings to mind a related notion, emerging from second language research; that is, the notion of *pushed output* as developed by Swain (1985).

The pushed output hypothesis is conceived as an addition to Krashen's acquisition hypothesis. In addition to comprehensible input, students need to be pushed to produce; they need opportunities for meaningful use of their linguistic resources, with their output being shaped by the assignments set and by feedback offered in response to these assignments.

This is consistent with the second kind of facilitative role for teachers outlined earlier: It is like the kind of guidance described both by researchers into everyday or situated cognition and those studying child language acquisition. In the former field, the term used is *guided participation* (Rogoff, 1990) and in the latter, *scaffolding* (as popularized by Bruner, 1978, and Cazden, 1979). Both terms suggest collaborative performance by the expert and the novice, a kind of cooperative interaction over the work in progress, with the teacher probing and responding tactfully where necessary, and giving over more and more responsibility to the learner as the learning progresses.

In the end, I am arguing against stand-alone GWSI classes. Instead, my claim is that writing can be more effectively taught in ways that supplement what is going on in the disciplinary classes—by setting up teaching contexts that are ancillary to, and supportive of, what is going on in the disciplinary class; for example, in writing centers, in sheltered courses, and in writing-intensive courses (cotaught with composition specialists).

Although all this sounds somewhat like writing across the curriculum (WAC), it is a specialized model of WAC. There are serious questions to be asked about stand-alone WAC classes in which the writing teacher independently teaches one section on sociology, one section on literature, and one section on biology. It is very difficult for those who are not in fact immersed in these fields, who are not themselves disciplinary specialists, to be sensitive to and to articulate the complex nuanced understanding of what counts as evidence or appropriate warranting, or what can be accepted as shared knowledge.

In the end, simulations of disciplinary writing tasks (like simulations of workplace tasks, see Freedman et al., 1994) are just rhetorical complications of the task; for example, pretending to write sociology for the composition teacher. All these carry with them the invidious possibility of causing inappropriate transfer when the student is confronted with the real thing.

CONCLUSION

In an earlier article (Freedman, 1993), I made the case against the value of the explicit decontextualized teaching of the underlying rules for specific genres as a way of enabling acquisition. (This is not to deny that there may be other reasons for explicating the rules of genre; for example, to satisfy linguistic scientific interest, to understand the ideologic forces at work, or to make decisions about which genres to privilege once they have been acquired.) By marshaling the available research evidence and by contextualizing the argument within genre studies and composition theory, I argued that explication of underlying rules is not a route to learning—except in very specialized instances. Increasingly such teaching has become the mainstay of composition teaching, and certainly forms an important part of GWSI. In fact, however, such explication does not facilitate acquisition, but often impedes it.

The focus in this chapter has been quite different. Rather than pointing to those kinds of teaching that are unlikely to succeed, I have been trying to discern, on the basis of various research undertakings, precisely what does facilitate learning. The combined evidence from many studies pointed compellingly to the powerful facilitative effect of establishing a richly textured and finely managed discursive context. This is what we saw typically in the disciplinary classes observed, where students did indeed learn to write, and learn to write extraordinarily well.

It may very well behoove us, as composition specialists, to look more closely at what happens in the disciplinary class where students learn to write—and to learn, ourselves, the appropriate pedagogic lessons, rather than taking our familiar stance of hectoring and proselytizing to the disciplinary specialists (e.g., "Use more journal writing" or "Encourage the use of active verbs.")

On the other hand, there is much that we can offer and that we can do. However, to accomplish these goals may very well require not just offering criticism of the institution from the safety of our classrooms, but in fact reconceiving the nature of our classrooms, of our teaching, and indeed of the institution of composition.

ACKNOWLEDGMENTS

I wish to thank Graham Smart, my "reader of choice," for his invaluable feedback to successive versions of this text, and to acknowledge my deep debt of gratitude to the Social Sciences and Humanities Research Council of Canada and to the Ministry of Education in Ontario for their handsome and generous support of the various research projects reported on here.

REFERENCES

Adam, C. (1994). *Exploring the exigencies of institutional reading practices: A comparison of reader responses in two settings.* Unpublished master's thesis, Carleton University, Ottawa, Ontario, Canada.

Bakhtin, M. M. (1986). The problem of speech genres. In C. Emerson & M. Holquist (Eds.), *Speech genres and other late essays* (V. W. McGee, Trans.). Austin: University of Texas Press.

Bereiter, C., & Scardamalia, M. (1987). *The psychology of written composition.* Hillsdale, NJ: Lawrence Erlbaum Associates.

Berkenkotter, C., & Huckin, T. (1993). Rethinking genre from a sociocognitive perspective. *Written Communication, 10,* 475–509.

Bitzer, L. (1960). The rhetorical situation. *Philosophy and Rhetoric, 1,* 1–14.

Brand, A. (1989). *The psychology of writing: The affective experience.* New York: Greenwood.

Brand, A., & Graves, R. (1994). *Presence of mind: Writing and the domain beyond the cognitive.* Portsmouth, NH: Boynton/Cook Heinemann.

Britton, J. (1980). Shaping at the point of utterance. In A. Freedman & I. Pringle (Eds.), *Reinventing the rhetorical tradition* (pp. 61–66). Ottawa, Canada: CCTE and L&S Books.

Bruner, J. (1978). The role of dialogue in language acquisition. In A. Sinclair, R. J. Jarvella, & W. J. M. Levelt (Eds.), *The child's conception of language* (pp. 241–255). New York: Springer-Verlag.

Burke, K. (1941). *The philosophy of literary form: Studies in symbolic action.* Berkeley: University of California Press.

Burke, K. (1966). *Language as symbolic action.* Berkeley: University of California Press.

Cazden, C. (1979). Peekaboo as an instructional model: Discourse development at home and at school. *Papers and Reports of Child Development, 17,* 1–29.

Devitt, A. J. (1993). Generalizing about genre: New conceptions of an old concept. *College Composition and Communication, 44,* 573–586.

Elbow, P. (1973). *Writing without teachers.* New York: Oxford University Press.

Foucault, M. (1977). *Discipline and punish.* (A. Sheridan, Trans.). New York: Vintage Books.

Freadman, A. (1987). Anyone for tennis? In I. Reid (Ed.), *The place of genre in learning* (pp. 91–124). Geelong, Victoria, Australia: Deakin University.

Freedman, A. (1987a). Development in story writing. *Applied Psycholinguistics, 8,* 153–169.

Freedman, A. (1987b). Learning to write again. *Carleton Papers in Applied Language Studies, 4,* 95–116.

Freedman, A. (1990). Reconceiving genre. *Texte, 8/9,* 279–292.

Freedman, A. (1993). Show and tell? The role of explicit teaching in learning new genres. *Research in the Teaching of English, 27,* 222–251.

Freedman, A. (in press). Argument as genre and genres of argument. In D. Berrill (Ed.), *Perspectives on written argumentation.* Cresskill, NJ: Hampton Press.

Freedman, A. & Adam, C. (1994, March). *Simulations and internships: Approximations of workplace genres.* Paper presented at the annual CCC Conference, Nashville.

Freedman, A., Adam, C., & Smart, G. (1994). Wearing suits to class: Simulating genres and simulations as genre. *Written Communication, 11,* 193–226.

Freedman, A., & Medway, P. (Eds.). (1994a). *Genre in the new rhetoric.* London: Taylor & Francis.

Freedman, A., & Medway, P. (1994b). New views of genre and their implications for education. In A. Freedman & P. Medway (Eds.), *Learning and teaching genre* (pp. 1–22). Portsmouth, NH: Heinnemann Boynton Cook.

Freedman, A., & Pringle, I. (1979). *The Carleton writing project part I: The writing abilities of a selected sample of grade 7 and 8 students.* Report prepared for the Carleton Board of Education, Nepean, Ontario. ED 217 412.

Freedman, A., & Pringle, I. (1980a). *The Carleton writing project part II: The writing abilities of a representative sample of grade 5, 8, and 12 students.* Report prepared for the Carleton Board of Education, Nepean, Ontario. ED 217 413.

Freedman, A., & Pringle, I. (1980b). Writing in the college years: Some indices of growth. *College Composition and Communication, 31,* 311–324.

Freedman, A., & Pringle, I. (1984). Why students can't write arguments. *English in Education, 18*(2), 73–84.

Freedman, A., & Pringle, I. (1989). Contexts for developing argument. In R. Andrews (Ed.), *Narrative & argument* (pp. 73–84). Milton Keynes, UK: Open University Press.

Gendlin, E. (1962). *Experiencing and the creation of meaning*. New York: Free.

Giddens, A. (1984). *The constitution of society*. Berkeley: University of California Press.

Gilbert, P. (1994). Stoning the romance. In A. Freedman & P. Medway (Eds.), *Learning and teaching genre* (pp. 173–191). Portsmouth, NH: Heinemann Boynton/Cook.

Giltrow, J., & Valiquette, M. (1994). Genres and knowledge: Students' writing in the disciplines. In A. Freedman & P. Medway (Eds.), *Learning and teaching genre* (pp. 47–62). Portsmouth, NH: Heinemann Boynton/Cook.

Green, B., & Lee, A. (1994). In A. Freedman & P. Medway (Eds.), *Learning and teaching genre* (pp. 207–224). Portsmouth, NH: Heinemann Boynton/Cook.

Hanks, T. (1991). Foreword. In J. Lave & E. Wegner (Eds.), *Situated learning: Legitimate peripheral participation* (pp. 11–21). Cambridge, UK: Cambridge University Press.

Heath, S. B. (1994, April). *Cracks in the mirror: Class, gender and ethnicity in multi-cultural education*. Paper presented at the annual meeting of the AERA, New Orleans.

Herrington, A. (1985). Writing in academic settings: A case study of the context for writing in two college chemical engineering courses. *Research in the Teaching of English, 19*(4), 331–359.

Hornung, A. (1987). *Teaching writing as a second language*. Urbana, IL: National Council of Teachers of English.

Hubbuch, S. (1989–1990, Winter). Confronting the power in empowering students. *The Writing Instructor, 35*–44.

Kaufer, D., & Geisler, C. (1989). Novelty in academic writing. *Written Communication, 6*(3), 286–311.

Krashen, S. D. (1984). *Writing: Research, theory, and applications*. Oxford, UK: Pergamon.

Lave, J., & Wenger, E. (1991). *Situated learning: Legitimate peripheral participation*. Cambridge, UK: Cambridge University Press.

Lefevre, K. L. (1987). *Invention as a social act*. Carbondale: Southern Illinois University Press.

McLeod, S. (in press) *Notes from the heart*. Carbondale: Southern Illinois University Press.

Miller, C. (1984). Genre as social action. *Quarterly Journal of Speech, 70*, 151–167.

Perl, S., & Egendorf, A. (1979). The process of creative discovery: Theory, research, and implications for teaching. In D. McQuade (Ed.), *Linguistics, stylistics, and the teaching of composition* (pp. 118–134). Akron, OH: L&S Books.

Peterson, C., & McCabe, A. (1983). *Developmental psycholinguistics*. New York: Plenum.

Petraglia, J. (1994). Mediated realism and the representation of a health care controversy. *Journal of Biocommunications, 21*(3), 10–17.

Petraglia, J. (1995a) *The role of affect in situating rhetorical cognition*. Unpublished manuscript, Georgia Istitute of Technology.

Petraglia, J. (1995b). Spinning like a kite: A closer look at the pseudotransactional function of writing. *Journal of Advanced Composition, 15*(1), 19–33.

Polanyi, M. (1964). *Personal knowledge*. New York: Harper & Row.

Popken, R. (1992). Genre transfer in developing adult writers. *Focuses, 5*(1), 3–17.

Pringle, I., & Freedman, A. (1985). *A comparative study of writing abilities in two modes at the grades 5, 8, and 12 levels*. Toronto, Ontario: Ontario Ministry of Education.

Reither, J., & Vipond, D. (1989). Writing as collaboration. *College English, 51*, 855–867.

Resnick, L. (1991). Shared cognition: Thinking as social practice. In L. B. Resnick, J. Levine, & S. Teasley (Eds.), *Perspectives on socially shared cognition* (pp. 1–21). Washington, DC: APA.

Rogoff, B. (1990). *Apprenticeship in thinking*. New York: Oxford University Press.

Schryer, C. F. (1993). Records as genre. *Written Communication, 10*, 200–234.

Stein, N. L., & Glenn, C. L. (1979). An analysis of story comprehension in elementary school children. In R. Freedle (Ed.), *New directions in discourse processing* (Vol. 2, pp. 53–120). Norwood, NJ: Ablex.

Sternberg, R. (1994, April). *The role of tacit knowledge in the professions*. Paper presented at the annual meeting of the AERA, New Orleans.

Swain, M. (1985). Communicative competence: Some roles of comprehensible input and comprehensible output in its development. In S. Gass & C. Madden (Eds.), *Input in second language development* (pp. 235–253). Rowley, MA: Newbury House.

Swales, J. (1990). *Genre analysis.* Cambridge, UK: Cambridge University Press.

Toulmin, S. R., Rieke, R., & Janik, A. (1979). *An introduction to reasoning.* New York: Macmillan.

Wertsch, J. V. (1991). *Voices of the mind: A sociocultural approach to mediated action.* Cambridge, MA: Harvard University Press.

Willard, C. A. (1982). Argument fields. In J. R. Cox & C. A. Willard (Eds.), *Advances in argumentation theory and research* (pp. 24–77). Carbondale: Southern Illinois University Press.

Wood, D., Bruner, J. S., & Ross, G. (1976). The role of tutoring ij problem solving. *Journal of Child Psychology and Psychiatry, 17,* 89–100.

Young, R., Becker, A., & Pike, K. (1970). *Rhetoric, discovery, and change.* New York: Harcourt, Brace, & World.

Creating Opportunities for Apprenticeship in Writing

Charles A. Hill
University of Wisconsin, Oshkosh

Lauren Resnick
University of Pittsburgh

Business and industry leaders often cite communication skills as one of the most important skills for their new employees to have, in the same breath reporting that the college graduates coming to work for them "can't write." It seems to be assumed that if writing instructors at the university just did their job better, students would enter the job market with all of the writing skills needed for their careers. However, it may be that college writing instruction, as it is now conceptualized and situated within the academy, will never be able to adequately train students for the rhetorical tasks they will face on the job. In other words, it may be that writing classes cannot really make a substantial difference in people's abilities to write well within their workplace contexts. If we want to help people develop these abilities, we may have to dramatically reconceptualize the task of preparing writers for the world of work.[1]

---

[1]Two points of clarification might be usefully set out here. First, our focus on preparing students for the workplace should not be construed as a lack of interest in other goals of a college education. We believe that a college education should also prepare students to participate in the democratic process and to take actions that may improve their lives outside of the workplace. Although many of the arguments that we present in this chapter apply to the accomplishment of these goals as well as to the goal of preparing for a career, a fuller discussion of these other goals is beyond the scope of this single chapter. The second point is that one may argue that courses in business writing and technical writing are designed to overcome the limitations of general writing skills courses in preparing students to enter the workplace. Again, many of our arguments describing the limitations of general writing skills instruction (GWSI) also apply to these more career-oriented courses, but we focus mainly on GWSI, because this is the type of writing instruction (and often the only type of writing instruction) that most university students encounter before entering the workplace.

Over the past decade, writing researchers have come to view writing as a social practice, one whose nature is profoundly affected by the social context within which it occurs. However, our newly acquired understanding of the social nature of writing is often not reflected in our writing pedagogy. If writing is seen as a social practice, then writing instruction may be most naturally seen as a process of socialization, of induction into a community of readers and writers working within particular contexts. However, in most colleges and universities today, the majority of the formal writing instruction still takes place within a series of "general" writing courses that are required for almost all students. Whether or not the writing sequence at a particular university or in a particular program includes courses in professional writing, this curricular structure seems built on the assumption that students can learn in the classroom much of what they need to know to write in professional contexts. In this chapter, we argue that writing instruction that takes place solely within the confines of the university—and, in particular, general writing skills instruction (GWSI)—can do little to prepare students for writing within the various professional contexts they will be entering after graduation, and that ameliorating the situation may call for radical revision of appropriate sites for writing instruction.

PREPARING STUDENTS FOR WRITING AT WORK

GWSI courses are largely designed to he lp students develop the rhetorical skills that they will need to analyze the particular rhetorical situations within which they will later try to operate, and to figure out how to respond to these situations appropriately. The pedagogical methods used to develop these skills are widely varied, of course, but a writing class designed to develop rhetorical skills will usually include some general strategies—perhaps in the form of the rhetorical "modes" (comparison/contrast, analysis, classification, etc.)—along with some practice analyzing rhetorical situations in order to determine which of the strategies should be applied.

In its most barren form, a skills-based writing class might consist largely of practicing each of the modes, treating them as formats or rhetorical genres, with some discussion of various rhetorical tasks (often assignments from content courses) in which it might be useful to apply each of the modes. However, most writing instructors today realize that the most difficult part of any real writing task is analyzing a complex rhetorical situation and deciding what combination of writing strategies would stand the best chance of accomplishing the writer's purpose(s) within that situation. For instance, in the workplace, a sales proposal might include some comparing and contrasting of the writer's product with products from other vendors; however, it might be best, within certain sales situations, to avoid such comparisons. An instructor wishing to help students heighten their rhetorical skills must somehow try to develop the students' abilities to make these kinds of decisions.

Instructors often develop hypothetical rhetorical situations in order to have students practice rhetorical decision making. A hypothetical situation might begin with a one-sentence description of a task: "As the Director of Library Resources, write a memo to the president of the university, explaining why you should be given the necessary funds to keep the library open 24 hours a day." The instructor will then guide the students through the process of addressing this task, asking questions such as, "What are the writer's goals?" and "What arguments and evidence might accomplish the writer's goals?" Some of these questions can be answered readily. For instance, the writer might supply some evidence that the library, if kept open all night, would be heavily utilized during the hours in which it is currently closed. This would make a nice segue into a discussion on survey methodology, and the students might "decide" that the best way to accomplish this rhetorical task would be to design and conduct a student survey—"Would you use the library during the night if it were kept open?" If the goal is to have students practice designing and administering surveys, such a task might have pedagogical merit. However, if the purpose is to practice analyzing and addressing rhetorical situations, such an assignment falls short on several grounds.

First, actual rhetorical situations usually involve a complex array of goals and purposes that may not be obvious to an outside observer. For instance, a library director writing such a letter might be already convinced that increased funding will not be forthcoming—however, having such a letter on file might increase the president's bargaining power at the next meeting with the Board of Regents. Or the letter might be an opening bid in a larger bargaining scenario; after being turned down, the director may make a smaller request—perhaps for funds to keep the library open an extra hour or two per day. Students who are not taught that the goals of transactional writing are often not the ones baldly stated in the document may not develop a full understanding of the situated and subtextual nature of such writing.

A library director writing such a letter would also be aware of constraints within the local situation that would surely affect his or her decision on the appropriate rhetorical techniques to utilize. For instance, the current fiscal situation within the university might have a great bearing on the rhetorical approach taken. Are many departments fighting over a steadily decreasing pool of funds? Did the library recently receive a large sum of money from the university for capital improvements? Did the president recently gain control of a large endowment that has not yet been spent? Research on writing within various organizations suggests that such writing is heavily dependent on such "local" knowledge about the particular organization within which the writing is taking place. Writers in professional contexts use their knowledge of the organization's procedures, of prior actions that have been taken on the matter at hand, and of attitudes and values that are widely shared within the organization in order to decide what content to include in their texts, and on how to present the content (Harrison, 1987; Odell, 1985; Odell & Goswami, 1982; Odell, Goswami, Herrington, & Quick, 1983). It is clear that that this type of local knowledge cannot be learned in a writing course. However, without the opportunity to bring such knowledge to bear, students may end up with an impoverished concept of the nature of rhetorical situations.

The "library director" assignment given might seem like a "ringer" because it is an extreme case—a hypothetical situation offered with no elaboration, no hypothetical background facts or "context" for students to use as they make their rhetorical decisions. But there is a good deal of evidence that such assignments are depressingly common (see Scharton, 1989). We would further argue that even the most minutely detailed hypothetical situations—such as the "cases" used in business and technical writing classes, or the "scenarios" used in mass writing assessments—can never be "complete" in the sense of replicating the complexity of purposes and constraints that a successful writer takes into consideration when working within a true rhetorical situation (Hagge, 1990). Anyone who has spent time in an organization has different personal relationships with various other members of the organization and has a wealth of personal experiences on which to draw—not only with the abstract rules of the organization, but with the various other individuals within it. Moreover, much of the "information" that is brought to bear on the writing task is tacit, embedded within the memories of these experiences. In contrast, hypothetical scenarios that strive for a high level of realism must include a large amount of explicit information. Students working with such scenarios do not have to retrieve relevant experiences and make inferences based on them, as writers facing genuine rhetorical tasks do. Rather, a student working with scenarios pulls information off of a page, where it is usually expressed in a way that highlights the "relevant" facts.

Finally, as with our example assignment, students responding to classroom writing assignments are usually required to respond within specific guidelines (e.g., "write a memo to the president of the university"). The instructor has already decided for the writer the mode of communication and the audience to whom it will be addressed. In actual rhetorical situations, however, the form of the response is usually not arbitrarily determined beforehand. In fact, the individual may decide that a full proposal, or perhaps a phone call or personal meeting, would be a more effective response—or that the president is not the best person to approach with this matter. Students responding to hypothetical scenarios will not have these options, and may not come to realize that outside of the classroom, rhetors employ written communication forms interdependently with telephone calls, personal meetings, and various other modes of communication in order to solve problems (Spilka, 1993a).

Rhetorical theorists have always understood the importance of understanding context for the production of successful texts. However, we have just recently begun to understand that the development of rhetorical abilities is also a highly contextualized process. In their discussion of genre theory, Berkenkotter and Huckin (1993) argued that rhetorical knowledge is developed through the writer's ongoing participation within specific discourse communities, insisting that such knowledge is "inextricable from professional writers' procedural and social knowledge" (p. 487). Writers in the workplace consistently report that they have learned more from their experience in the workplace than in their college writing courses (Anderson, 1985; MacKinnon, 1993). When MacKinnon interviewed new bank employees about their writing development on the job, he found that "a critical aspect of the participants' development appeared to be learning a good deal about the social and organizational context in which they wrote" (p. 45). These new professionals apparently thought, when they began their careers, that they would not need to improve their writing skills on the job because they had done well in college writing courses. They did not realize how different writing on the job would be from the types of writing they were asked to do in the university; they were later shocked by the vast differences between the demands of workplace writing and the demands of their academic writing. As one of MacKinnon's participants succinctly put it, moving from the classroom to the workplace context was "like going to China" (p. 50).

Similarly, Anson and Forsberg (1990) found that students beginning professional internships were surprised to find that their success in college writing classes did not translate into an easy transition into the kinds of writing that they were being asked to do on the job. The interns that Anson and Forsberg observed all seemed to pass through a stage of disorientation and frustration with their new professional writing tasks, even when they had done similar writing in their college classes. Anson and Forsberg (1990) concluded that:

> While certain surface-level writing skills are "portable" across diverse contexts, such skills are less important to making a successful transition as a writer than coping with the unfamiliar epistemological, social, and organizational characteristics of a new context. A writer in such a context is

in many ways "illiterate" until he or she begins to understand these characteristics and their manifestations in written texts (p. 201).

Given a view of writing as a social activity, one that is dependent on the assumptions, values, and expectations of the community within which it is being performed, it is clear that rhetorical knowledge—by this, we mean the specific knowledge about the workings of the community that will enable the writer to function effectively within it—can be effectively learned only within the community in which the writing task is situated. Rhetorical knowledge is, by its nature, complex and local; rhetorical contexts appear to vary greatly across organizations (Harrison, 1987). Rhetorical constraints may even change within a single rhetorical task over time—the manager who will be reading the revised proposal tomorrow will have different expectations and assumptions than he or she did when reading the earlier draft last week. Researchers have found such a wide range of variability in the writing requirements and constraints across organizations, and even among different job categories within organizations, that making generalizations that could be used effectively in the writing classroom may not be possible.

No matter how "genuine" instructors try to make classroom writing, there are intractable differences between the purposes of the classroom and of the workplace, and these differences continue to make it difficult for students to make the transition from school to work. MacKinnon (1993) wrote that the new bank employees in his study, all recent university graduates, "were writing, perhaps for the first time in their lives, to an audience with real needs-to-know and in order to make things happen. Instead of writing to display mastery of knowledge as they had done in school, they were writing, as they came to understand over time, to promote action and to inform decision making" (pp. 51–52). Although they had been successful writers in school, the writers in MacKinnon's study did not come to understand the rhetorical nature of writing until they began their careers: "Some participants seemed to come to an explicit understanding, perhaps for the first time in their lives, that audience counts" (p. 52).

We have argued to this point that writing instructors may not be able to provide students with the specific rhetorical *knowledge* that they will need to acquire within the various contexts within which they will be writing, and that building the rhetorical *skills* needed to analyze these contexts may therefore be problematic. It may, however, be possible to develop within students a rhetorical *awareness*—that is, an awareness that writing is a situation-based activity, that what counts as "good writing" depends on the audience being addressed, the writer's goals, and the values and assumptions of the community within which the written communication is taking place. If writing instruction in the university can accomplish nothing else, then it should be able to develop within students an appreciation of the fact that "audience counts." If students come to realize this, then they will also realize that even the best writers in school will have much to learn when they leave the writing classroom and begin writing within other contexts. They will come to understand that "learning to write" is a never-ending process. Every task brings its particular goals, problems, and constraints. Students should know that an effective writer is one who will realize this and not try to complete every writing task using the same strategies that were learned in school.

Developing rhetorical awareness in students is a goal that most writing instructors already take seriously, although, here as well, the school environment poses some obvious problems. For instance, a common technique for developing such awareness is having students write for a variety of hypothetical audiences and identify a purpose for each writing assignment. In order to help students "construct" a purpose for each assignment, many composition textbooks give examples of "genuine" purposes from which the students may draw. In these textbooks, "we get the spectacle of students literally being told what their own motives for writing might be" (Smith, 1994, p. 205). Outside of the classroom, Smith pointed out, motives for writing exist before the thought of writing occurs. "People write because they want to accomplish something that requires communicating. . . . Absent these feelings, they don't write" (p. 206). Outside of the writing classroom, no one has to devise a purpose to write or think of a "genuine" audience that an assigned document might plausibly be addressed to. Given these discrepancies between classroom writing and any other context in which writing might occur, it is unlikely that such practices will give students a heightened awareness of the situated nature of genuine written communication. On the contrary, these attempts to make writing in the classroom more "genuine" merely serve to highlight its artificiality, which may confuse students about the "audience" they are supposed to be addressing (they know it is the teacher, but they have to pretend it is someone else) and do nothing to teach students about the situated nature of writing practices (Petraglia, 1995).

MAKING CONNECTIONS BETWEEN SCHOOL AND WORK

The problem of making classroom work more relevant to the demands of the workplace is not limited to the field of writing. Across the educational community, there is a growing awareness that the work being done in classrooms is not adequately preparing students for the demands of the workplace. The apprenticeship programs being initiated within many school districts and on some college campuses are just one manifestation of this awareness (see Cantor, 1993; Hamilton, 1990). In the area of writing, a variety of approaches are being taken on various campuses to make the work that students do in the writing classroom more relevant for the types of writing tasks they will be faced with after they leave the university. These include going into the business community to get samples of tasks for students to work on and models for them to examine (Lauerman, Schroeder, Sroka, & Stephenson, 1985), and setting up formal collaborations with industry, in which business leaders serve on committees that develop curricula and assessment procedures (Couture, Goldstein, Malone, Nelson, & Quiroz, 1985). These approaches, though, do not adequately take into account the inherent differences between writing that is done in the classroom and writing that is accomplished in workplace contexts. In short, they do not serve to replicate or take advantage of the socialization process in which discourse forms are learned on the job, and the translation from genuinely transactional task to classroom assignment may leave students with little appreciation of the real constraints under which such tasks normally must be accomplished.

Viewing writing as a situated social activity implies that the development of writing skills must take place while the writer-learner is working with a genuine task, in response to a rhetorical exigence (Freedman, 1993a, 1993b). In a discussion of rhetorical genres, Freedman (1993b) argued that, "as social actions governed by social motives within recurrent socially-constructed contexts, genres can only be learned when that social motive is experienced by the rhetor; and that experiencing can only take place within the relevant context" (p. 273). In a similar discussion, Berkenkotter and Huckin (1993) argued that rhetoric is a form of "situated cognition"—that rhetorical knowledge can only be developed by engaging in genuine experiences within the community, not in classroom replications of such experiences (Brown, Collins, & Duguid, 1989). This does not necessarily mean that universities should have no part in this learning process. It does mean, though, that students need to have access to experiences outside of the writing classroom—experiences that will inform the nature of the rhetorical task at hand—and that those experiences should be integrated into their classwork.

One attempt to provide such experiences was described by Mansfield (1993). Working largely on her own initiative, she had students do some work for a college committee, putting together a survey questionnaire, analyzing the results, and writing a report. The students also wrote an "academic" paper reporting on the experience, and on how it differed from their academic assignments. Many examples of such "homegrown" apprenticeship projects can be heard about at conferences and read about in journals and newsletters. For instance, other instructors have had their students create textbooks, guides for local museums, brochures and pamphlets for local charity organizations, and so on. These are not hypothetical or "practice" texts, but texts that will suit a real need, and that will perform a genuine function in the community outside of the classroom.

A more formalized program at the University of Illinois was described by Williams and Colomb (1993). In this program, students take on writing projects provided by "University Partners"—"corporations, small businesses, civic organizations, charities, and others with writing projects that students can plausibly attempt" (p. 259). The students in the program work with the Partners to investigate the particular needs of the Partners' organizations, and the students' documents are "almost always" used when finished. The key here is that the outside organizations, once recruited by the university, work closely with the students, providing information about the constraints of the organizational structure, perhaps expecting a useful document to result from the transaction.

Of course, even programs such as these have their limitations. For instance, much of the work—writing as well as discussion of writing—may still be done within the classroom, away from the people who are interested in using the final product. Evaluation of students may also be problematic. In Mansfield's project, students were instructed to communicate with committee members about the project through memos as the need arose. The idea was to have students engage in real, practical, self-initiated writing. However, because Mansfield collected and graded these memos, students complained that they had to write the memos in ways that they thought would satisfy the instructor, and this imposed a set of criteria on these writing tasks that had nothing to do with their own purposes for writing them. One student complained of the dissonance of working "with" the instructor who was playing the role of collaborator on the committee project, but whose main job as instructor was to evaluate the students' writing along "academic" criteria. How can students treat an instructor as a true collaborator—that is, one who shares equally in the benefits and/or consequences resulting from the project—when the students know that the instructor will be giving the students grades based on the final product? Also, how much input (if any) should the outside "client" have in the evaluation process? What if a student seems, from the instructor's viewpoint, to have successfully accomplished all of the goals of the assignment, but the clients report that the product is inadequate for their purposes?

Programs such as these, although they may do much to develop students' rhetorical awareness, may not always constitute true apprenticeships. In traditional apprenticeships, participants get to see the effects of their work by seeing how the product is accepted into, and influences, the community—the marketplace, the organization, and so on. Apprentices also, presumably, share in the benefits when the product is successful and the consequences when it is not. Perhaps most importantly, in traditional apprenticeships, the apprentices are motivated to learn as much as they can about their new community because they expect to someday attain expert status within that community, and supervisors are motivated to spend time and energy teaching the apprentice, who they expect to stay within the organization for a long period of time. In short-term internship programs, these aspects of the typical apprenticeship experience may be missing (Anson & Forsberg, 1990).

A more radical type of educational solution would go even further toward integrating classroom work with the world of work. This solution would concentrate not on bringing aspects of the workplace into the classroom, but on taking the expertise of writing researchers and scholars into the workplace (MacKinnon, 1993). The traditional process of apprenticeship learning—that is, picking up tacit information through long-range exposure to experts in the workplace context—is effective, but it is also slow and inefficient. The new professional must work hard to discern the tacit values and assumptions of the workplace society in which he or she is attempting to operate. Because these assumptions are tacit, the individuals who hold them, and who ultimately hold the new members of their community responsible for them, have difficulty expressing them and probably do not see the need for making them more explicit. The apprentice has to figure out the rhetorical constraints of the new community on his or her own, based on the feedback received and on interactions with other community members (MacKinnon, 1993; Paradis, Dobrin, & Miller, 1985). It is as yet unclear whether making the tacit values and expectations of the workplace culture more explicit would greatly facilitate the process of socialization into a new discourse community (Sullivan & Porter, 1993). However, this is a promising area that more writing specialists should be working in—trying to make the on-the-job apprenticeship process more efficient and less frustrating for the rhetorical apprentice by trying to bring tacit assumptions and values to the surface for examination.

This is a challenging prospect for many reasons. First, it would require writing instructors to step outside of the classroom boundaries and venture into unfamiliar contexts. In the process, it would entail a change in the role of the writing specialist. Rather than being the one who students look to for the answers, the specialist's job would be to bring together the experts—who have information and experiences that we do not—with the novices—who will be facing a set of tasks and constraints that we can only guess at. (Those of us who have ventured into other university departments through local writing across the curriculum initiatives have some sense of what this can feel like. In the case of going beyond the university—into business and industrial settings—the dislocation can only be more severe.) By bringing together experts and novices, asking the right questions of each, and giving them time and opportunity to talk about their writing projects, we might be most helpful to students as they enter new discourse communities. These discussions might occur physically inside the workplace or inside the classroom; what is important is that students are working on texts that are meaningful to them and that are initiated outside the classroom—in other words, they should be texts that the students would be working on even if the university did not exist.

Rather than go to great lengths to bring "genuine" writing tasks into the classroom, it might make more sense to admit that this level of writing instruction can most effectively take place only once the students have begun their initial careers—that is, once they have genuine tasks to accomplish. Having students practice producing professional documents in the classroom before they have ever engaged in such writing "for real" almost guarantees that there will be little transfer from the school-based writing instruction to the world beyond school. As Freedman (1993b) pointed out, a growing body of research in "everyday cognition" suggests that this is true, not just of writing, but of much of the work that students do in school (Brown, Collins, & Duguid, 1989; Lave, 1988; Lave & Wegner, 1991; Rogoff, 1990; Rogoff & Lave, 1984). Such transfer is possible, but only if the work being accomplished and the instruction designed to inform that work are far more integrated than the current system normally allows. In short, the relationships between work and school must be radically rethought.

CONCLUSION

The central concept that we have been addressing (although hardly mentioning it by name) is *transfer*. A growing body of research in social cognition suggests that tasks performed in school do not transfer well to the world outside of school (Brown, Collins, & Duguid, 1989; Lave, 1988; Lave & Wegner, 1991; Rogoff, 1990; Rogoff & Lave, 1984). More specifically, studies of writing outside of school suggest strongly that writing instruction is not fully preparing students for the types of writing they will later face (Anson & Forsberg, 1990; Harrison, 1987; Kogen, 1989; Odell & Goswami, 1985; Spilka, 1993b).

It is simply naïve to think that students will learn all that they will ever need to know about writing (or about anything else of importance, for that matter) by taking a few courses. However, this does not excuse us in the field from continuing to look for ways to make our efforts more effective. If we are spending most of our time and energy on tasks that do not transfer into contexts outside of the writing classroom, then we need to find ways to redirect these efforts. Given the writing field's increasing awareness of the social nature of writing and of learning, we believe that the way to improve writing instruction is to embed the instruction as much as possible into the genuine rhetorical situations in which writers find themselves—not to "create" classroom tasks that approximate such situations on a surface level. To accomplish this will require some fairly creative ideas about the way the university operates—perhaps taking instruction into the workplace, or at least postponing some of our writing instruction until students have begun their careers. The current assumption that the university's job ends once the student's career begins needs to be rethought.

Again, we have not forgotten that a college education has other purposes besides preparing students for their careers. Although educators may argue about the meaning of the term, most of us still believe in the concept of *liberal education*—that is, that a university education should help students participate more fully in the social and political institutions that shape their own lives—whether their reason for participating is to try to improve U.S. society, the neighborhood they live in, or just their own lot in life. However, we believe that nearly all of the reasons we have discussed for the failure of writing courses to prepare students for workplace writing also work to undermine the efforts of writing instructors to help students learn how to operate within the society's larger political and social institutions. Specifically, universities are structured to "educate" students about the workings of these institutions within a relatively isolated environment, and then to send them away, hoping that they paid attention and that they will be motivated to participate in meaningful ways. In order to have a real impact on students' lives, we may have to follow them out of the academy and spend some time working with people as they write in various other settings. Isolated individuals in our field are already going out into the community, helping people to better their lives and participate in the political process through writing. Given the structure and expectations of most universities, projects like these are the exception; we are suggesting that they should be the rule. If we really want to help people as they use writing to try to improve their lives, we need to find ways to work with people as they initiate, agonize over, and struggle to complete the kinds of writing tasks that matter to them as they are facing them.

REFERENCES

Anderson, P. V. (1985). What survey research tells us about writing at work. In L. Odell & D. Goswami (Eds.), *Writing in nonacademic settings* (pp. 3–83). New York: Guilford.

Anson, C. M., & Forsberg, L. L. (1990). Moving beyong the academic community: Transitional stages in professional writing. *Written Communication, 7,* 200–231.

Berkenkotter, C., & Huckin, T. N. (1993). Rethinking genre from a sociocognitive perspective. *Written Communication, 10,* 475–509.

Brown, J. S., Collins, A., & Duguid, P. (1989). Situated cognition and the culture of learning. *Educational Researcher, 18,* 32–42.

Cantor, J. A. (1993). *Apprenticeship and community colleges.* Lanham, MD: University Press of America.

Couture, B., Goldstein, J. R., Malone, E. L., Nelson, B., & Quiroz, S. (1985). Building a professional writing program through a university-industry collaborative. In L. Odell & D. Goswami (Eds.), *Writing in nonacademic settings* (pp. 391–426). New York: Guilford.

Freedman, A. (1993a). Show and tell? The role of explicit teaching in the learning of new genres. *Research in the Teaching of English, 27,* 222–251.

Freedman, A. (1993b). Situating genre: A rejoinder. *Research in the Teaching of English, 27,* 272–281.

Hagge, J. (1990). Review of writing in the business professions. *Journal of Advanced Composition, 10,* 169–175.

Hamilton, S. F. (1990). *Apprenticeship for adulthood: Preparing youth for the future.* New York: The Free Press.

Harrison, T. M. (1987). Frameworks for the study of writing in organizational contexts. *Written Communication, 4,* 3–23.

Kogen, M. (Ed.). (1989). *Writing in the business professions.* Urbana, IL: National Council of Teachers of English & Association for Business Communication.

Lauerman, D. A., Schroeder, M. W., Sroka, K., & Stephenson, E. R. (1985). Workplace and classroom: Principles for designing writing courses. In L. Odell & D. Goswami (Eds.), *Writing in nonacademic settings* (pp. 427–450). New York: Guilford.

Lave, J. (1988). *Cognition in practice: Mind, mathematics, and everyday life.* Cambridge, UK: Cambridge University Press.

Lave, J., & Wegner, E. (1991). *Situated learning: Legitimate peripheral participation.* Cambridge, MA: Cambridge University Press.

MacKinnon, J. (1993). Becoming a rhetor: Developing writing ability in a mature, writing-intensive organization. In R. Spilka (Ed.), *Writing in the workplace: New research perspectives* (pp. 41–55). Carbondale: Southern Illinois University Press.

Mansfield, M. A. (1993). Real world writing and the english curriculum. *College Composition and Communication, 44,* 69–83.

Odell, L. (1985). Beyond the text: Relations between writing and social context. In L. Odell & D. Goswami (Eds.), *Writing in nonacademic settings* (pp. 249–280). New York: Guilford.

Odell, L., & Goswami, D. (1982). Writing in a non-academic setting. *Research in the Teaching of English, 16,* 201–223.

Odell, L., & Goswami, D. (Eds.). (1985). *Writing in nonacademic settings.* New York: Guilford.

Odell, L., Goswami, D., Herrington, A., & Quick, D. (1983). Studying writing in non-academic settings. In P. V. Anderson, R. J. Brockman, & C. R. Miller (Eds.), *New essays in technical and scientific communication: Research, theory, practice* (pp. 17–40). Farmingdale, NY: Baywood.

Paradis, J., Dobrin, D., & Miller, R. (1985). Writing at Exxon ITD: Notes on the writing environment of an R&D organization. In L. Odell & D. Goswami (Eds.), *Writing in nonacademic settings* (pp. 281–308). New York: Guilford.

Petraglia, J. (1995). Spinning like a kite: A closer look at the pseudotransactional function of writing. *Journal of Advanced Composition, 15,* 19–33.

Rogoff, B. (1990). *Apprenticeship in thinking: Cognitive development in social context.* New York: Oxford University Press.

Rogoff, B., & Lave, J. (Eds.). (1984). *Everyday cognition: Its development in social context.* Cambridge, MA: Harvard University Press.

Scharton, M. (1989). Models of competence: Responses to a scenario writing assignment. *Research in the Teaching of English, 23,* 163–180.

Smith, J. (1994). Against "illegeracy": Toward a new pedagogy of civic understanding. *College Composition and Communication, 45,* 200–219.

Spilka, R. (1993a). Moving between oral and written discourse to fulfill rhetorical and social goals. In R. Spilka (Ed.), *Writing in the workplace: New research perspectives* (pp. 71–83). Carbondale: Southern Illinois University Press.

Spilka, R. (Ed.). (1993b). *Writing in the workplace: New research perspectives.* Carbondale: Southern Illinois University Press.

Sullivan, P., & Porter, J. E. (1993). On theory, practice, and method: Toward a heuristic research methodology for professional writing. In R. Spilka (Ed.), *Writing in the workplace: New research perspectives* (pp. 220–237). Carbondale: Southern Illinois University Press.

Williams, J. M., & Colomb, G. G. (1993). The case for explicit teaching: Why what you don't know won't help you. *Research in the Teaching of English, 27,* 252–264.

Philosophical Issues in Writing
and Writing Instruction

Creative Experience and the Problem With Invention on Demand

Daniel J. Royer
Grand Valley State University

> The doctrine of the philosophy of organism is that, however far the sphere of efficient causation be pushed in the determination of components of an [experience]—its emotions, its appreciations, its purposes, its phases of subjective aim—beyond the determination of these components there always remains the final reaction of the self-creative unity of the [experiencer].
>
> —Whitehead (1929, p. 47)

The effort to take experience seriously is characteristic of a variety of movements in 20th-century philosophy.[1] Smith (1970) reminded us that "whereas pragmatism began as a theory of meaning and as definitive of a new method for approaching philosophical problems, it also contained a *metaphysic of experience,* an account of the general structure and status of experience in reality" (p. 129). For Alfred North Whitehead in particular, this account involved an effort to describe experience in a way that was as inclusive and adequate as possible.

Composition's prevailing theories of invention—modernist and postmodernist—are more or less inadequate to experience. Elucidating this thesis is one goal of this essay. The accompanying goal is to point out how Whitehead's metaphysics, understood as a theory of experience, offers a more adequate understanding of the writing experience of invention and

---

[1]I am indebted to Jorge L. Nobo for many insights regarding Whitehead and process philosophy. I wish to thank him for his thoughtful readings and criticisms of this essay. Nobo (1986), the author of a book on Whitehead's metaphysics, is currently writing a book for SUNY Press that rallies several movements in philosophy under the banner "taking experience seriously."

creativity than the prevailing theories. One outcome of my analysis is the claim that the general writing skills instruction (GWSI) classroom is not large enough to accommodate the kind of experience that genuine invention requires. As the unacknowledged cornerstone of the GWSI framework, invention on demand, I argue, is to various degrees implicit in both modernist and postmodernist approaches to writing. With the richer, more adequate notion of invention suggested by Whitehead's theory of experience comes a challenge to the very idea of the GWSI classroom: Invention as creative experience disallows invention on demand and requires an environment that places the goal of rescuing classroom-sized views of invention out of the reach of even the best efforts of modernists and postmodernists.

Where modernist theories of the inventing subject have been challenged or replaced with postmodern theories on the grounds that these new theories better account for the writer–reality–audience–language relationship, something called *lived experience* has been overlooked. Lived experiences, or simply experiences, are the existential or phenomenological occurrences that constitute our lives. Throughout this chapter, I draw attention to the significance of this kind of experience for understanding invention. It is important to note that experience, as my point of departure for understanding invention, is not equated with sense experience only. As James (1902/1985) explained, there is more to reality than is revealed by the senses: "It is as if there were in the human consciousness a *sense of reality, a feeling of objective presence, a perception* of what we may call '*something there*,' more deep and more general than any of the special and particular 'senses' by which the current psychology supposes existent realities to be originally revealed" (p. 55).

Whitehead (1927) developed a similar distinction between sensuous and nonsensuous perception. The former he described as handy, vivid, well-defined, superficial, and derivative: "It halts at the present, and indulges in a manageable self-enjoyment derived from the immediacy of the show of things" (p. 44). The latter is massive, primitive, underived, and "however insistent, is vague, haunting, unmanageable . . . heavy with the contact of the things gone by, which lay their grip on our immediate selves" (pp. 43–44). These two modes of perception are brought together in the complex experience of *symbolic reference*, the correlation of these two modes resulting in what the actual world is for us. This phenomenological analysis of experience is prereflective and prelinguistic, although enhanced by both.

Hence, my view of invention as creative experience joins forces with what Gleason (1993) described as self-reflective, phenomenological investigations in composition. Gleason made this distinction:

> From the perspective of deconstruction (as a philosophy laid out by Derrida), it would not make sense to talk about reflecting on one's own thinking or on

experience; in fact, it would not even be appropriate to speak of reflecting on language since language which has a will of its own, is not subject to the control of language users. Thus does phenomenology (as philosophy of consciousness) position itself in opposition to deconstruction (as philosophy of language), with each leading to separate, highly consequential conclusions about the act of writing, the writer, and, indeed, the field of composition. (p. 61)

Whitehead's theory of experience anticipates some of these consequences. His metaphysics, like phenomenology, stresses that we have prelinguistic, precognitive experience of reality, experience that is partially but not wholly structured by language. In short, this chapter initiates an effort to show how Whitehead's metaphysics, as a theory of experience, can guide our phenomenology of invention.

MODERN AND POSTMODERN INVENTION

A tension characterizes composition's prevailing views of invention. On the one hand, a lingering or tacit modernism in composition perpetuates the view that language provides an unproblematic medium for representing reality (making invention a matter of simply finding the right match between content and words). Crowley (1990) wrote:

> The modern model required a double assurance—that human understanding could be brought into direct contact with the things of the world and that the syntactic order of language corresponded in some essential fashion with the ordering of things in nature. Locke grounded this double set of representative relationships in the primacy of sensation: the senses handed over accurate information about the world, which the operations of the mind translated into ideas. (p. 9)

Crowley described the current-traditional application of this model that "trivializes the process of knowledge acquisition—any subject whatsoever can be read up on and mastered for the occasion" (p. 164).

Invention, according to modernism, draws on a model of the self or mind that is assumed to be an independent "substance," to use Descartes' language, requiring nothing other than itself in order to exist. When this view of the independent subject is coupled with the modernist identification of experience with sense experience, what follows from this model is a mechanical view of invention: The senses hand over the sense data to the mind; the mind transforms this data through such operations as association, generalization, comparison, contrast, and similar modes of thought. Modernism not only promotes the view of knowledge as a commodity as Crowley (1990) pointed out, it also fosters the view that invention itself is a singular set of independent operations rather than, as I argue in this chapter, a way in which the full experiencing life of the writer comes together in discursive patterns.

On the other hand, Berlin's (1988) postmodern argument holds that "the perceiving subject, the discourse communities of which the subject is a part, and the material world itself are all the constructions of an historical discourse, of the ideological formulations inscribed in the language-mediated practical activity of a particular time and place" (p. 489). For this social epistemic perspective, invention is a "social act" (LeFevre, 1987), a constructive emergence out of the dialectical interplay of the various linguistically constructed components of the rhetorical triangle. Our language, according to this view, indeed frames the limits of our knowledge claims. As Berlin (1988) claimed, "The observer, the discourse community, and the material conditions of existence are all verbal constructs. This does not mean that the three do not exist apart from language: they do. This does mean that we cannot talk and write about them—indeed we cannot know them—apart from language" (p. 488).

Language, as this view is understood by postmodernists in composition, does not correspond to the real world. As Berlin (1988) summarized, "It creates the 'real world' by organizing it, by determining what will be perceived and not perceived, by indicating what has meaning and what is meaningless" (p. 775). Unlike the modernist view that burdens the isolated and private subject with the sole responsibility for invention, prevailing postmodern views take the subject itself to be an epiphenomenon of the inventive process. The burden of invention is therefore placed on the social, communal relations that identify or constitute the plural subject.

Like modernism, this postmodern view is also beset with difficulties, but in this case, not merely with the coherence of the theory per se (invention understood as finding or creating something previously unknown must be nonsense, or alternately, invention is some sort of mysterious team gestalt), but—most importantly for my approach—in overlooking prelinguistic experience, that feeling of solitary creativeness and the emergence of originality from within that gave rise to and sustained for many centuries what constructionists now deride as the "Columbus complex" or the "myth of the atomistic discoverer" (LeFevre, 1987, p. 26).

INVENTION AND EXPERIENCE

Both modernist and postmodernist approaches to invention capture some aspects of experience. Modernist views of invention direct our attention to the subjective enjoyment of our experience as the primary starting point of our understanding of experience but end up affirming a mechanical relation (the methodical memory) and a stubborn dualism between the knower and the known. Postmodern views of invention direct our attention to the broad cultural and linguistic contexts of the inventing writer and the power of those contexts to shape experience but end up affirming a Kantian-like separation of a real world from the world of language (or the reduction of the world to language), which creates a skepticism about the very lived-through experience that phenomenology takes as the necessary starting point for the investigation of invention.[2]

Whitehead's philosophy in certain ways subsumes both of these aspects of modernism and postmodernism. However, his philosophy is also an alternative to both. Whitehead has been called a "constructive" postmodern philosopher: He is postmodern because he rejects Locke's (and successive modernists') identification of perception with sense perception; however, he does not accept the deconstructive postmodern claim that there is no bottom layer of experience common to humanity, the more deep and more general "something there" described by James. His postmodernism, for example, rejects Rorty's (1982) claim that we have such intuitions because "we have been educated within an intellectual tradition built around such claims" (pp. xxix–xxx). As Griffin (1993) commented, "accordingly, in his [Rorty's] version of what pragmatism is, he recommends 'that we *stop having* such intuitions,' as if they were culturally conditioned through and through" (p. 27).

Whitehead, as what is now called a *process philosopher*, understood experience, not in the usual sense of the accumulation of memories, sensations, consciousness and so forth, but as the event itself in which all these things occur.[3] Process philosophers have tried to construct, or contribute in some way, to a neoclassical metaphysics understood as a "theory of experience."[4]

---

[2]I have discussed some of the implications of this Kantian dualism in an earlier essay (Royer, 1991).

[3]Browning (1965) included among the group of philosophers of process William James, Charles Sanders Peirce, Henri Bergson, Lloyd Morgan, John Dewey, and Alfred North Whitehead.

[4]*Process philosophy* has become the standard term to point to, as Hartshorne (1965) said, "a profound change which has come over speculative philosophy or metaphysics in the modern period in Europe and America" (p. v). This kind of metaphysics avoids the attacks suffered by classical metaphysics as a foundationalist metanarrative. These attacks are advanced, for example by Rorty (1979) and simplified, for example, by Crowley (1990, pp. 165–167). Lucas (1989), a respected authority on process philosophy, provided the following descriptive list of categories familiar to both disciples and critics of the process tradition:

> Process philosophy is customarily delineated through the specification of a series of descriptive categories, stressing in particular the central metaphysical importance of time and change; the ontological primacy of events in place of underlying and static substance; flux, becoming, novelty, and finite freedom or partial self-creativity; internal relatedness, organicism and holism; a doctrine of critical realism that emphasizes the phenomenological interconnections of subject and object, knower and known; and a doctrine of "experience" understood as coextensive throughout the whole of nature rather than as inexplicably limited to an arbitrarily narrow range of entities. (p. 20)

A theory of experience can deepen composition's conceptual understanding of invention and illuminate the way that writers invent or become creative. This claim can be developed largely from Whitehead's (1929) seminal theory of experience, what he called the "philosophy of organism" (p. 18). Whitehead's theory of experience, as I apply it to composition studies, does more than subsume the insights and correct the oversights of modernist and postmodernist views of the subject and invention. It also develops a unique understanding of the nature of invention as creative experience. In other words, as a speculative theory of experience, Whitehead's philosophy serves not only as a philosophic critic of existing theories, offering an abstract alternative, but also as a guide to phenomenological investigations and hence can help in the development of the theory and practice of writing—especially regarding invention and creativity.

Before showing how the application of Whitehead's metaphysics helps to guide phenomenological investigation and develop a theory of invention, it will be helpful to review the importance of experience to the development of different approaches to rhetoric and their theories of invention. Each of the views I draw attention to takes up experience to a greater or lesser degree, and accordingly, each view conceives of invention somewhat differently. There already exist several important surveys of the relation of invention to rhetorical theory in general; my purpose is to draw attention to the relative importance of experience among each of these views. This overview highlights the significance of various aspects of human experience in developing a theory of invention. With this significance in mind, I believe that the value of Whitehead's theory of experience to invention will be made more evident.

Invention in classical rhetoric involves using language as the more or less unproblematic medium of thought. In current-traditional rhetoric, invention is ignored, viewed instead as the more proper province of science and sense perception or musing poetic genius. For cognitivists, invention means using cognitive structures that allow the writer to overcome the problems or obstacles that militate against the fluent composing process familiar to good writers. For expressivism, invention involves self-reflection and allowing one's authentic voice to emerge through the obstacles of language. The insights of each of these views are obviously more complex than this brief outline suggests. For example, Crowley's (1990) take on classical rhetoric provides a much more elaborate framework for invention than I can develop here. And Flower's (1993) evolving theory of the "social/cognitive process of making meaning" (p. 177) explores the promising territory of accounting for the relation between cognition and social context in the construction of purposes and meaning in writing.

My point is that none of the prevailing views of invention have taken experience seriously enough. Classical rhetoric, to the extent that it attempts to discover the best available means of persuasion, may eschew experience in its reliance on either rational products or topics of invention given prior to experience. Current-traditional rhetoric tries to ignore inventive experience completely if we take this paradigm to stand for the belief that the proper goal of rhetoric is merely to present ideas derived from other disciplines.

Cognitive rhetoric, in its early forms, charted the thought processes of writers writing, recording think-aloud protocols that captured a particular layer of "thinking experience." Formalizing cognitive structures clearly involves paying attention to experience, but the cognitivists' proper domain has been limited to a high-level, abstract experience, those structures of experience that emerge into consciousness and become articulated in language protocols. The formalization of these protocols produces an abstraction of just one (albeit an important one) component of experience: the unity that can be schematized from the welter of activity and process of human cognition.

Expressivist rhetoric has been attuned to James' "something there" in experience and the creative potential of the writer in dealing with it. As Stewart (1972) said, "the fault of present-day teaching methods is that they teach students how to *judge* their finished work but not how to *produce* it." (p. xi), and the response to this conviction in the expressivist camp involves encouraging students to tap into the dynamics of creation through journal writing, freewriting, meditation, or other prewriting methods. Although some may discount it because of the Platonic epistemology it espouses, none of the critics of expressivism has examined the reasons in experience that gave rise to Plato's epistemology in the first place. One might think that 2,000 years of philosophy ought to be able to improve on Plato's theory of knowing, yet the Platonism we know as expressionism gets its significance and staying power from its appeal to subjective experience. For example, Murray (1989) may ignore the philosophical antecedents of expressionism, for he has the phenomenological evidence reported by writers writing, which itself is sufficient reason to continue to tap the value of this kind of experience.

Unfortunately, expressivist rhetoric did not sustain its early theoretical interest in cognitive psychology and creativity studies as seen in Rohman (1965). Its continued application in the classroom has been sustained by practitioner lore and its methods disseminated piecemeal to other rhetorical approaches. Freewriting, for example, gained much of its impetus from the expressivism of Macrorie and other advocates of prewriting. It is now a staple in our profession, but as Belanoff, Elbow, and Fontaine (1991) pointed out in their anthology on freewriting, "It doesn't have a literature.

There is little theory and even less data" (p. xii). Freewriting has thrived on the sheer phenomenological evidence and experience that supports it; however, without a guiding theory of experience (such as I believe Whitehead's metaphysics could provide), it has a groundless quality, seeming suspect to some and often degenerating into gimmickry as usually happens when lore becomes institutionalized in textbooks.

The varieties of epistemic rhetoric represent postmodern views of rhetoric and invention. Whether psychological epistemic or social epistemic, these views claim that as we study the ways discourse is generated we are studying the ways that knowledge comes into existence. Language is the grounding for existence, and according to social epistemic positions, language not only shapes our perceptions and our world, but it constitutes that world.

According to either epistemic position, invention is dynamic: It occurs as dialectical relations are established and exploited. The social view of rhetoric, including epistemic rhetoric, has focused on a certain kind of experience, or rather interpreted social experience in a certain kind of way. Faigley's (1986) effort to point out the basic assumption of this approach seeks to be general enough to do justice to the diversity of the social view. He wrote, "It rejects the assumption that writing is the act of a private consciousness and that everything else—readers, subjects, and texts—is 'out there' in the world. The focus of a social view of writing, therefore, is not on how the social situation influences the individual, but on how the individual is a constituent of a culture" (p. 535). Hence, in terms of the analysis of experience, the social view of rhetoric balances cognitive rhetoric in that it focuses on the "plural I," the subject as many, and the multiplicity that composes the experience of the writer-subject.

THE HARMONY OF EXPERIENCE, THE SUBJECT, AND LANGUAGE

The prevailing views of invention suggest two kinds of experience that need to be accounted for: the personal agency of the inventing writer, and the influence of cultural and linguistic givens that shape, color, limit, and make possible new understanding. Modernists have taken the former experience as the most pressing and fundamental experience to account for and learn about, postmodernists the latter. As Flower (1988) insisted, "We need a theoretical language that can recognize the shaping power of language and context and still respect and explain individual, human agency" (p. 528). Whitehead's theory of experience promises to satisfy this need.

The theory of experience in Whitehead's constructive postmodern philosophy provides a conceptual framework that harmonizes these two aspects of experience and explains them both in terms of a more general theory. The tension that exists between these two poles of experience is relieved in Whitehead's account of experience.

Whitehead (1933) reminded us that "the doctrines which best repay critical examination are those which for the longest period have remained unquestioned" (p. 177). First among these doctrines is that of personal unity. Descriptions of a substantial soul are as old as Plato and Epicurus. They are developed in Christian thought and in Descartes. As Whitehead (1933) noted about this history, "evidently there is a fact to be accounted for" (p. 186). However, this is not the whole story. As Whitehead (1938) also pointed out, we are all subject to the powerful sway of language: "Mentality and the language of mankind created each other. If we like to assume the rise of language as a given fact, then it is not going too far to say that the souls of men are the gift from language to mankind. The account of the sixth day should be written, He gave them speech, and they became souls" (pp. 40–41).

One of the great feats of Whitehead's metaphysical scheme involves his development of a general theory of experience that accounts for both of these features of human experience as abstractions from something more fundamental. This accomplishment hinges on a metaphysical hypothesis that revises the received understanding of mind and matter, and posits instead a more fundamental actuality—*actual occasions*—from which mind and matter are but two abstractions. The soul, according to Whitehead, is a linear series of "ego" occasions, a soul thread that emerges out of, and is harbored by, the lower grade occasions that compose our body. Whitehead (1933) wrote, "Wherever a vicious dualism appears, it is by reason of mistaking an abstraction for a final concrete fact" (p. 190). Where some contemporary thinkers have avoided the impasse of Cartesian dualism by avoiding "philosophy" (cf. Rorty), Whitehead conquered this impasse with a close examination of experience. Understood as an occasion or an event, the basic components in experience exhibit a structure that offers clues that help us to better understand our human experience as writers trying to be inventive.

For example, central to Whitehead's speculative description of experience is his analysis of the way that various moments come together in experience. Whitehead's description of "concrescence" is a description of this process. According to Whitehead, new ideas are formed out of a rich diversity of precognitive experience. What emerges into consciousness builds serially on preceding moments. Ideas may occur all of a sudden, but mostly they occur across a series of many moments in experience; this takes time, and at the very least, it requires imaginative thought. It is more like what Perl (1983) called "drawing on felt sense" (p. 47) than like proficient memory. Perl's description of this process is very Whiteheadian and anticipates similar patterns in Phelps' description presented in the next section. Perl (1983) wrote:

> There seems to be a basic step in the process of composing that skilled writers rely on even when they are unaware of it and that less skilled writers can be taught. This process seems to rely on very careful attention to one's inner reflections and is often accompanied with bodily sensations. When it's working, this process allows us to say or write what we've never said before, to create something new and fresh. . . . The basic process begins with paying attention. If we are given a topic, it begins with taking the topic in and attending to what it evokes in us. There is less "figuring out" an answer and more "waiting" to see what forms. (p. 47)

There are two key points in Perl's description that relate directly to Whitehead's metaphysics. First, the process of creating something new and fresh happens in active experience, not in a static cognitive domain. There is nothing mechanical about it because the processes that sometimes result in something new are more like the functioning of an organism than like a computer. Teachers cannot simply assign students the task of invention. Invention is a process that forms, one that grows out of a certain way of entertaining experience even at a bodily level. For these reasons, the common practice of "assigning invention" in the GWSI classroom appears to recur to views of discovery that emphasizes mysterious inspiration or, in its contemporary, demythologized guise, divergent thinking.

In his more detailed descriptions of concrescence, Whitehead used the term *subjective aim* to describe that "drive" to make something of and for itself in every occasion of becoming. This purpose or aim is partly inherited from a selection of past occasions in experience, but it also includes the capability of each actual occasion to entertain the worth or values inherent in possible alternatives. I am suggesting that in everyday experience, invention involves sorting through the world as given and selecting what is valuable for the subjective aim of the moment and the anticipated aim of that moment's relevant future. Techniques really have very little to do with it. Finding a topic is not the real problem: The task of invention involves sorting through experience and determining how we might form our subjective aim amidst the given past and the anticipated relevant possibilities. In terms of formal education, topics might as well be given to students so long as they lend themselves to this kind of moment. Students are impatient with typical invention strategies because these strategies bypass so much of what is described here as the structure of this basic experience.

Accordingly, invention should be understood as a response to both the world as it is given and to the lure of possibility. The world given in experience may not be given to consciousness, but rather consist of a vague feeling—pressure or anxiety to perform well, the excitement of learning, the possibility of pleasing one's teacher, hope for a good grade, or perhaps an honest desire to persuade or entertain—but what is given in experience is all that we can respond to. From the teacher's point of view, teaching rhetorical sensitivity becomes teaching students to pay close attention to these real exigencies within the student's own experience.

Although Whitehead's view of the subject does not support a view of persons as isolated souls that transcend the contingencies and exigencies of their environment, his theory of experience nevertheless makes it clear why we experience ourselves as singular, self-fashioning, sometimes original beings—even as atomistic discoverers. The self is not a singular originator of ideas, but it is an enduring object. The conscious self, although pluralistic in its origins, is an ongoing achievement obtained by the welter of feeling presented by the world that grows together (in concrescence) and then presents itself back to that world as a simplified and unified edition of this reality. For Whitehead, the self is both "subject," in the literal sense of "thrown under" its antecedent occasions of experience, and "superject," meaning it throws itself beyond to the world of subsequent occasions of experience.

However, personal agency is just one fact to be explained. There is also the experience of cultural and linguistic factors that limit, shape, and make possible new understanding. Although Whitehead's view of language stands in opposition to prevailing postmodern views that make language the source of the landscape of our lived experience, he would agree with many aspects of constructionist doctrine. Language, according to Whitehead, shapes our experience and thus our world, making language a powerful, generative tool. It is a mistake, however, to view what is generated by language as ontologically prior to the experience out of which it emerges. Language refers symbolically to prior moments in experience, eliciting feelings about the world and luring or promoting in others certain possibilities in experience. Invention, according to this view, means learning to harness language to isolate, evoke, or promote new possibilities in experience—in ourselves or others. In this way, the social and collaborative aspects described by epistemic rhetoric are accounted for; also explained, however, is the way that language use by a solitary writer works to elicit possibilities within that writer's personal experience. Whitehead's theory of experience suggests a view of composing that is adequate to both modernist and postmodernist descriptions of that experience.

A GUIDED PHENOMENOLOGY

The notion of a guided phenomenology introduces a qualification to the method of inquiry known as "pure" phenomenology introduced to philosophy by Husserl (1913/1962).[5] Whereas phenomenology in the pure sense seeks to describe experience without presuppositions and theories, a guided phenomenology describes or calls attention to certain aspects of experience guided, in a sense, by metaphysical presuppositions.[6] A guided phenomenology offers writing professionals interested in phenomenological inquiry a way to steer a course through what Elbow (1991) called the "dangerous territory" (p. 204) of feeling and experience. Elbow wrote, "When we get more careful phenomenological research, I suspect that one result will be to give us more respect for this suspect business of being excited, aroused, carried away, 'rolling'" (p. 205). A guided phenomenology uses a theory of experience to interpret our phenomenological reports; the theory may also make us aware of aspects of our experience that were previously unnoticed.

What follows is a Whiteheadian appraisal of Phelps' (1985) self-study of her own composing life. My intent is to demonstrate the way that a certain kind of experience—feeling and nonsensory perception—become active in our writing experience. I focus special attention on the way that Whitehead's metaphysics guides us to a better understanding of Phelps' experience of invention.

Phelps' (1985) study, although she recognized the impossibility of a "pure" phenomenology, is a straight-ahead effort toward the ideal of phenomenological description. She wrote, "What I am trying to do here—a beginner's effort—is to intensify that self-reflective attitude to approach the level and quality of phenomenological description, which involves not only intuiting, analyzing, and describing particulars of composing in their full concreteness, but also attempting to attain insight into the essence of the experience" (p. 243).

This approach and goal was much like Whitehead's (1929) philosophic starting point. He wrote, "Our datum is the actual world, including ourselves; and this actual world spreads itself for observation in the guise of the topic of our immediate experience. The elucidation of immediate experience is the sole justification for any thought; and the starting-point for thought is the analytic observation of the components of this experience" (p. 4). Whitehead's (1929) broad aim at "synoptic vision" and the "divination of the generic notions which apply to all facts" (p. 5) requires that he interrogate a much wider range of experience than just composing events, but the starting point in these approaches is similar.

[5]The notion of a "guided phenomenology" is introduced to philosophy by Nobo (1986, pp. 387, 415). His description gives a fuller account of this notion.

[6]Guided phenomenology also offers the opportunity to improve on what Murray (1989), Phelps (1985), Gleason (1993), Perl and Egendorf (1979), Elbow (1991) and others have accomplished in their phenomenological descriptions by supplying a metaphysical theory of experience that allows one to generalize more fully his or her discoveries by corroborating his or her descriptions with a general theory of experience.

Phelps (1985) identified herself as a "composer" (p. 242). She recognized the variety of forms experience takes: For the musical composer there is the tune in the head and for her, the "sounds and images of language in my head crystallize[ing] periodically into texts" (p. 242). Underneath it all is the "continuous language experience of the literate person," "semiotic environment," "symbolic energy," transforming "experience into a personal stream of verbal activity" (p. 242). For Phelps, the "slow, deep rhythms and texture of the composing life" are stranded and braided, conscious and unconscious, intense and peaceful. Ultimately she conceived composing "as constructed from a more diffuse and confused experience" (p. 244). As Whitehead's theory suggests should be the case, Phelps conceived of the composing process as embedded in rich and penumbral experience.

Out of this diffuse and confused experience, Whitehead's causal efficacy, Phelps (1985) identified two kinds of activity "whose conjunctions and opposition construct its fundamental rhythm" (p. 245). She described these as two impulses: "the *generative*, a desire to link information and feeling into more and more densely connected and layered networks; and the *discursive*, a drive to formulate meaning in precisely articulated, highly textualized, and rhetorically addressed sequences of meaning" (p. 245). These two impulses, she said, run below the surface of her everyday composing mind. To illustrate the power of Whitehead's theory of experience to guide a phenomenology of writing, I would add that these generative and discursive impulses correspond to his metaphysical distinction between the becoming of an *actual entity* and the becoming of an *enduring entity*, impulses that reside together in tension because the latter is a function of the former.

Without allowing the technical detail of Whitehead's metaphysics to obscure the importance of this point for my purpose here, suffice it to say that the concept of an actual entity is central in Whitehead's system. Actual entities, also called *actual occasions*, are the "final real things of which the world is made up." Whitehead (1929) called his philosophy, the "philosophy of organism" (p. 18), because of the principle of relatedness of all actual entities. His theory claims that "every item of the universe, including all the other actual entities, is a constituent in the constitution of any one actual entity" (p. 148).

The becoming of an actual entity involves the inheritance of all the past entities in the universe and its anticipation of at least the immediate future. The becoming of the actual entity aims at its own subjective satisfaction, feeling no obligation to limit itself with a serial link to its own past. It is related to its own past but that relation lacks the constraints or limitations of serial order. On the other hand, enduring entities are characterized by a unique personal order that limits their novel and creative possibilities but enables defining characteristics such as we associate with personalities or things. This explains the source of tension felt in our efforts to be inventive and original, for enduring entities resist when presented with possibility. Whitehead (1929) said, "Life [i.e. nature, not just the biological] is a bid for freedom: an enduring entity binds any one of its occasions to the line of its ancestry" (p. 104). Phelps' generative impulse is that bid for freedom; or as she wrote, "resistance to order, hierarchy, selection, definition" (p. 245).

Whitehead's becoming of actual entities is Phelps' generative impulse: "the piles of paper that rise around the house in little puddles," the "mute and unrealized patterns of understanding" (p. 246). It is Phelps' "endless multiplicity of the concrete activity of making meanings" (p. 257). Whitehead's actual entities make up moments in our experience that are guided by their own subjective aim at satisfaction. Invention is a species of this moment of concrescence.

Whitehead's becoming of enduring entities is Phelps' discursive impulse: "hierarchy, selection, definition," "sequences of meaning," "thinness," "the loss of depth and richness of meaning" (pp. 244–245). The sacrifice of depth and richness incurred by the discursive impulse does not come as a surprise to Whitehead's (1933) metaphysics. He wrote, "Mentality is an agent of simplification; and for this reason appearance is an incredibly simplified edition of reality. There should be no paradox in this statement. A moment's introspection assures one of the feebleness of human intellectual operations, and of the dim massive complexity of our feelings of derivation" (p. 213).

When these contrasting impulses—the generative and the discursive—are observed from the perspective of Phelps' phenomenological view, it is clear that the rhythm of the two together in experience is necessary for a satisfying termination of the experience. Phelps (1985) wrote, "The push and pull of generative and discursive impulses is not just a brute force struggle; they enact a true dialectic rhythm. Without the generative urge the drive toward form would be empty; without the possibility of writing them out these patterns of understanding would remain mute and unrealized" (p. 246).

According to Whitehead, the tug of dull repetition is inherent in all occasions of experience, which suggests why writing requires effort to overcome inertia, or on a grander scale, why Whitehead (1933) said "a race preserves its vigour so long as it harbours a real contrast between what has been and what may be; and so long as it is nerved by the vigour to adventure beyond the safeties of the past. Without adventure civilization is in full decay" (p. 279). Phelps' (1985) composing life is this adventure; she concluded, it "not only feeds on the vitality of life but illuminates and changes its possibilities" (p. 257).

INVENTION AS CREATIVE EXPERIENCE

According to the prevailing modernist and postmodernist assumptions about the writer-subject, invention can be assigned, it can be insisted on, or it can be completed as take-home school work. Views that take invention as an addition to experience, for example, as assigned heuristic strategies, brainstorming, or listing—or invention taken as mock social experience like small-group discussion work, sharing ideas, collaborative problem solving—they all fail to take seriously the full experiential nature of invention.

This guided phenomenology, as already illustrated, provides what I think is a balanced perspective on experience. I have used this phenomenology as a guide through what Elbow (1991) called the "dangerous territory" of feeling and experience. What we learn from this analysis is a central tenet of Whitehead's metaphysical theory of experience: Creativity resides in the very structures of experience, in the welter of precognitive experience out of which consciousness, language, and thought emerge. Invention is best understood as a concrescence—a synthesis of contrasts that emerge as possibilities are entertained and anticipated against the backdrop of given experience. Invention must be understood, therefore, as the originality or creativity that emerges within, and not as an addition to, writing experience. The notion of invention as creative experience, according to this view, should subsume the narrower notions of invention as reflection and invention as social dynamic. Inventing is not retrieving information or merely finding the right word; neither does invention just happen merely by using language in a social context. It is not best understood as a technique at all. It is a feature of all experience that writers can learn to wait for, anticipate, and exploit.

Invention is a natural component of all zestful experience: In the secondary school, for example, the basketball player and the student in the school wood shop know this truth. Both students can be proudly inventive, and in fact, they hardly need to be taught how. Yet the zestful experience that makes invention what it is in composing writing is more voluminous than what the writing classroom will hold or permit, for relative to each inventive moment, "the whole antecedent world conspires to produce a new occasion" (p. 164). This is Whitehead's (1938) language: It is understood, I would suggest, as the view that what makes some writers capable of invention is in their experience and this experience is bigger than what invention on demand naïvely assumes. A classroom cannot be an isolated site of inventive experience. The experience, if it is fully developed, takes up time and space.

LeFevre (1987) recognized this fact in her suggestion that we begin thinking about "invention across the curriculum" (p. 137) as an alternative to the social and intellectual vacuum of the GWSI classroom. The value of this idea, I suggest however, goes deeper than the argument that knowledge is constituted by language. From the point of view of writing as creative experience, invention thrives on more than just language, invention also needs physical space: the library, the outdoors, conversations, pacing, waiting, driving, and books. Invention needs space not only to supply material for syntheses, but to harbor the social experience of composing—not because knowledge is merely a social construction—but because in the world of people and things, writers find value, possibility, hope, and excitement.

The experience of invention does not end with the whole antecedent world conspiring to produce a new occasion. As Whitehead (1929) also said, "there always remains the final reaction of the self-creative unity of the [experiencer]" (p. 47). All of what is given in experience comes together in some special way in the inventive writer. Elbow (1973) was correct to describe this experience as "the interaction of contrasting or conflicting material" (p. 49). In Phelps' terms, these contrasts and conflicts are harbored in the generative and discursive impulses.

Although all experience is genuine, per se, Whitehead reminded us that dull repetition dominates most kinds of experience in nature. The bid for freedom—the anticipation of possibility that characterizes inventiveness and originality—can only be achieved as the writer steps into experience with both feet, as the writer participates in the felt structures of the composing life and learns to live those experiences through to the successful completion of a composition. In his early work, Elbow (1973) described the entertainment of the possibilities of these experiences as the "believing game" (p. 147). In order to play that game, students need to learn what many writing professionals have said all along: that writing is thinking. Students also need a greater awareness that writing is living, that the composing life is an integral part of the experience of being an educated and participative citizen. It seems to me that, in part, this broader sense of what it means to live as a writer is what the push for portfolio assessment and writing across the curriculum has been all about.

There are all kinds of problems inherent in the notion of GWSI that militate against invention as creative experience. One of the greatest hindrances may be the GWSI classroom itself. Such classrooms encourage students to concoct their creativity and, in doing so, undermine any genuine appreciation of the generative capacities of the imagination. The teacher-instigated performances Petraglia (1995) termed *pseudotransactions* seem to be, at best, an excrescence on any real composing life our students might enjoy. If we accept that invention occurs in the tensions and contrasts of preconscious feeling, it is easily imagined why being told to "think up" a purpose for writing, "invent" an argument to publish as next week's editorial, or "discuss" for 30 minutes in your small group the pros and cons of school locker searches—however much good intention accompanies the teacher's effort to find assignments and topics that are meaningful—simply will not substitute for creative experience.

Invention as creative experience is not esoteric and thus need not be learned as, say, the neophyte learns the practice of Eastern meditation from the master. On the other hand, like in Buddhist practice, students can learn how to trust their experience: They can be encouraged to step into their experience and have faith that the structures of creative experience will work in their favor. Students can be prompted into this experience, ideally, by the exciting possibilities of learning, although there may be as many lures as there are good teachers. In short, in order to be inventive, writers must have a received context and feel imaginative possibilities. The structure of our schools should provide this much, even if the writing classroom cannot. The bid for freedom must sometimes pay off.

REFERENCES

Belanoff, P., Elbow, P., & Fontaine, S. I. (1991). *Nothing begins with n: New investigations of freewriting.* Carbondale: Southern Illinois University Press.

Berlin, J. A. (1988). Rhetoric and ideology in the writing class. *College English, 50,* 477–494.

Browning, D. (Ed.). (1965). *Philosophers of process.* New York: Random House.

Crowley, S. (1990). *The methodical memory: Invention in current-traditional rhetoric.* Carbondale: Southern Illinois University Press.

Elbow, P. (1973). *Writing without teachers.* New York: Oxford University Press.

Elbow, P. (1991). Toward a phenomenology of freewriting. In P. Belanoff, P. Elbow, & S. I. Fontaine (Eds.), *Nothing begins with n: New investigations of freewriting* (pp. 189–213). Carbondale: Southern Illinois University Press.

Faigley, L. (1986). Competing theories of process: A critique and a proposal. *College English, 48,* 527–542.

Flower, L. (1988). The construction of purpose in writing and reading. *College English, 50,* 528–550.

Flower, L. (1993). Cognitive rhetoric: Inquiry into the art of inquiry. In T. Enos & S. C. Brown (Eds.), *Defining the new rhetorics* (pp. 171–190). Newbury Park, CA: Sage.

Gleason, B. (1993). Self-reflection as a way of knowing: Phenomenological investigations in composition. In A. R. Gere (Ed.), *Into the field: Sites of composition studies* (pp. 60–71). New York: Modern Language Association of America.

Griffin, D. R. (1993). Introduction. In *Founders of constructive postmodern philosophy* (pp. 1–42). Albany: State University of New York Press.

Hartshorne, C. (1965). Introduction. In D. Browning, (Ed.), *Philosophers of process* (pp. v–xxii). New York: Random House.

Husserl, E. (1962). *Ideas: Introduction to a pure phenomenology.* (W. R. Boyce Gibson, Trans.). New York: Collier. (Original German edition published 1913)

James, W. (1985). *The varieties of religious experience.* Cambridge, MA: Havard University Press. (Original work published 1902)

LeFevre, K. B. (1987). *Invention as a social act.* Carbondale: Southern Illinois University Press.

Lucas, G. R., Jr. (1989). *The rehabilitation of Whitehead: An analytic and historical assessment of process philosophy.* Albany: State University of New York Press.

Murray, D. M. (1989). *Expecting the unexpected: Teaching myself—and others—to read and write.* Portsmouth, NH: Boynton/Cook-Heinemann.

Nobo, J. L. (1986). *Whitehead's metaphysics of extension and solidarity.* Albany: State University of New York Press.

Perl, S. (1983). Understanding composing. In J. N. Hays, P. A. Roth, J. R. Ramsey, & R. D. Foulke (Eds.), *The writer's mind* (pp. 43–51). Urbana, IL: National Council of Teachers of English.

Perl, S., & Egendorf, A. (1979). The process of creative discovery: Theory, research, and implication for teaching. In D. McQuade (Ed.), *Linguistics, stylistics, and the teaching of composition* (pp. 118–134). New York: Queens College, City University of New York.

Petraglia, J. (1995). Spinning like a kite: A closer look at the pseudotransactional function of writing. *Journal of Advanced Composition, 15*(1), 19–33.

Phelps, L. W. (1985). Rhythm and pattern in a composing life. In T. Waldrep (Ed.), *Writers on writing* (Vol. 1, pp. 241–257). New York: Random House.

Rohman, D. G. (1965). Pre-writing: The stage of discovery in the writing process. *College Composition and Communication, 16,* 106–112.

Rorty, R. (1979). *Philosophy and the mirror of nature.* Princeton, NJ: Princeton University Press.

Rorty, R. (1982). *Consequences of pragmatism (essays: 1972–1980).* Minneapolis: University of Minnesota Press.

Royer, D. J. (1991). New challenges to epistemic rhetoric. *Rhetoric Review, 9,* 282–297.

Smith, J. E. (1970). *Themes in American philosophy: Purpose, experience, and community.* New York: Harper & Row Publishers.

Stewart, D. C. (1972). *The authentic voice: A pre-writing approach to student writing.* Dubuque, IA: Brown.

Whitehead, A. N. (1927). *Symbolism: Its meaning and effect.* New York: Fordham University Press.

Whitehead, A. N. (1929). *Process and reality: An essay in cosmology* (corrected ed.). D. R. Griffin & D. W. Sherburne (Eds.). New York: The Free Press.

Whitehead, A. N. (1933). *Adventures of ideas.* New York: The Free Press.

Whitehead, A. N. (1938). *Modes of thought.* New York: The Free Press.

Writing Dialogically: Bold Lessons From Electronic Text

Fred Kemp
Texas Technological University

It was during my seventh or eighth year of teaching writing that I realized that I was not teaching writing but was instead teaching a form of basket weaving, and not doing a bad job of it. The baskets my students learned to weave were sturdy, prosaic affairs that could hold just what I expected them to carry, and no more, but not much less either. If you saw these baskets lined up alongside the road, you would grudgingly compliment them on their uniformity and minimal structural integrity and the diligence that went into the weave and, most of all, the sheer persistence required of anyone who would submit to the mindless discipline of twisting the straw here and there, here and there, for something that was not a whole lot different from what had gone before, and promised to be little different from what would come after. Just follow the form, I told them. What you end up with will be able to do the job.

However, what I was teaching could not do the job, mainly because I had never understood what the real job was. Nor did those colleagues from whom I had learned the most about teaching understand what the real job was; we had taken for granted what our teachers had taken for granted and their teachers had taken for granted before them: that words and the forms within which we carefully laid the words had the single important function of communication. If communication is the goal of writing, as was universally presumed among my practitioner peers, at least, then the vehicle must be as sturdy as tradition has molded it, and the forms of the ancients were undoubtedly the best master. How foolish it would be to question the collective accomplishments of great men (and a few great women) who seemed to say in every word they wrote that it was the transmission of what they knew (and what the reader did not) that constituted the central dynamic to writing. Writing's only failure would be to leak or spill meaning during the maneuver of transmission, and hence cheat the reader of the writer's full magnanimous offer. To ensure a safe passage, the text must be constructed firmly and formally, reducing risk by reducing idiosyncracy and anomaly. Nobody wants an aqueduct designed and built by an iconoclast.

The container model of writing, and the general writing skills instruction (GWSI) curricula devised to support it, revealed a subtle bifurcation to the universe that I had not previously considered, at least for those first 7 or 8 years. The world was divided into writers and readers, or more directly, into knowers and unknowers, senders and receivers. The categories were contextual, of course, because a knower in one knowledge domain could be (and probably was) an unknower in another, and therefore be at the same time a writer about one thing and a reader about another. However, the world in general, and certainly the educational system, was fairly clear about assigning the roles of knower and unknower in specific arenas, at least, and in my writing class the composition textbook writer was a knower and the student an unknower. The textbook writer sent and the student received, and it was up to writer to send with as little transmission noise as possible, and it was up to the student to make something approximating the barest minimal effort (as a student) to receive the professionally delivered goods. Writing can communicate to the self as well. As Faigley (1992) noted, "Since the beginning of composition teaching in the late nineteenth century, college writing teachers have been heavily invested in the stability of the self and the attendant beliefs that writing can be a means to self-discovery and intellectual self-realization" (p. 15).

Accepting this bifurcation, I had taught the students to construct the vehicle within which to carry meaning but had never given them any chance of actually becoming writers, because I had never provided a way by which they might understand what meaning itself is. I had swallowed whole a conception of meaning that, I would discover, could do nothing other than inhibit writing and articulation, and the very skills I intuited were so important in the modern world.

FROM CONTAINER TO CONVERSATION

Gadamer (1962) wrote that "Language has its true being only in conversation, in the exercise of understanding between people" (p. 32). Wachterhauser (1986) said Gadamer was implying that "deep adequate views of things cannot in a strict sense be guaranteed at all, even by 'method,' but can be worked out only in conversation. Talk, 'mere talk' is the source of our growing awareness of how things really are in the world" (pp. 32–33). Rorty (1979) said much the same thing when he wrote, eschewing an attempt to derive "certainty" from either a scientific accuracy of perception or a mathematical purity of formula, that "our certainty will be a matter of conversation between persons, rather than a matter of interaction with nonhuman reality" (p. 157), and again, "If we see knowledge as a matter of conversation and of social practice, rather than as an attempt to mirror nature, we will not be likely to envisage a metapractice which will be the critique of all possible forms of social practice. So holism produces . . . a conception of philosophy which has nothing to do with the quest for certainty" (p. 171).

Bruffee (1993) quoted Oakeshott's view of education as "a conversation which goes on both in public and within each of ourselves. . . . And it is this conversation which, in the end, gives place and character to every human activity and utterance" (p. 113). Bruffee went on to comment that Oakeshott reversed the common foundational understanding of the relationship between thought and conversation that was eloquently stated in a recent defense of conversation as the mode of education at St. John's College: "Conversation is the public complement to that original dialogue of the soul with itself that is called thinking" (p. 113). The position taken in this statement is that we can talk with one another because we can think. Oakeshott's position and the position taken in this chapter is the contrary, that we can think because we can talk with one another.

Conversation, or highly interactive verbal exchange, here takes on a primacy not afforded it in modernist thinking, as that which not merely displays conceptual deep structures but actually constitutes them. The implication is that if we are to understand how things really are in the world, we cannot achieve this understanding by attempting to appropriate the carefully modulated (as in written formally) concepts of an individual. Yet it was "method" in writing that assumed principal authority in modernist concepts of writing and especially in the teaching of writing. Crowley (1990) described traditional concepts of what school writing accomplished: "The constant study and practice of discourse could be justified on the grounds that it immersed its students in the exercise of method; method in turn exercised the mind along its natural lines and thus strengthened it" (p. 126). This athletic view of writing presupposes meaning as essentially a function of individual perception and mental processing, and privileges the transmission or communication model of writing. Yet, ironically, the essay as it is typically constituted in academic thinking may be the most oppressive, inhibiting, and actually misleading form of writing we can impose on our students, a principal constituent in what Nelson (1981) the father of hypertext, has called "an era of school-induced stupor" (p. 3).

Seen in this light, GWSI reflects not so much an ineffective pedagogy as a pedagogy effective at producing the wrong results, results that directly inhibit the kind of knowledge making that most of those who think about it seriously would promote in the young, and results that mask what we should be seeking in the first place and therefore comfort us in our unambitious intentions. Clearing away the clutter of all the usual academic presumptions regarding writing was no easy matter for a person as embedded in traditional practice as I was. However, computer technology, so often presumed to be the foe of deep understanding and intellectual illumination, provided me the experiences with a kind of writing that I call *dialogic writing,* which showed me how and why even very good writing teachers see themselves as persistently frustrated in what they want to accomplish, and what they can do about it.

THE CONVERSATION ON COMPUTER

Dialogic writing is largely a function of the digital revolution that occurred in the 1980s. The digitalizing of text in a word processor can transform an understanding of what words are and do. For me, most influencing was the constant, reoccurring evidence of how extraordinarily fluid the letters and words existed before my eyes, as I cut and pasted and inserted and deleted and merged and indented. What I was watching on that monitor was not the loading of my ideas into the text the way stevedores load a freighter, but an organic process of growth, microbes spawning beneath the electron microscope. I was experiencing a new portal into my own writing, not a magnification so much as a view I had previously been incapable of making sense of and so had ignored for many years. In societal terms, Heim (1987) described what was happening to me as a manifestation of "transformation theory," the notion "that basic intellectual changes acompany widespread innovation in symbol manipulation" (p. 97). Lanham (1989) made the point more fiercely: "What happens when text moves from page to screen? First, the digital text becomes unfixed and interactive. The reader can change it, become writer. The center of Western culture since the Renaissance—really since the great Alexandrian editors of Homer—the fixed, authoritative, canonical text, simply explodes into the ether" (p. 143).

The *canonical text* is the literary equivalent to Holy Scripture, the fixed transmission of a transcendently accurate truth, one that necessarily suffers from the ambiguities of language, the impossible-to-avoid "noise" of the medium of text. The hope was always to find, as Toulmin (1990) called it, "the scratch line, to serve as a starting point for any 'rational' philosophy" (p. 178), and it was the transcendent characteristics of individual authors, their genius or good luck, that provided them the insight to define where "the scratch line" lay. So what was important in writing was the conceptual baggage that the text carried, the presentation of that scratch line. As Bolter (1991) put it, the printed text was "as an unchanging artifact, a monument to its author and its age [that magnified] the distance between the author and the reader, as the author became a monumental figure, the reader only a visitor in the author's cathedral" (p. 3).

As such, an "authoritative" canonical text models for all writers the implicit and undeniable nature of writing as an inevitably flawed communication. Electronic forms of text, on the other hand, as Heim (1987), Landow (1992), Bolter (1991), and Lanham (1989) insisted, undermine not just the literary canon but static models of writing as primarily communication, a communication that necessarily works against the deep-structure truths it must convey. Electronic texts, and especially extended e-mail conversations, tend to diminish the authority of the writer in favor of the authority of the writing itself and thereby reduce the competition between the conceptual freight and the medium of transmission.

Not until I had labored for some time as a mistrustful computerist could I come to see what had been before me all the time. The typewriter had always fixed text as a palpable reality, so that the physical text became a set container for its cargo of ideas, and the ideas themselves became anchored to their own manifestations in a way that denied the flexible and constructive nature of writing. Writing, and especially revision, seemed like a process of fixing faults and lapses, ironing out glitches and bridging gaps, and the text itself always seemed to be damaged goods seeking repair. Pre-electronic forms of writing promote an almost Baconian mistrust of all the ways writing corrupts true meaning, the meaning that existed prior to the act of writing.

What I saw on the computer screen displayed a different opportunity altogether. The temporality and fragility of those words frightened me at first. If I kicked the plug loose or the current experienced a slight power flux, the words would be gone forever. The words could be made more permanent by saving them to a diskette or hard disk, but not much more permanent. I was at first considerably bothered at this lack of fixedness and this insecurity, and I know by experience that it vastly troubles new users and contributes to the tentative nature with which they approach word processing.

However, what was originally a curse began to reveal itself as a blessing. Freed from the assumption that writing must progress in these semipermanent stages on paper drafts, I began to see revision as less a curing or fixing of the text and more of a growing of the text, a growing process that can only exist outside the mind in a medium more permanent than neural activities but less fixed than ink and paper. The mutability of screen text encourages, over a period of time, the understanding that print and manuscript may not be writing in some foundational sense, but may be only manifestations or variations of writing, and perhaps not the most useful or facilitating manifestations or variations. To those who have invested intellectual capital in a culture that cherishes the stability of inscribed knowledge, the perception that writing may actually do something other than transmit and preserve knowledge or may actually be something other than an efficient means of communication is likely to be disorienting in profound ways.

AN ALTERNATIVE PEDAGOGY

It was not until I began teaching students in network-based computer classrooms in the late 1980s that my ideas regarding electronic text began to aggresively challenge my previous understanding of writing as principally communication, either communication with a reader or communication with the self. At that time, and since, I have extensively used software in networked classrooms that allows a number of students to write messages in a "chat" format: One of the two windows on each computer screen is an editing window in which the student can compose and send a comment, and the other window displays all the students' comments in chronological order. It becomes an easy matter for several or all of the students to engage in a real-time written conversation, in which the transcript of the conversation is shared at the same time by everyone who is logged on.

This process creates a mode of discourse that is not speech and not what we normally think of as writing. It is not speech because the participants are able to compose their remarks in writing, edit them carefully, and either distribute the comments or cancel them at will. Further, the usual collatoral aspects of face-to-face orality are missing, including gestures, appearance, tone of voice, and oral emphasis. On the other hand, it is not what is usually thought of as writing because the comments are delivered interactively, each responding to a context that changes as the "discussion" proceeds. Faigley (1992) a user of such computer-mediated discussion since 1988, calls this "a hybrid form of discourse, something between oral and written, where the conventions of turn-taking and topical coherence are altered" (p. 168). The dictates of form, organization, and reflection that direct the usual writing process must be ignored, for the participant has to keep up with the flow of ideas and does not have the luxury of providing extensive support or editing at length. The type of writing that appears in written conversation is necessarily first-draft writing and hasty. Having performed its function, it will never see a second draft.

It is a form of writing, in other words, that seems perfectly appalling to those who embrace a model of writing defined largely as a means of preserving or distributing valuable ideas, the commentary across time and space of great minds, what I have described earlier as the container model. Often those who espouse the container model condemn written conversation and e-mail as sloppy, witless, and even corrupting. But here, the medium that always first appears in a "broken" condition is not fixed, nor is it intended to be fixed, and the utter disregard for the purposely cracked communication of those who promote and use written conversation comes across as an affront to traditional sensibilities. The attitude of the critics is that writing is not being managed as it is supposed to be, and in an educational situation such a thing is not so much negligence as malfeasance.

However, those who use written conversation see it as highly functional, highly revealing, even revelatory, as it demonstrates interactive writing to be as fluid and liberating in contrast to expository prose as screen text is in contrast to physically inscribed or inked text. What displays itself in written conversation is a strata of human utterances delivered into chaos that emerges and grows into a self-structured system of meaning. The point of focus here is not the individual comment, the single message, or even a string of messages from a single discussant. In traditional forms of writing, most often if not always, text is judged as divorced from a constructing context and as a measure of the individual who wrote it. This is reasonable, because most formal or serious writing is written precisely to be divorced from context, to be cut free from the constraints of time and place in an attempt to attain an objective or acontextual validity. If writing's purpose is to transmit the content of an individual consciousness, then a text's value resides in what it has carried from the writer. Consequently, the uninitiated who read a written conversation grasp a message or a string of messages from an individual and attempt to discover an acontextual quality of conceptualization; but a single written comment delivered in an interactive stream of comments is necessarily abbreviated, highly contextual, and often incomprehensible. Read in a traditional way, the comments of an individual in a written conversation contain just about every flaw as communication as what is usually considered dysfunctional text.

A computer-based written conversation can only be read as a written conversation, and its scheme of development from beginning to end (although beginning and end have little meaning in such a format) is nothing approximating the scheme of development an individual would use in presenting a structure of ideas. Here there can be no forethought, no foreshadowing, no controlling thesis, no disciplined pattern of exposition, no managed rhetorical elements, no introduction or conclusion, or no reoccuring motif; not even a consistent tone, purpose, or audience awareness. None of the criteria normally applied to judge a piece of serious writing can be applied to written conversation.

Written conversation suggests that the criteria normally applied to judge a piece of serious writing may be myopic in terms of what writing really is and does. What experts and intellectuals have determined to be writing, the most serious writing, may be only a subset of what writing is and does in society. Consequently, there may be a more valuable reason to teach writing in K–12 and postsecondary institutions than the traditionally accepted one, which is that writing communicates the expressed concepts of the individual. If, as Geertz said, "Human thought is consummately social . . . social in its origins, social in its function, social in its forms, social in its applications," (cited in Lefevre, 1987, p. 119), then instructional processes should support that "consummately social" nature. Writing, rather than expressing the individual mind, may be in fact be a constituent of growth, incrementally unimportant but holistically of the greatest importance in supporting the values and belief structures of a community.

This may not, at first, seem an exceptional statement. It is generally held that writers contribute to, if not construct, the cultures to which they belong. The point here is that it is not the writers who contribute to the written conversation; it is their writing. The writers individually, and their comments, exist in importance only as constituents of the system of meaning their comments contribute to. The claim that writers can be separated from their writing may seem disingenuous; it can be demonstrated clearly only in the context of a computer-based written conversation. That which is offered from the periphery in a written conversation is quickly reconstructed as it enters the common stream and becomes an aspect of a significance impossible for any of the discourse participants to have originated or foreseen. Electronic writing therefore becomes the principal element of what Bolter (1991) called "the network culture" in which "the network has replaced the hierarchy." This "culture of interconnections both reflects and is reflected in our new technology of writing" (pp. 232–233).

WHY VALUE WRITTEN CONVERSATION?

The transition to network culture, to an appreciation of written conversation, has been and will be a difficult one. A written conversation does not "transmit" anything other than its own organic self-construction. There is no constitutive singularity generating the text, no deep structure seeking a clear and adequate surface structure, no controlling intelligence struggling for translation into words, and in fact, no competition between thought and word at all. This is so because the "thought" that the written conversation engenders is purely a product of the conversation itself, not a pale, reconstituted (always imperfectly) copy transmitted from one brain to another. As such, this description resembles Faigley's (1992) description of a postmodern theory of text, which "decisively rejects the primacy of consciousness and instead has consciousness originating in language, thus arguing that the subject is an effect rather than a cause of discourse. Because the subject is the locus of overlapping and competing discourses, it is a temporary stitching together of a series of often contradictory subject positions" (p. 9).

So how does a written conversation differ from a transcribed oral discussion? The written nature of the interaction provides a reflective and compositional character that deepens the discourse at every stage and strengthens its self-structuring effect. Each individual's contribution can be examined and reexamined at length by the participants, as can entire series of comments. The discussant need not depend on short-term memory in order to appropriate ideas, positions, and supports, but may rely on the evolving transcript for constant review. The comments themselves benefit from the advantages of writing, rewriting, and reflecting, although the nature of the dialogic interaction limits how long a discussant may take to prepare a comment. Long and carefully prepared comments are often ignored, because the discussion may have moved past the point of the long comment as it was being written and it will be seen as irrelevent or too taxing to be responded to. An ignored comment, although certainly existing in the final transcript, has not supported a discussion thread (having led nowhere) and exists as an excluded element of the written conversation.

The value of written conversations and extended e-mail exchanges (such as found in Internet discussion lists and on NetNews discussions) lies in the organic and open-ended nature of knowledge making they display, not in their transmitted factual increments, which are usually, and crudely, termed *information*. This "coming to knowing" is made manifest by the processes and results of written conversation in a way impossible or at least much more difficult otherwise. In a sense, knowledge and the manner in which knowledge is made is "scheduled" openly in a written conversation, but not by a single manager or according to any conscious script.

About the only way to understand this is as another manifestation of much wider cultural shifts variously characterized as the movement from modernism to postmodernism, or from a physics-based to a biological or organic model of how human beings make meaning. We have come from searching out the scratch line, as Toulmin characterized it, to realizing that "there *is* no scratch" (p. 178). "In both science and philosophy, then, the intellectual agenda obliges us to pay less attention to stability and system, more attention to function and adaptability (p. 192). In Lanham's (1993) terms:

> What seemed to be happening in the sciences was a movement from the "philosophic" thinking of Newtonian physics to the "rhetorical" thinking of molecular biology or nonlinear physics. Physical science had spent three hundred years looking for its lost keys under a Newtonian lamppost, not because it had lost them there but because, as the old joke has it, the light was better. (p. 869)

Chaos, the "new science" that emerged primarily from computer-generated perceptions of dynamic processes, throws into question the nature of knowledge itself and how we learn. The modernist presumption, drawing on an inherent positivism that deducts surface-structure behaviors from deep-structure, a priori principles and characteristics, has assumed that knowledge is primarily a transmitted set of identities and relationships; identities and relationships that were originally codified as an accumulated wisdom over time by men and women of extraordinary talent with the rare ability to perceive and report the deep structure of things. The ruling supposition has been that one learns primarily by receiving such transmitted knowledge, primarily through the act of reading.

Complexity theory, an outgrowth of chaos theory, suggests that systems that are "complex, in the sense that a great many independent agents are interacting with each other in a great many ways" (Waldrop, 1992, p. 11) cannot be reduced to simple formulations. Such systems do not respond to basic principles of organization or design, what Waldrop (1992) called *paranormal guidance* or principles that can be isolated and reduced to laws and formulas. The agents within such systems interact in such a massively complex fashion that prediction and hence control is impossible; "the very richness of these interactions allows the system as a whole to undergo spontaneous self-organization" (p. 11). What allows complex systems to self-organize is easy communication, massive interactivity, and ready response to feedback.

The dynamics of complex organisms may apply equally well to an understanding of how people learn. Doll (1989) adapted the work of Prigogine, a Nobel Prize winner in chemistry and a leading figure in complexity theory, to what Doll called a "postmodern" instructional theory. Doll proposed that a modernist or static model of instruction assumes the necessity of, in Waldrop's terms, a paranormal guidance or transmitted knowledge informing the learner. Postmodernism, on the other hand, as Doll (1989) quoted Prigogine and his colleague Stengers saying, allows us to develop "a new dialogue with nature" in which "our vision of nature is undergoing a radical change toward the multiple, the temporal, and the complex" (p. 3). The "multiple, the temporal, and the complex" suggests a rhetorical over a philosophical interpretation of reality, or an approach that stresses adaption and function over ontological truths and foundational first principles.

The principal difference, therefore, between traditional instruction and a postmodern instruction is that, unlike traditional instruction that stresses discipline, consistency, and internal coherency, postmodern instruction realizes the functionality of "external pertubations" or disequilibrium introduced into a system in order to excite its feedback mechanisms and allow it to evolve. "A far-from-equilibrium structure is one in the process of becoming" (Doll, 1989, p. 4). Complex systems reach equilibrium only when they die or atrophy; disequilibrium is a condition of life and growth. Traditional instruction seeks a facilitating control of the student, more for the purposes of mass processing than for anything that encourages the individual student to grow, and the process purposely excludes as many disequilibriating influences as possible. Doll (1989) posited "three facets of post-modern thought . . . which have radical implications for curriculum. . . . (1) the nature of open as opposed to closed systems, (2) the structure of complexity (as opposed to simplicity), (3) transformatory (as opposed to accumulative) change" (p. 4).

All three facets are displayed in electronic written discussion. The writing (viewing the discourse as a whole) is obviously open-ended: There can be no beginning, middle, or end to a transcipt that is not controlled by a singular purpose or authority. Those who contribute to written discussions act as independent agents seeking a validity within the communal discourse, largely through feedback. Those who contribute to a written discussion and who ignore feedback suffer the fate of having their posts ignored and their participation negated. An open-ended electronic discussion, therefore, operates as a complex system that structures itself without paranormal guidance or imposed hierarchical principles.

So how does the openly manifested "coming to knowing" of written conversation, the openly displayed schedule of communal knowledge making, benefit the participant? Certainly not as a source for acquiring the usual table of facts or event narratives that provide the participant a kind of personal guidance in future decisions. Written conversations do not usually agree on such things, a constant source of irritation for those who seek a modernist value to the texts they engage with. A written conversation is almost always internally inconsistent and self-contradicting, but not in the debilitating, static manner of an argument between two people holding fixed positions. Written conversations are perpetually in negotiation as participants build less off of their own internal representations and more off of the textual contexts of the conversation itself. This movement away from responding from personal, internal representation to the contexts of the text stream itself is a function of the short-message, highly interactive nature of written conversations. Long journal pieces and 20-minute conference papers, although obviously and necessarily constructed out of disciplinary context and responding to the issues and conflicts within a professional domain, tend to be playbacks of internal, previously framed personal constructions, and hence support the container model of text. Written conversations operate too much "on the fly" to validate such playbacks. Each e-mail must build on previous e-mail in order to be accepted within the communal discourse thread, and because e-mails arise out of a mix of positions, personalities, and experiences, the participant who attempts to bend the discourse thread into a singularly coherent representation of a theory or issue—in effect force the previous organic complexity of the discourse into a coherently structured mental scheme—simply signals an irrelevency and places himself or herself outside the discourse thread.

Such self-exclusion is certainly not the result of any conscious exclusion by other participants and often is not even noticed by anyone but the person who has attempted to influence the discourse in terms of his or her own internal representations. The self-excluder's message or messages have simply been ignored. The reason for ignoring those messages is never articulated, hardly even considered. If questioned as to why the self-excluder's mail was not responded to, other participants would probably indicate that the e-mails were too long, too complicated, too "stuffy," too "pretentious," or too "rigid."

The written conversation denies the validity of any individual internal representation and ignores it when it tries to intrude too blatantly on the discourse, which has in effect become an externally manifested representation whose "consistency" (if that is the right word), is the result of organic, self-structuring processes independent of any individual consciousness. It is not hard to understand the outrage of traditional, modernist intellectuals when confronting written conversations. The presumed purpose of discourse, especially academic discourse, seems thwarted by the lack of individual control, the lack of academic validation, and the sheer lack of beginning, middle, and end. There is no closure.

The validity of closure itself, even as the product of a single author, is being consistently challenged as postmodernists attack the traditional notion of, as Landow (1992) described it, the "unitary text," and seek to "replace it with conceptions of a dispersed text," or a "dispersed field of variants" (p. 56). Landow quoted Morgan as suggesting that a new emphasis on the intertextuality of writing, "as a structural analysis of texts in relation to the larger system of signifying practices or uses of signs in culture," in Landow's words, "shifts attention from the triad constituted by author/work/tradition to another constituted by text/discourse/culture" (p. 10). This is not a startling notion; Barthes (1971) presented the idea that the text writes the writer, that the various signifying codes in a text (cultural, semantic, proairetic, symbolic, hermaneutic) are the real producers of a text and the writer (ironically, considering the usual perception of text as merely a conduit) is simply the vehicle of transmission, or the slate on which the culture writes itself. The "difference among texts is not some complete, irreducible quality (according to a mythic view of literary creation), it is not what designates the individuality of each text; on the contrary, it is a difference which does not stop and which is articulated upon the infinity of texts, of languages, of systems: a difference of which each text is the return" (Barthes, 1971, p. 3). The "difference which does not stop" seems a specific counter to a presumed need for closure and the packaging of concepts that closure implies.

The point is that what is gained from the text, from the act of reading, is an act of engagement with acculturating forces, not the reception or utilization of specific data or concepts. This engagement has no ontological placement, no value in terms of clicks up the scale of progress or degrees of ascending levels in some "tank" of knowledge. What is gained from the text is a holistic appropriation of one's culture, a subliminal map of beliefs and values that situate the reader within a field of aspirations and achievement. All texts do this, but some more capably than others.

The electronic written conversation displays this writerly characteristic of texts more profoundly than any printed text, either written by an individual or a combination of individuals, and indeed more than even hypertexts that link hundreds and—through the Internet's World Wide Web—potentially hundreds of thousands of writers. Texts that build on hypertext links leading into vast complexities of conjoined meaning promise an amazing "external neural network" for society, Nelson's (1981) "docuverse" of equally massively distributed information. The links that tie together discrete bundles of text or information, even when readers are allowed to write their own links, or even, in "constructive" hypertext, when readers are allowed to add text itself and become cowriters of the hypertext, nevertheless do not constitute a defining interactivity or a truly constructive intertextuality. The link that leads from my page to that on another campus or in another country does not necessarily lead back to me, and rarely does.

The written conversation, however, unlike a hypertext, is multiply interactive. The text is sequential, a "stream," so that a reader has no choices in navigating it other than the usual ones to skip or stop. However, the writers are intermittently engaged, so that they are responsible to their various cowriters in complex ways. Challenges, corrections, and disavowals are endemic. Apologies and reversals are common. Although Barthes' concept of a text writing the writer may not be obvious to those unfamiliar with literary theory, it is certainly obvious to just about anyone who contributes to electronic written conversations, for they are under the persistent scrutiny of co-contributors and have no opportunity to manage or repair their texts behind the scenes. The entire process of presentation is delivered in the transcript. The authority of the text over the authority of each writer is irrepressible and obvious.

The result is an unmitigated freedom for the reader, who reads not to decode the mental representations of presumably more capable or more insightful people, or people more favored by the gods, but instead experiences in terms of personal negotiation ideas that are under the reoccurring management of people who, like him or her, have not successfully completed what Dewey attacked as (the title of his 1929 Gifford Lectures) "the quest for certainty." Participating in an electronic conversation as reader and writer is similar to stepping out of the crowd and joining the parade, and not simply because one can actually send comments. The dialogic nature of written conversation melds text and writer profoundly and irreversibly, unplugging both the tyranny of the writer and the subservience of the reader.

Not without cost. Basket weaving has long enjoyed a mythical, if not actual, history as therapy for the mentally infirm. Much of U.S. writing instruction has thrived on the passivity of its classroom students, who have learned to give up their personalities and even their minds (temporarily, but leading to habit) to get an easy A, a "school-induced stupor." The comforting myth that writing is an esoteric presentation device for the especially talented permeates the student consciousness, leading to dull competence in a few and outright somnambulism in many. The sheer lack of engagement in anything resembling a real-world writing act for both writing teachers and writing students permits both to engage in a collusion of diminished effort.

The end result of all education is "meaning," in two senses. First, in the sense of creating knowledge structures that include the elements of one's experience—one's world picture—that affect success and failure, happiness and unhappiness, and the myriad decisions that negotiate the extremes. The second is "meaning" in the sense of "meaningful," or personally important. Dialogic writing, or writing that arises from the interactive engagement of participants negotiating, without closure, the concepts that constitute those things that make life worth living, compels meaning in both senses. Dialogic writing, unlike monologic writing or writing as transmitted truths, is complex, open-ended, and transformatory. Computer-mediated communication encourages both the disequilibrium and the process of feedback inherent in committed intellectual growth, but undoubtedly at the expense of traditional clarity and method.

REDISCOVERING REASONS TO WRITE

Ken Burns' celebrated PBS series, *The Civil War*, provided moving examples of exquisite writing from soldiers with fourth and fifth grade educations. This writing skill did not demonstrate, as some of my colleagues would have it, that school was more rigorous and effective in the first half of the 19th century than it is now (hinting darkly of a return to a draconian past), but that the written word was the singular means of entertainment and distance communication for the literate population. Writing meant something to that population much different from what it does to a population steeped in radio, television, movies, interstate highways, VCRs, video games, and—above all—the telephone. Writing was not a strange activity conducted almost entirely in classrooms, but something that liberated people from a crushing separation from those they loved and the ideas they respected. Writing was a cherished tool to all who possessed the skill, and it was lovingly exercised. It appears that it may again be lovingly exercised, on the Internet, but in ways whose value will take years to articulate.

The digital revolution is showing us that writing is not something that can be codified in classroom assignments or glorified by romantics as windows into Platonic truth. Even *Time* magazine ("Technology," 1994) remarked how the phenomenal growth of electronic mail and the Internet represents "for millions of people, a living, breathing life of letters" among those not inclined to submit to the formalisms of academia. The often proclaimed death of the novel and poetry, the deterioration of a cultural coherency, and even the decline of general literacy is more a report of the self-fixated concerns of those who hold very narrow definitions of what writing and literacy are than any indications of a significant deterioration in what writing itself is or does for people.

The GWSI approach to writing presumes that writing accomplishes something universally recognized and validated, and that all that remains for the schools is to provide the means to teach this legitimated skill. Unfortunately, writing as it is taught is not universally validated as one of life's important abilities, and students often see a general skills approach as little more than busy work. Dialogic writing, on the other hand, benefits from immediacy, relevancy, and commitment. Students grow intellectually as they participate in writing interactive texts. Being able to see this, being able to move beyond presumptions regarding writing that are so deeply embedded as to be assumed inherent, is the challenge facing writing teachers during this time of technological transition.

REFERENCES

Barthes, S. (1971). *S/Z: An essay*. New York: Hill & Wang.
Bolter, J. D. (1991). *Writing space: The computer, hypertext, and the history of writing*. Hillsdale, NJ: Lawrence Erlbaum Associates.
Bruffee, K. A. (1993). *Collaborative learning: Higher education, interdependence, and the authority of knowledge*. Baltimore: Johns Hopkins University Press.
Crowley, S. (1990). *The methodical memory: Invention in current-traditional rhetoric*. Carbondale: Southern Illinois University Press.
Doll, W. E. (1989, May). Foundations for a postmodern curriculum. *Journal of Curriculum Studies, 21*(3), pp. 243–253.
Faigley, L. (1992). *Fragments of rationality: Postmodernity and the subject of composition*. Pittsburgh, PA: University of Pittsburgh Press.
Gadamer, H.-G. (1962). Hermeneutik und Historismus. *Philosophische Rundschau, 9*, 422.

Heim, M. (1987). *Electric language: A philosophical study of word processing*. New Haven: Yale University Press.

Landow, G. P. (1992). *Hypertext: The convergence of contemporary critical theory and technology*. Baltimore, MD: Johns Hopkins University Press.

Lanham, R. (1993). *The electronic word: Democracy, technology, and the arts*. Chicago: University of Chicago Press.

Lefevre, K. (1987). *Invention as a social act*. Carbondale: Southern Illinois University Press.

Nelson, T. H. (1981). *Literary machines: The report on, and of, Project Xanadu concerning word processing, electronic publishing, hypertext, thinkertoys, tomorrow's intellectual revolution, and certain other topics including knowledge, education and freedom*. South Bend, IN: Theodor Nelson.

Rorty, R. (1979). *Philosophy and the mirror of nature*. Princeton, NJ. Princeton University Press.

Technology: Would Shakespeare have sent Email? (1994, July 4) *Time, 144*(1), p. 66.

Toulmin, S. (1990). *Cosmopolis: The hidden agenda of modernity*. New York: The Free Press.

Wachterhauser, B. R. (1986). Introduction: History and language in understanding. In B. Wachterhauser, (Ed.), *Hermeneutics and modern philosophy* (pp. 5–61). Albany: State University of New York Press.

Waldrop, M. M. (1992). *Complexity: The emerging science at the edge of order and chaos*. New York: Simon & Schuster.

Alternative Conceptions of Writing Instruction

10

Discourse, Interdiscursivity, and Composition Instruction

David A. Jolliffe
DePaul University

College composition instructors and administrators miss an opportunity to contribute substantially to their students' liberal education by not thinking critically about what students should read and write about in general writing skills instruction (GWSI) courses. When educators think of basic skills in GWSI, they rarely think of issues involving subject matter. To most educators, the idea of basic skills lies largely in the areas of the form, structure, and correctness of whole texts, paragraphs, sentences, words, and mechanics. Educators maintain this limited formalist–structuralist view of basic skills even though it stands in sharp contrast to two obvious facts. First, the subject matter of student writing has come to play an important, if ill-defined and underinvestigated, role in composition studies. Indeed, one of the principal emphases in GWSI for the past three decades has been to teach students how to learn about subject matters by writing about them and to draft and revise compositions filled with clear, rich, well-developed substance. Second, there can actually be no such thing as a subject matter-free GWSI course: As they learn about writing, students must write about something. Thus, the questions instructors must address about the subject matters of student compositions are directly related to issues of liberal education: What do we want to teach students about the relationship between writing and learning? What subject matters do we want them to learn about through writing? Why are these important subject matters?

When composition scholars do consider the subject matter of their students' papers, they frequently think about it in ways that suggest a kind of intellectual unidirectionality. That is, some scholars think that the subject matter of compositions must come solely from the students' own spheres of experience and observation and that students will learn to write "out of"

197

their own personal realms into the worlds of material that they encounter in school and life beyond the academy. Conversely, other scholars believe that they can provide the subject matter for students' compositions and when students write "into" this body of material, it is solely the provided subject matter that students use in their papers. A few scholars aim to achieve a kind of via media between these two positions, guiding students to take up subject matters and read and write about them from the perspective of their own experiences and observations. However, even these scholars generally must approach questions of the subject matter of student compositions haphazardly. Although their curricula ask students to engage with relatively universal subject matters—adolescence, education, popular culture, gender, the mass media, and so on—there is no way these instructors can guarantee that students will be grounded in the subject matters presented.

None of these positions on the subject matter of students' compositions is as simple as it appears. Within all three positions—the student centered, the teacher mandated, and the blended compromise—composition students are being asked to undertake the tremendously complicated tasks of formulating, enunciating, contrasting, and accommodating different discourses, or intricate patterns of ideologically loaded and coded thought and language. In order to help students learn how to select and develop vital, challenging subject matters, composition scholars need, I believe, a clearer understanding of what discourse is, how discourses constitute both writers and subject matters, and how composition pedagogy can either harness or (at its peril) ignore the interdiscursive tensions that students experience. This chapter is designed as an initial contribution to this understanding. Before moving to define discourse and illustrate how discourse analysis can shape composition curricula, I raise some questions about two prominent features of the GWSI terrain: the claim that writing is a mode of learning and the notion that students should write about "their own ideas."

CAN GWSI REALLY TEACH WRITING TO LEARN?

Composition scholarship since the mid-1960s has gradually effected a change in what GWSI seems to be about, a change that most academics in other fields as well as the general public seem to have ignored. These academic and public circles apparently think the most important thing GWSI should accomplish is to teach students how to write well-organized compositions that evince no errors of standard written English. Composition scholars, on the other hand, have seemed convinced, at least for the past 20 years, since Emig (1977) published her seminal article, "Writing as a Mode of Learning," that an important—if not the most important—purpose of composition instruction is to teach students how to use writing to learn challenging, complex subject matters and to produce compositions that embody rich, engaging ideas. Emig's article aimed to demonstrate the "unique correspondences between writing and learning" (p. 124), namely that both successful learning and writing involve and integrate multiple representations of the subject matter at hand, benefit from immediate and long-term feedback, rely on synthetic and analytic conceptualizations, and are active, engaged, personal, and self-rhythmed. In simpler terms, both when you learn successfully and when you write, you conceive your subject matter from many perspectives and try to integrate them; you see what you are doing immediately by looking at the text at hand, and you leave a "paper trail" that documents at least the surface of your process; you take your subject matter apart and put it back together again; and you become actively involved with your subject matter and work at a pace you establish. In the process pedagogy world that Emig's article spoke to (and still does, nearly two decades later) no instructor would assume that students simply had (or has) these multiple perspectives on their subject matters, perspectives enriched by the writers' personal commitments and habits of analysis and synthesis. It was (and many believe still is) the purpose of composition instruction to teach students to generate challenging ideas, to engage in a substantial process, to practice analysis and synthesis, and to demonstrate a personal commitment to the ideas in their papers.

Although Emig's article focused the issues of writing to learn in order to produce rich ideas in compositions, she was clearly no voice crying in the wilderness on this issue. Even a cursory glance through the literature from composition studies' "Wonder Bread" years, when the process movement was being established as the dominant pedagogical paradigm, shows that its scholars saw successful instruction as being primarily interested in promoting robust thinking and not as interested as it once was in inculcating habits of conventional and correct arrangement, style, and usage. Consider just a few, randomly chosen, examples: In Diederich's (1964) study of the factors that readers from English departments and other fields believed were responsible for improved writing ability, "the largest cluster was influenced primarily by the ideas expressed: their richness, soundness, clarity, and development" (p. 42). In Flower and Hayes' (1980) groundbreaking efforts to define a model of the cognitive process of composing written texts, they assumed that the "act of *creating* ideas, not finding them, is at the heart of significant writing" (p. 22). In Sommers' (1980) study of revision strategies of students and experienced adults, she concluded that competent adult writers "seek to discover (to create) meaning in their engagement with their writing" (p. 386). In Knoblauch and

Brannon's (1984) treatise on their vision of a new rhetoric, they lauded the student writer who is "in pursuit of a significance that matters" (p. 12).

Even though writing to learn as an avenue toward rich ideation has been a staple of GWSI for many years, the concept demands more careful scrutiny than it has received. Neither composition scholarship nor composition instruction has carefully considered the question, "Writing to learn what?," and as a result, I believe has not succeeded in teaching students useful principles about how writing leads to learning and, in turn, to producing rich, substantial ideas in their texts.

Composition scholarship has paid such scant attention to issues of what students write about that Kaufer and Young (1994) coined an accurate term to describe a tradition in GWSI that they call "Writing-WNCP," for "Writing With No Content in Particular" (p. 78). Within this tradition, students rarely engage in extensive inquiry into subject matters in order to write about them. Instead, they generally are directed to write about whatever interests them, often writing about a new topic for every assignment they undertake. Kaufer and Young argued that two assumptions undergird Writing-WNCP. First, there is an assumption that the content of students' compositions plays an "instrumental" role rather than "an intrinsic one" (p. 78). That is, the function of the content is to provide the raw materials on which the students are to practice the concepts, abilities, or skills that their instructor wants them to learn—invention, arrangement, style, prewriting, drafting, revising, text/paragraph/sentence structuring, or whatever. Second, there is the assumption that "pretty much the same skills will develop no matter what content is chosen" (p. 78). That is, if students are trying to learn, say, how to write a topic restriction illustration paragraph, they may do so whether they are writing about "How to Make a Peanut Butter and Jelly Sandwich" or "A Comparison of the Differences Between Wendy's and McDonald's," two topics I discovered in the same section of first-year composition at a public 2-year college near Chicago.

When GWSI allows students to write about no content in particular, I believe that what vitiates the prospect for teaching students to learn by writing and to produce substantial ideas is the pedagogy's failure to distinguish, in Kaufer and Young's terms, "between *content* and *subject matter*" (p. 79). They explained further:

> A subject matter . . . consists of a content that has been discussed in recurring and public rhetorical situations. "What I Did Last Summer" can be a content, but it is unlikely to be a subject matter. Because subject matters have publicly shared histories and have usually been analyzed from the perspective of abstract writings called "theory," a writer who tackles a subject matter (the Civil War, rhetoric, Romantic poetry, biology) must first engage in learning

this history and theory and sifting through relevant information to the extent necessary for credibility. (p. 79)

Given that students usually write about whatever they choose as their content and rarely about subject matters, Kaufer and Young maintained that "the emphasis in the tradition of Writing-WNCP is on personal expression in interpersonal rhetorical transactions" (p. 79). In other words, students in most GWSI courses are, willy-nilly, encouraged to learn by writing, but what they learn about is generally just what their content means to them personally, and usually not what any public conversation about the content has established as salient, relevant, or controversial about it. As Kaufer and Dunmire make clear (chap. 11, this volume), creating an awareness of the public dimension of writing is central to teaching writing.

GWSI has nearly always bought into the trope of tranference. It is assumed that whatever students learn about writing in GWSI courses they will be able to apply when they are asked to write in other settings, either within academia or beyond. My question is this: If students have not been taught to write in order to learn and produce substantial ideas about subject matters in GWSI, will they be able to do so when they write for courses in their majors or their jobs? I fear the answer is no. Thus, composition scholars should think long and hard about the kinds of ideas that students should read and write about in their courses.

SHOULD STUDENTS WRITE ONLY ABOUT THEIR OWN IDEAS?

When students write papers for GWSI courses, where do their ideas—their substance, their subject matters—come from (see Royer, chap. 8, this volume, for an extended discussion of this question in terms of invention)? The simplest response to this question would offer a dualism that many instructors and most students apparently believe is legitimate: Either students retrieve and generate ideas from their own realms of observation and experience, or their instructors propose subject matters for students to learn and write about. Indeed, this dualism is so generally accepted that many colleges and universities have built their required composition curriculum on it. At these schools, students in the first course write about "their own" ideas, observations, and experiences; in the second course, they read others' ideas and write "research papers" from "sources."

As administratively convenient as this dualism seems, it too demands the same level of careful scrutiny as the notion of writing to learn. Both sides of the dichotomy are troublesome. It is problematic to ask students to write solely about their own ideas, observations, and experiences for two related reasons. First, to do so begs a question that initially sounds impertinent: Do students really have any of their own ideas? Notice that the question is not whether students have any ideas. Of course they have plenty, and they are potentially rich and challenging. However, as a number of composition theorists (e.g., Berlin, 1994; Faigley, 1992) have recently argued, students are inextricably bound up in the ideologies of the cultures in which they participate—their families, homes, jobs, religions, social classes, ethnicities, and so on—and what they perceive as their own ideas are actually the manifestations, the intertextual products, of the texts of these cultures in which students are immersed. Second, asking students to write solely about their own ideas, observations, and experiences is troubling, because it encourages them to write, as suggested earlier, about content, not subject matters, and thus to miss out on opportunities to learn about challenging ideas by writing.

It is equally problematic to require students to write solely from sources other than their own ideas, observations, and experiences, a practice that people often mistakenly believe is a central component in pedagogies that aim to teach "academic discourse." Two aspects of this practice are also troublesome. First, it is difficult for students who must write only to summarize, analyze, or synthesize others' ideas to feel a sense of ownership, or to feel invested in their subject matters. As a result, they often produce compositions that seem more like responses to examination prompts than independent, self-sufficient essays. Second, and perhaps more nettlesome, instructors assume when they direct a class to learn and write about some prescribed subject matter that the students' responses will be only about that material. Just as students, because they are immersed in the ideologies of cultures in which they participate, are ultimately unable to express any ideas that are completely their own, so for the same reason they are finally incapable of writing solely about other people's ideas.

Let me try to illustrate the slipperiness of this distinction between the students' own ideas and other people's ideas by examining two positions on the subject matter of student writing, one from the exemplars of process pedagogy and one from composition research, but research that has an analog in teaching. In process pedagogy, perhaps no one speaks more forcefully for the students' right to their own ideas than Murray. In an article entitled "What, No Assignments?," Murray (1974/1982) stated unequivocally, "Students will write well only when they speak in their own voice, and that voice can only be authoritative and honest when the student speaks of his own concerns in his own way" (p. 129). Murray suggested in the article that his advice to students, "Find your own subject" (p. 134), stands in contrast to the pedagogical practice prevalent at the time, asking students to write papers about "common knowledge" topics or about themes in literature. Murray's advice might have run counter to common practice at that time, but now it is status quo thinking among many process-oriented composition teachers and scholars. In a column in the *Chronicle of Higher Education* protesting a plan at the University of Texas at Austin to have students in GWSI courses write about court cases involving racial and sexual discrimination, Hairston (1991) echoed Murray: "[W]e know students develop best as writers when they are allowed to write on something they care about. Having them write about other people's ideas doesn't work well" (p. B1).

When instructors teach that students should write only about their own ideas—that writing "about other people's ideas doesn't work well"—these instructors do little to move their students, as Dillon (1981) put it, from producing "utterance" to producing "text," a transition that Dillon saw as GWSI's principal contribution to liberal education. Students generally come to college producing utterance, he argued; we want them to learn to produce text. Among the several distinctions he drew between utterance and text, Dillon proposed that "[u]tterance expects speakers to reproduce accepted wisdom, attitudes, and values; cogency and assent are based on conformity to received opinion and common sense," whereas "[t]ext expects writers to produce novel, even counterintuitive, facts and viewpoints; cogency and assent are based on logical consistency and evidence" (p. 28). When utterance-oriented students are directed to write about ideas, Dillon suggested, they "think of them as preformed things (like 'opinions on a subject') rather than processes or the results of processes" (p. 29). Even with intensely personal topics (Dillon recounted his experiences having students write about "The Type of Person I Am"), he asserted that students tend to "apply conventional categories uncritically," to "accept value judgments attached by their immediate culture," and to buy into "perfect exemplars of a full-blown stereotype" (p. 29). In other words, when instructors urge students to write about their own ideas, the students' default move is to find those ideas not within their own minds or psyches, but embedded in the cultures that immerse them. It seems they must write about other people's ideas.

Just as it seems difficult to conceive of students' writing about their own ideas without appropriating and incorporating material developed in the cultures that surround them, so it is problematic to believe that when an instructor directs students to write about specific ideas from sources other than their own realms of experience, that is all they write about. To be sure, in some rhetorical situations, writers do need to rehearse and present only the specific information and data that the situation organizer—whoever assigns or will evaluate the writing—calls for. Prompted to write an examination essay about, say, the causes of the Peloponnesian War, the successful writer will list and explain these causes and that is all. However, when directed to produce something that can be read as a self-sufficient, self-framing text, one that does not require readers to know the wording of the prompt—in other words, the kind of texts that students in composition courses usually produce—and even when the content of these texts is specified by the situation organizer, writers will invariably write about more than simply the mandated subject matter.

Penrose (1992) validated this phenomenon in a study that "explore[d] the assumption that writing is a way to learn by examining the influence of task interpretation on writing and studying as learning aids" (p. 465). The subjects in Penrose's study, college freshmen, were given two texts to read, one a description of how hurricanes form and the other an extended definition of paternalism. Half the students were instructed to "write a report" about one of the texts; the other half were directed to "study for a test" on one of the passages, "using whatever study strategies they deemed appropriate" (p. 470). Among the many features Penrose analyzed in the students' think-aloud protocols and their actual texts, one "elaboration strategy" is noteworthy. This is the strategy of "extending source material," where the student "adds or constructs new meaning," including "substantive inferences, questions about content," and "prior knowledge connections" (p. 473). Penrose discovered that students working with both passages "extended" the source text when they were assigned when directed to "write a report" about it. However, they elaborated more on the paternalism text than on the hurricane passage. "The fact-laden hurricane passage encouraged a less constructive interpretation of the writing task," Penrose noted, "whereas the paternalism passage apparently offers more opportunities for constructive elaborating and/or more encouragement to do so" (p. 490).

Although Penrose's student writers operated in a carefully controlled experimental setting, both her method and the conclusions she drew have analogs in the settings of GWSI courses. Some instructors do indeed give students a data source—readings, observations, statistics, whatever—and direct them to write about that source. However, because the data source is processed through the individually and culturally conditioned schemata of the writer—a commonplace finding in decades of psychological and educational research in schema theory—the writer invariably extends the data source by tapping into prior knowledge and drawing inferences. In other words, it is just as impossible to write solely about other people's ideas as it is to write only about one's own ideas.

Many composition scholars, of course, recognize this one's own ideas versus other people's ideas distinction for what it is: a phony dualism (the process advocates' devotion to the students' own ideas notwithstanding). Most GWSI instructors seem to think that students should not write solely "out of" their own reservoir of observations, ideas, and experiences, nor "into" the subject matters mandated by assignments. Instead, a prevalent intellectual strategy in GWSI assignments—perhaps the predominant strategy in most curriculums—is to have students read a text or otherwise learn about some realm of subject matter and then write about how that material speaks to their own worlds of experience, observation, and thought. Two masters of incorporating this strategy in challenging courses are Bartholomae and Petroskey (1986, 1987) whose curriculum for a basic writing course at the University of Pittsburgh was explained conceptually in *Facts, Artifacts, and Counterfacts* and then widely promulgated in the successful textbook, *Ways of Reading*.

Bartholomae and Petroskey (1986) told their basic writing students that the class would be "modeled after a course for advanced graduate students," in which "students are expected to develop their own ideas and theories on a subject . . . and to report what they learned to others" (pp. 47–48). As they read and write about "Growth and Change in Adolescence," Bartholomae and Petroskey forecast, the students will in essence create "a new research center at the University of Pittsburgh" (p. 48). Barthomolomae and Petroskey explained further:

> We're interested . . . in what you can find to say over 15 weeks' constant study of a single subject; we're more interested in that than in your ability to study and remember the ideas of some accepted, "official" group of scholars. We don't expect you to become experts on adolescent development—at least not as the university defines such expertise. We do, however, expect you to become expert enough to begin to understand the work (not the genius or inspiration) of those the university does acknowledge as expert. (p. 48)

Apparently a major strategy toward developing this understanding is to read challenging texts and reflect on how their ideas reverberate for the writer personally. For example, the first writing assignment asks the students to read a chapter from Margaret Mead's autobiography, *Blackberry Winter*, and to address these questions:

> 1. We'd like you to describe as carefully and completely as you can the important point or points you see Ms. Mead making about her experience at DePauw.
>
> 2. Would you then write about whatever in the chapter seems most important or most significant to *you*? And would you be sure to explain why you feel it is important or significant? (p. 52)

A later assignment in the course reflects the same strategy, this time applied to Richard Rodriguez's *Hunger of Memory*:

> Review *Hunger of Memory* . . . and select a section from each chapter that in some way represents the "heart" of that chapter. Use the selections you've chosen to explain what you see to be Rodriguez's view of his development from childhood to adulthood. When you have done this, reread what you

have written, and go on to explain the key ways in which Rodriguez did and did not have what you have come to think of as a "typical" adolescence. (p. 69)

Bartholomae and Petroskey's curriculum represents a sensible middle ground between urging students to write solely about their own experiences and observations and having them write summaries and reports of other kinds of source materials. Two features of the curriculum are praiseworthy. First, it attempts to capitalize on a realm of subject matter that first-year college students may be interested in. Second, it works to acquaint students with the rigor of academic work that will be expected from them as they proceed to more advanced courses in the curriculum.

Three features surrounding the Bartholomae and Petroskey curriculum, however, keep it from being the ideal model for planning what students should read and write about in GWSI courses. First, it assumes that the students have a strong, active enough interest in the problems and issues surrounding "growth and change in adolescence" that they are willing to spend 15 weeks reading and writing about it. Second, it assumes that finally the teacher—the situation organizer—is ultimately the person who sets the subject-matter agenda for the student writers to follow. Third, and most problematic, it is too easy for most GWSI instructors to see the Bartholomae and Petroskey curriculum as simply asking students to read and write about a complex and difficult subject matter for 15 weeks. At its best, a subject matter-focused GWSI course should do more than that: It should teach students how all writing—their own "basic" writing as well as writing done by "experts" in the university—embodies and reflects discourse. Students cannot learn this by solely writing about their own ideas. They can learn it by operating with a curriculum that resembles Bartholomae and Petroskey's. However, as the next section illustrates, when instructors themselves understand principles of discourse and use discourse analysis to plan their teaching, they can develop curricula that permit the student writer to select a subject matter to write about extensively and that lead to a negotiation between instructor and student about how exactly the student writer will develop this subject matter.

DISCOURSE AND INTERDISCURSIVITY IN GWSI

Talk of introducing composition students to "academic discourse" is certainly nothing new in the profession. However, discussions of academic discourse frequently conceive discourse as merely the surface features of students' texts—their invocation of key terms in a discipline, their use of sophisticated transitional words or phrases, and their adherence to certain formatting conventions. Discourse is a much richer phenomenon than this typical portrayal. It is not simply something that writers produce; it is something that produces writers. It is not merely a reflection of a domain of subject matters; it constitutes this domain.

An extremely clear perspective on discourse and discourse analysis, and one that I believe holds great promise for composition scholarship, can be found in the work of the British critical linguist Fairclough (1992). Merging the scholarship on discourse analysis from Anglo-European linguistics, especially that of Halliday, with contemporary French social theory, especially that of Pecheux and Foucault, Fairclough defined *discourse* as "language use as a form of social practice" (p. 63). Fairclough described "a dialectical relationship between discourse and social structure":

> On the one hand, discourse is shaped and constrained by social structure in the widest sense and at all levels: by class and other social relations at a societal level, by the relations specific to particular institutions such as law or education, by systems of classification, by various norms and conventions of both a discursive and a non-discursive nature, and so forth. . . . On the other hand, discourse is socially constitutive. . . . Discourse contributes to the constitution of all those dimensions of social structure which directly or indirectly shape and constrain it: its own norms and conventions, as well as the relations, identities and institutions which lie behind them. Discourse is a practice not just of representing the world, but of signifying the world, constituting and constructing the world in meaning. (p. 64)

Particularly, Fairclough noted that discourse contributes to the construction of "what are variously referred to as 'social identities' and 'subject positions' for social 'subjects' and types of 'self'"; it also "helps construct social relationships between people," and it "contributes to the construction of systems of knowledge and belief" (p. 64). Fairclough provided an example to clarify these constitutive categories. The "speech of the classroom" helps to construct not only the identities of teachers and pupils but also a social relationship in which the teachers orchestrate the pupils' activities and evaluate their performances. Ideologically, this relationship generally reproduces a society's systems of knowledge and belief about the nature of schooling, but it is also "open to transformations which may partly originate in discourse" (p. 65). Fairclough noted that ideology is constituted primarily by a process of "hegemony": "constructing alliances, and integrating rather than dominating subordinate classes, through concessions or through ideological means, to win their consent" (p. 92).

Although the features of discourse that help to constitute subject positions, social relations, and ideologies can be analyzed as static entities, Fairclough (1992) was more interested in elucidating the ways discourse contributes to social change—that is, the way discourse alters subject positions, social relations, and ideologies. Accordingly, he examined constitutive discourse features as they are organized by *interdiscourse*, a cognitive construct that he defined as "the complex interdependent configuration of discursive formations" that serves as "the structural entity (underlying) discursive events" (p. 68). Interdiscourse, in turn, is manifest in two kinds of intertextuality: *manifest intertextuality*, in which "other texts are explicitly present in the text under analysis"; and *constitutive intertextuality*, or *interdiscursivity*, which is "the configuration of discourse conventions that go into (a text's) production" (p. 104). Suppose, for example, that a news story reports that the emergence of a victorious party in an election amounts to a brave new world for U.S. politics. This sentence is intertextual with both Miranda's exclamation in *The Tempest* and with the title of Aldous Huxley's dystopic novel. Suppose that the same story explains that the victorious politicians "scored a knockout punch" at a particularly successful rally. This sentence is interdiscursive with the discourse of sports reportage.

According to Fairclough (1992) four specific text features are analyzable under the rubric of interdiscursivity; each feature capitalizes on an interdiscursive relation to help construct identities, social relations, and ideologies. The first feature is *genre*, "a relatively stable set of conventions that is associated with, and partly enacts, a socially ratified type of activity" (p. 126). As Fairclough explained, "A genre implies not only a particular text type, but also particular processes of producing, distributing, and consuming texts" (p. 126). Consider, for example, the genre of the "infomercial," a type of television program one finds during off hours on many television stations. The program's purpose is to sell whatever product has bought the air time, and it exploits its interdiscursive similarity to the genre of documentary programs produced by legitimate news organizations. Ideologically, this interdiscursivity invests the infomercial with a sense of importance and credibility, whether warranted or not. Genre, to Fairclough, is a superordinate category that draws together all four features he analyzed under the rubric of interdiscursivity.

The second feature is *activity type*, or "the structured sequence of actions" and "the participants involved in the activity—that is, the set of subject positions which are socially constituted and recognized in connection with the activity type" (p. 126; for an overview of a related framework, Vygotskian activity theory, see Russell, chap. 3, this volume). Consider, for example, a kind of advertisement that runs in the sports sections of many newspapers. It looks just like a news story (a generic interdiscursivity) with boldface headlines and small columns of one-sentence-per-paragraph exposition, except it has "advertisement" written in small type at the top. The headlines announce: "Latest Scientific News: Male Pattern Baldness Cured." To create an impression of novelty and importance, this text exploits an interdiscursivity with the "news report" activity type (see Fairclough, 1992, p. 129) in which an anonymous reporter gives the news receiver the gist of a story in headlines, then a slightly longer gist in the lead, then a development of details.

The third feature is style, which Fairclough divided, following Halliday, into *tenor*, or "the sort of relationship that obtains between participants in an interaction"; *mode*, or "whether texts are written or spoken or some combination of the two"; and *rhetorical mode*, which "can be classified with terms such as 'argumentative,' 'descriptive,' and 'expository'" (p. 127). Fairclough's explanation of the phenomenon he called synthetic personalization provides a useful example of the interdiscursivity of style. *Synthetic personalization* is "the simulation of private, face-to-face, discourse in public mass-audience discourse" such as "print, radio, television" (p. 98). When, say, a bank's advertisement says, "Trust us—we want to be your friend," it is capitalizing on interdiscursivity with friendly, spoken, generally expressive discourse between people.

The fourth feature is *discourse* used as a count noun, for example "a discourse" or "these discourses" (p. 128). "Discourses correspond roughly to dimensions of texts which can traditionally been discussed in terms of 'content,' 'ideational meanings,' 'topic,' 'subject matter,' and so forth," Fairclough (1992) wrote (pp. 127–128). Thus, for example, one can analyze textual examples of "techno-scientific medical discourse" or "feminist discourses of sexuality" (p. 128) and analyze the effects the texts achieve by exploiting this interdiscursivity.

Fairclough's three constituent elements—identities, social relations, and ideologies—combined with his four analyzable text features—genre, activity type, style, and discourse—can generate a three-by-four grid of heuristic questions, useful for analyzing any text, including those produced by students in GWSI courses. For any text, one can ask the following about genre: Is this text a recognizable genre? What type of person produces such a genre? Who reads it? How could one characterize the type of interaction between writers that this genre fosters? What kinds of ideological positions does this genre seem particularly suited to establishing, and how does it do so? One can ask the following about activity type: Is there a structured sequence of actions in this text? What roles do the writer and the reader play in these actions? How could one characterize the social relations among these participants? What kinds of ideological positions does this activity foster and how does it do so? One can ask the following questions about style: How could one characterize the tenor, mode, and rhetorical mode? What do the tenor, mode, and rhetorical mode reveal about the writer and readers? About the relations among them? About the ideological positions being established? One can ask the following question about discourses that might be present in the text: Who are the typical participants in such discourses? How are they positioned vis-à-vis each other? What kinds of ideological positions inhere within this kind of discourse and how does this text reveal those positions?

These questions offer insight into the ways any text both manifests and constitutes subject positions, social relations, and ideological positions. As valuable as they are in their own right, however, I have found these analytic questions additionally provide a useful entry into students' early, "diagnostic" compositions in a GWSI course. By examining these texts for both intertextual and interdiscursive manifestations, I have been able to initiate with students a discussion of what they are genuinely interested in reading and writing about—in other words, about what discourses they are currently positioned within. Beginning with these conversations, the students can contract to write a series of compositions that lead them not only to write about a meaningful subject matter but also to learn how to recognize the ways discourse helps to constitute their worlds.

Let me illustrate how discourse analysis leads to conversations about meaningful subject matters using an early, diagnostic, "react-to-a-reading" essay from a first-year composition course at the University of Illinois at Chicago. The students were asked to read an excerpt from Allan Bloom's essay, "Our Listless Universities," which appeared in the *National Review* as a prelude to his popular book, *The Closing of the American Mind.* For purposes of analysis, here is the student's paper in full:

> In Bloom's essay, "Our Listless Universities," he attempts to argue as his main point that university students don't believe in anything, and that the universities are not doing anything to help, nor can they. He claims that the universities are not doing anything to help rejuvenate our agnostic students and as a result a portion of the blame deserves to go to the universities.
>
> He claims as one of his supporting points that the reason why this is happening to students is that their heads are being filled with "jargon," and this jargon is taking the place of "real experience and instinct." He also claims as his supporting point that the students have replaced their real souls with artificial ones, ones filled with abstract ideals. The funny thing is, he claims, is that these students are not truly aware of the true implications of these ideals, like "values, ideology, identity." An example for these points, evidence, was the "Sixties." This time was filled with "jargon," which the students promoted.
>
> The next supporting point he makes is that students have not gotten anywhere due to the universities. He says that the "university has no vision, no view of what a human being must know in order to be considered educated." He feels that one of the problems are the types of courses being taught. He thinks that they don't apply to being "liberally educated." As evidence, he says that the "Natural Sciences" do nothing to help enlighten a

student. Another one is the social sciences. He claims that there is nothing fresh about it, "theoretically barren."

He claims that the universities should concentrate on humanities and philosophy. These classes offer insight into the soul, "the soul's furniture," "soul's food."

Another supporting point on why our students are listless is due to Books. He claims that students don't read books anymore for pleasure. For evidence, he says that people now read literature and philosophy only for information, because they feel it doesn't apply to this time. Next he claims as a supporting point that music is another big cause of decay. Music has caused separation among society, given students too much freedom and expression to their emotive soul.

Finally he claims as his supporting point that the sex roles are a big blame. The new feminist movement and "desexualization" of society has distorted the natural order of things.

In conclusion, this essay is a bunch of "crok!" I enjoyed his arguments in Part I and II, but during the IIIrd part, I got furious reading it. He seems to be telling us to live our life according to the "great" books, a fantasy world. Not possible, Bloom.

This text is clearly interdiscursive with the relatively traditional "summarize-and-respond" composition type often found in GWSI courses. However, reading it analytically using the template generated by Fairclough's theory of intertextuality and interdiscursivity reveals several strata of subject matters that the student and the instructor could use to begin negotiating an area of inquiry for future compositions. This school-based genre establishes two identities: The writer is positioned as an isolated, perhaps even idiosyncratic, reader of the primary text at hand; it is his or her job to summarize the theses and supporting points and then to agree or disagree with them. The agreement or disagreement is hardly ever couched in terms of any collective, public conversation on the issues raised. Often in such papers, one finds the writer defining himself or herself with such phrases as, "Well, it's only my opinion, but. . . ." The reader in this genre, on the other hand, is positioned in three roles: as an evaluator of the clarity and correctness of the prose, as a coach calling for additional development of the ideas, and as a potential collaborator with, or antagonist to, the writer's distinctive reactions to the theses.

In terms of social relations, the first and third of these roles coalesce into a power dynamic between writer and reader: The reader/evaluator/instructor checks the composition for clarity and presence of error, but he or she also is in the position either to praise the position the writer takes in reaction to the theses and thus raise the writer's stock in the class; or, conversely, to take issue with the writer's reaction and thus potentially imperil the writer's standing with the instructor. Given this power relationship, it is not unusual in this genre to find the reaction to the theses tucked in at the end and coming as something of a surprise. Notice how suddenly the writer of the response to Bloom announces that "this essay is a bunch of 'crok.'" The writer is obliged to react but wants to do so quickly and then get out. Ideologically, this genre as it is practiced in school settings casts nonfiction as something to be agreed or disagreed with, but not necessarily processed. First-year writing courses typically offer college students their first critical exposure to nonfiction prose other than textbooks. Not only have the students had no experience in writing about their phenomenologically developing responses, but I have also found that instructors rarely teach them to observe and record such reactions.

In terms of activity type, this paper capitalizes on interdiscursivity with book reviews, as young writers have frequently experienced them. In this activity, the writer is the presenter—the speaker, the critic; the auditors play no role except to listen. The social relations in this activity derive from this presentational setting: The writer as critic is in the position to stake out his or her position and take the risk of the auditors' disagreeing with him or her. Ideologically, the strength of the critical position taken is vital, but again the writer as critic is under no obligation to process—to justify, to explain—the critical stance, simply to announce it.

The influence of this activity type is evident in the style of the composition. Although the language embodies the spirit of a distinctive discourse, as I argue momentarily, the tenor of the piece is relatively subdued and matter-of-fact until the final paragraph, when the writer announces the rather emotional reaction. The mode, similarly, is typically written exegesis until the final paragraph, when colloquialism, "a bunch of 'crok,'" carrying its residue of spoken language, intrudes. The rhetorical mode, as well, is strictly expository until the final paragraph, when the writer proposes to be argumentative but clearly does not develop an argumentative case.

Most importantly, the text displays interdiscursivity with a distinctive discourse that can provide a starting point for the student and instructor to negotiate a potential subject matter for future compositions. This is the discourse of evangelicalism. Notice that the writer perceives Bloom to be saying that universities should "help rejuvenate our agnostic students," who have "replaced their real souls with artificial ones." Humanities and philosophy courses "offer insight into the soul, 'the soul's furniture,' 'soul's food.'" Popular music has "given students too much freedom and expression to their emotive soul." The text represents a highly intertextual and even more intensely interdiscursive summary of the Bloom excerpt. Nowhere did Bloom use the verb *rejuvenate* or refer to contemporary students as *agnostic*. Bloom (1991) did suggest that "modern thought has produced an artificial soul to replace the old one supplied by nature" (p.

57). The allusions "the soul's furniture" and "soul's food" are freely adapted from Bloom's sections on the roles of books and popular music in contemporary youth culture. Bloom wrote, "The Bible and Plutarch have ceased to be a part of the soul's furniture" (p. 62); he asserted that rock music has been "[f]rom the time of puberty the food of their [young people's] souls" (p. 62). Thus, whereas the text reveals actual, manifest intertextuality to a limited degree, to a larger degree it represents an interdiscursive manifestation of a discourse that, as the student writer admitted to his instructor in a conference, is extremely strong in his life: He considers himself a born-again Christian, and he sees how his faith influences his readings in many of his classes.

How exactly could an instructor use such an analysis and the conversation that grows from it to help students determine subject matters they could profitably write about? Over the past several years, I have been developing a curriculum-generating device that I have labeled the *inquiry contract* (see Jolliffe, 1994). The inquiry contract, which has its roots in the aims of discourse proposed by Kinneavy (1971) in *A Theory of Discourse*, generates a sequential, cumulative series of four papers. Before beginning work on the first, students write a domain statement, in which they propose subject matters to write about. The assignment asks the students to (a) name the subject matter, (b) describe how they got interested in it, (c) explain, in a paragraph or so for each, two things they already know about the subject, and (d) list two important questions they would still like to address about the subject. Next, the instructor meets with each student to plan his or her sequence. For the first paper, students write largely to themselves (and any consultant readers they deem appropriate) clarifying what they already know, think, feel, or believe about the subject. For the second paper, students follow this self-clarification exercise by purposefully undertaking to learn something new about the subject. This paper may involve research ranging from interviewing people on the subject to observing some site or phenomenon to consulting books or periodicals. I frequently urge students to consult some other source of expertise than printed materials; I think students need to learn how to interview people and collect oral history and commentary. Some instructors, however, use this assignment to teach students how to conduct a selective, evaluative review of available literature on the subject. The second paper, then, asks writers to inform their readers—their peers in the class or the general community of an academic field—of what they have discovered that is new to them.

The third paper returns the writers to a questioning mode. Here they attempt to tear their subject matter apart by raising as many sensible questions about it as possible and proposing as many plausible answers to each question as they can. This exploratory paper can take the form of a traditional essay, but it need not. Some instructors ask students in this part of the contract to write dialogues involving several "characters" connected to their subject matter or simply to list strings of questions and multiple answers.

After clarifying, learning and informing, and exploring, the students are finally ready to engage in argument. For the fourth and final paper, then, they write in order to demonstrate a thesis or to persuade people to think or behave differently about their subject matter. The fourth paper consciously builds on the previous three. The writers have focused on key issues, gained background on them, and anticipated potential objections to the points they will now offer and develop. The final paper grows out of a miniature research program, an imitation—but a respectable one—of the kind that motivates the reading, research, and writing of more experienced mentors.

The inquiry contract offers no simple, infallible heuristic for generating reading and writing assignments; it requires relatively intensive conferencing with students, and it demands that both the students and the instructor be flexible enough to allow the assignments, especially the third and fourth, to emerge from the investigation. Even with these faults, however, I have found that inquiry contracts generate rich, challenging, engaged writing from students when they grow from the discourses that the students' own texts reveal, intertextually and interdiscursively. Here is how I might negotiate an inquiry contract with the author of the Bloom critique. In my first-term GWSI course, I frequently ask students to propose a sequence of compositions that deal generally with the nature and purposes of higher education. After reading the student's response to Bloom, I might work with him to construct a contract that would lead him to inquire into the roles that evangelical, moral edification might play in public higher education. His first paper would clarify for himself what he already thinks, feels, knows, and believes about evangelicalism's ideal place in higher education and would list questions he would still like to address about the subject. For his second paper, I would urge him to pose these questions in interviews with several people on campus—a dean of students, a campus chaplain, the leaders of student religious organizations from several faiths, not just evangelicals—and to write back informing his classmates (or members of a writing group, which I usually establish in such classes) of what he learned. For the third paper, I would meet with the student again, and help him craft a paper on the subject that uses an exploratory structure that Kinneavy (1971) adapted from the work of Kuhn. This structure asks the writer to review status quo thinking on a subject, to determine a need to change the status quo, to argue that the time is right for such a change, and to propose and critique more than one alternative to status quo thinking and action. This paper requires the student to balance what he has written in his first paper with the information he has discovered in writing the second. This third paper, notice, offers several potential paths of action. For the fourth paper, then, the student would propose a specific plan for a specific audience to think or act differently than they currently do concerning his subject matter. The fourth paper is thus primarily persuasive, but it has the benefit of embodying the myriad viewpoints that the interviewees provided in the second paper and of choosing the best plan from the several alternatives generated in the third.

I have found that such sequences, when they grow out of the discourses one finds emerging from students' early writing in a course, lead the student to learn a great deal about a subject matter by considering it as being constituted by a public conversation. Students learn to write in order to create rich, challenging ideas—not just their own, and not just others' but ideas generated by a complex dialectic of status quo thinking and original discovery.

CONCLUSION

Informal critics of the inquiry contract have expressed a predictable qualm about its use as a generator of curricula in GWSI courses. "You have stopped teaching writing," the critics contend, "and in its place you have taken to teaching little seminars on the students' subjects." I disagree. When students and faculty generate reading and writing projects using the contract—especially when the contract grows from an analysis of the discourses within which students are unconsciously positioned—the instruction that follows is consummately writerly. Students and their instructors now have real, challenging subject matters with which to study methods of invention and strategies of prewriting. Instruction in arrangement, genre, style, and correct usage emerges naturally from the varying audience and purpose dimensions of the four projects within the contract. Revision becomes integral to instruction because students write a sequence of papers in which the subject matter develops from one composition to the next.

Using the inquiry contract, moreover, students not only learn to write, but they also learn two valuable lessons about writing. First, they learn about the ways writing has already inscribed them into identities, social relations, and ideological structures, and in doing so, they are provided with an opportunity to gain critical awareness of writing's constitutive power. The contract provides a second lesson by showing student writers how their own writing can, in turn, contribute to the shaping of identities, relations, and ideologies. For these reasons I cannot think of a more valuable contribution to a student's liberal education than a "basic" course like GWSI could make.

REFERENCES

Bartholomae, D., & Petroskey, P. (1985). *Facts, artifacts, and counterfacts*. Upper Montclair, NJ: Boynton/Cook.

Bartholomae, D., & Petroskey, P. (1987). *Ways of reading: An anthology for writers*. Boston: Bedford.

Berlin, J. A. (1994). Poststructuralism, cultural studies, and the composition classroom: Postmodern theory in practice. In T. Enos & S. C. Brown (Eds.), *Professing the new rhetorics* (pp. 461–480). Englewood Cliffs, NJ: Blair Press.

Bloom, A. (1991). Our listless universities. In D. A. Jolliffe et al. (Eds.) *Purposes and ideas: Readings for university writers* (pp. 57–66). Dubuque, IA: Kendall-Hunt.

Diederich, P. (1964). Problems and possibilities of research in the teaching of written composition. In D. H. Russell, E. J. Farrell, & M. J. Early (Eds.), *Research design and the teaching of English: Proceedings of the San Francisco conference* (pp. 52–74). Champaign, IL: National Council of Teachers of English.

Dillon, G. L. (1981). *Constructing texts: Elements of a theory of composition and style*. Bloomington: Indiana University Press.

Emig, J. (1977). Writing as a mode of learning. *College Composition and Communication, 28,* 122–128.

Faigley, L. (1992). *Fragments of rationality: Postmodernity and the subject of composition*. Pittsburgh, PA: University of Pittsburgh Press.

Fairclough, N. (1992). *Discourse and social change*. Cambridge, UK: Polity Press.

Flower, L., & Hayes, J. R. (1980). The cognition of discovery: Defining a rhetorical problem. *College Composition and Communication, 31,* 21–32.

Hairston, M. C. (1991, January 23). Required writing courses should not focus on politically charged social issues. *Chronicle of Higher Education,* B1–B2.

Jolliffe, D. A. (1994). *Writing, teaching,and learning: Incorporating writing throughout the curriculum*. New York: HarperCollins.

Kaufer, D., & Young, R. (1993). Writing in the content areas: Some theoretical complexities. In L. Odell (Ed.), *Theory and practice in the teaching of writing: Rethinking the discipline* (pp. 71–104). Carbondale: Southern Illinois University Press.

Kinneavy, J. L. (1971). *A theory of discourse*. Englewood Cliffs, NJ: Prentice-Hall.

Knoblauch, C. H., & Brannon, L. (1984). *Rhetorical traditions and the teaching of writing*. Upper Montclair, NJ: Boynton/Cook.

Murray, D. M. (1982). What, no assignments? In *Learning by teaching: Selected articles on writing and teaching* (pp. 129–134). Upper Montclair, NJ: Boynton/Cook. (Original work published 1974).

Penrose, A. M. (1992). To write or not to write: Effects of task and task interpretation on learning through writing. *Written Communication, 9,* 465–500.

Sommers, N. I. (1980). Revision strategies of student writers and experienced adult writers. *College Composition and Communication, 31,* 378–388.

11

Integrating Cultural Reflection and Production in College Writing Curricula

David S. Kaufer
Carnegie Mellon University

Patricia L. Dunmire
Kent State University

Although it can be demonstrated that actuaries, accountants, and insurance adjusters write on the job, no one seriously designs writing programs with the tasks that cross their desks each day. As a tool of the professions, writing retains a quality that makes it seem more generic, more encompassing, less circumscribed, and more ambient and vague, than more conventional tools of professional practice. There is, further, a disanalogy between what differential equations means for the engineer and what writing means for the generic professional. For the engineer, critical paths of the profession would not be crossed without differential equations. For the professional in general, critical paths often get crossed even with poor writing, albeit not without some anxiety and social discomfort, perhaps.

The so-called "writing problem" on campus has been sustained by this anxiety. No institution wants to graduate students with writing skills that remain under suspicion. The symbol of a university asleep at the wheel is one that graduates such students. Not wanting to be caught napping, administrators are willing to put resources into the problem. What they seek to redress is not a problem in the classic sense; only an ill-defined anxiety that their students will be "caught" performing below standards.

The obvious way to meet the problem (were it a clean problem) would be to define criteria and see that students meet them. The reason the problem remains, at best, an anxiety is that no standards are easy to come by or uncontroversial to sustain. We are still at square one when it comes to defining the legitimate social goals of a writing program. Writing, after

217

all, remains a mixed bag when it comes to goals beyond the classroom. In the culture at large, writing is seen as a vehicle for purging dishonesty and self-deceit, for legal documentation, for blackmail, for gaining friends and selling them out, for social repression and titillation, for worthy and worthless subversion, for intellectual exploits and fraud, for sending journalists to jail, and for rehabilitating the inmates already incarcerated. Given such mixed cultural images, the question of goals for a college-level writing curriculum are nontrivial.

If writing programs are to be more than administrative stress pills, the question of a college writing program's goals and cultural legitimation has to be answered better than we have so far answered it. Although answering this question is outside the scope of our chapter, we do offer a perspective that will contribute to the inquiry and debate needed for moving us closer to an answer. Underlying our project is a view of language use and writing instruction that challenges the view held by programs characterized by Kaufer and Young (1993) as "writing with no content in particular," a tradition that has dominated the thinking of most English departments and the university community in general. On this view, language and content are dichotomized, with language functioning solely as a neutral medium for presenting knowledge discovered through inquiry. Such a reductive view characterizes writing as a body of general skills resulting in the tradition of general writing skills instruction (GWSI).

Our thesis challenges this tradition by arguing that there are cognitive, social, and public dimensions to writing that are worth knowing and that most students probably would not be fully aware of were they not taught in college. We complicate this thesis, moreover, by suggesting that if students are to effectively pursue these dimensions during their college years they must be taught to approach them from a reflective stance rather than from just a narrowly productive one. Students can learn what writing knowledge is and how it can be deployed in contexts of written production. Yet it is unrealistic to think that, in the span of the 4-year curriculum, much less a single course of GWSI, students will take great strides in performing up to the highest standards of the art.

We describe the gap between reflection and production in terms of a gap between learning conventions and historicizing conventions in practice. The rules of chess are conventions that everyone can learn. The strategies of the grand master of chess are not. One cannot learn to be a grand master by learning the rules, but one can bootstrap one's way into more masterful strategies by playing games and associating historical playing situations with the capacities of the pieces as defined by the conventions. Expert players learn how the capacities of the pieces—the conventions—define historical playing situations and are in turn defined by them. The conventions and the situations, after a long period of training, become seamless pieces of reasoning. A writing program cannot always provide this time, but it should provide students with a clear understanding of what writing performance can be if they use their time strategically. Perhaps because the "writing problem" has festered more as an anxiety than a well-defined problem, the tolerance for reflection–production gaps has been low in writing programs. Such programs are expected to guarantee a certain level of student performance in an unrealistically compressed amount of time, one reason perhaps why so many programs focus on the seemingly "contained" problems of grammar and usage. Writing programs that stress reflection (i.e., talk and inquiry about written expression itself) are often questioned as to whether they teach writing at all. In some cases, the criticism may be legitimate because a reflective theory of writing must bring a strong enough theory of production to work, over the long term, in making a student a higher functioning writer. At the same time, a writing curriculum that promises high-level production is doomed to produce students whose performance will be disappointing, the kind of illegitimate disappointment one would feel after teaching novices the rules of chess and discovering that their games fall short of Bobby Fisher's. Such curricula, ironically, only exacerbate the very anxiety they were put in place to reduce.

In this chapter we address the anxiety induced by the disjunction between the reasonable goals and the high-level expectations of a 4-year writing program. Relieving this anxiety, we argue, requires both that realistic goals of a curriculum be defined and that interactive theories of production and reflection be introduced that have a serious chance, in the long term, of moving students to higher levels of performance. Despite the recent interest and research in composition as an intellectual process, writing programs continually promote a GWSI approach, thereby reducing composition to the level of productive skill. This reduction occurs in spite of the understanding that we as professionals hold toward writing as a complex, involved undertaking that relies as much on activities of reflection as it does on activities of production.

In the first section of the chapter we elaborate the multiple dimensions of writing that a college writing program can and should present to students. We argue that for these dimensions to be effectively conveyed and understood they must be incorporated into writing pedagogies through integrated theories of reflection and production. We focus the second half of the chapter on the freshman curriculum currently in place at Carnegie Mellon University, a curriculum designed to realize the dimensions laid out in the first section.[1] Although the curriculum has been effective for our

---

[1]For a detailed explanation of the curriculum see Geisler and Kaufer (1989), Kaufer and Geisler (1990), Kaufer, Geisler, and Neuwirth (1989), Kennedy (1992), and Kennedy, Neuwirth, Straub, and Kaufer (1994).

students in many areas (e.g., providing them methodologies for representing an author's line of argument in their reading and writing and for representing the various argumentative paths different authors take through a particular issue), it has been less effective in others. Specifically, our concern here is with the unit of the course called analysis. In the final portion of our chapter we use a text of psychologist Sylvia Scribner to introduce and demonstrate the concept of *knowledge design* as an approach for teaching students the intricacies of analysis and analytic writing and, more generally, as a framework for integrating reflection and production in college writing curricula.

DIMENSIONS OF WRITING AS RHETORICAL BEHAVIOR

Although the cultural purposes of writing are varied, we suggest that as rhetorical behavior, writing is a multidimensioned intellectual endeavor that advanced schooling can strengthen, regardless of the specific purpose to which it is put. We now review what we believe are the most important dimensions that should be presented to college students through direct instruction in writing.

Cognitive Dimension

One such dimension along which advanced schooling can seem to benefit students is cognitive. Along this dimension, advanced schooling in writing can benefit students' reasoning, can extend their awareness of thoughtful communication in a new medium, and their understanding of writing as a series of parallel behaviors.

Writing as Reasoning.   Writing is not simply linear patterns of strings on the page assembled through rules of grammar. It is also constituted by more or less explicit chains of reasoning, from premise to conclusion. Premises and conclusions can be more or less true or false and the inferences binding them can be more or less deductively valid or inductively probable. Reasoning, of course, is not unique to the modality of writing but writing, leaving a visible and frozen trace of reasoning, makes it easier to isolate reasoning for instructional feedback. Significant for the development of mature literacy, reasoning chains that sustain writing must be planned beyond single sentences and paragraphs to the thematic level in order for the writing to have coherence as a whole text. At the secondary level, students typically have not benefited from feedback on the reasoning chains they produce at the whole text. An important goal of advanced schooling in writing is to give students practice planning and then sustaining chains of reasoning at the thematic level.

Writing as Thoughtful Action at a Distance. Because of the fixity of writing, the chains of meaning that sustain a whole text can survive intact beyond the immediate context. This gives writing a power of potential "distance" not found in face-to-face interaction. Although the audience of the writer may contingently be the same as the familiar audience of the speaker, to make them the same is to reduce greatly the potential of writing. For the majority of college-bound students, the potential of writing as a medium of distance is not well understood. College-ready students are not likely to appreciate that in making meaning for familiar and sympathetic audiences, they are also constructing more or less "plausible" worlds that can rise to the challenge of accommodating anonymous and skeptical audiences as well. Writing that rises to this challenge has a potential audience—a potential reach—far in excess of any audience that comes in the range of simple talk. Another goal of advanced schooling is to help students rise to this challenge and so understand the potential reach of writing as a medium of distance; to help them understand that writing is not simply talk on the page but rather language readied for print, a subtle difference suggesting that the written register must be prepared with the care required to connect with audiences farther removed in time, space, and culture. This care is minimal if the chains of reasoning constituting writing are to be judged probable and valid for a mass or quality audience outside the classroom. Although it is too abstract and lofty a goal to assume that advanced schooling can teach students how to publish, it is not unreasonable to assume that such schooling can teach students about the long-distance requirements of language readied for print, which in turn houses a good many implicit assumptions about requirements for publishing.

Writing as Parallel Behavior. Writers who do well in any genre are doing many things well. Research in writing is now only beginning to scratch the surface of what these many things are: exercising reasoning skills, whole text organization, paragraph and sentence-level organization, audience sensitivity, affect, the historical context of author–audience interaction, the control of discourse conventions and registers, grammar, usage, and much more. Yet the awareness of writing as a complex, highly parallel activity has yet to penetrate most of our college writing programs, where simple factors of "good" or "bad" writing endure as the holy grail of assessment. A myth that perpetuates the search for this grail, held by most college-ready students, their parents, college administrators, and even faculty is that writing is a monolithic skill assessable on a single dimensioned scale. With a research literature in writing still so new, it is too much to expect a writing program to "crack" all the levels of parallelism that go into the assessment of good or bad writing. Yet such programs can reasonably expect to give students an accurate cognitive understanding of the parallelism they must deal with when they deal as writers. Operationally stated, such an understanding would make teachers and students alike impatient with the judgment of "bad writing" if it does not go on to isolate what factors are nonetheless going well; and impatient with the judgment of "good writing" if it does not isolate areas for improvement. Many college writing programs formed to address the writing problem are doomed to fail if only because their definition of the writing problem withdraws from the formidable challenge posed by parallelism.

Social Dimension

A second dimension along which advanced schooling can seemingly benefit writing is social. Writing takes place in the head of the writer but what goes on in the writer's head must sensitively adapt to changes in the larger environment for writing. Changes in social variables must be accompanied by changes in the writer's cognitive environment and vice versa. Let us consider some of the more obvious and important social variables at issue.

Variable Audiences. Audiences vary. Some are individuals with faces; others may be helped by thinking of individual faces but are in fact delimited by mental constructs with a few constrained attributes (e.g., males between 18 and 34 who drink beer). Still others consist of highly differentiated audiences with attributes ranging over such a wide set of values that the writer's best advice, as in a mass circulation mailing, is to isolate and avoid only the blatantly objectionable, to aim "not to offend."

Because writing is a medium of greater potential distance than talk and because college-ready students are not likely to have experimented with this distance, they are also likely not to have much practice varying audience parameters as writers. Students are likely to come to college only having written to an audience with a single face: a friend, parent, or teacher. In cultural terms, students might be thought of as proximate agents, interacting mainly if not exclusively with those who share the same space, time, and culture. Students are not likely to have written to a group, much less a group dispersed in time, space, or culture and constructed abstractly, from some shared attributes.

Giving students lessons in varying audience as writers helps them transcend their status as proximate agents and makes them aware of the values added and achieved when audiences are reached at a distance. As many students are now learning through the Internet, there is much value added when one can reach others around the world with the same cultural interest in, say, chess or computer games. In addition, the interests of many groups cannot be realized or furthered without the grant of licenses, permissions, resources, or coalition support from groups removed in culture as well as space. A student group cannot expect to have their interests furthered on AIDS testing on campus without making contact with officials who have the power to vote on or restrict such testing; or without making contact with coalition groups removed in culture (e.g., the ACLU) that happen to share a common interest on the local issue. As the social theorist Giddens (1984) indicated, power in modern technological cultures has everything to do with the capacity to marshal resources from audiences at a distance. This means, as a first step, learning to talk to culturally differentiated audiences. Lessons in helping students write to variable audiences are, finally, lessons in cultural power.

Variable Registers.   The labor leader George Meany was widely admired for being able to adapt to the level of his audience. He was as comfortable talking to presidents and foreign dignitaries as to the high school dropouts in his own union. He not only spoke at the educational level of his audience, but he spoke in the way they spoke. He understood that the language a person speaks and the manner in which he or she speaks it captures a way of life that needs to be affirmed, without condescension, if the audience is to accept the speaker as its own. Let us call this adaptive skill the skill of variable registers, the ability to regulate vocabulary, formality, attitude, tone, jargon, clichés, slogans, and slang as used within a particular group.

Students understand and practice this skill in their daily life. They speak one way to their parents, another to their teachers, and still another to their friends. None of these registers is more real or phony than the others. The variability of registers simply reflects the fact that a person plays many roles in a social world and these roles are tied to different communicative settings, discourse conventions, and audience expectations. For students, these multiple roles are still very much anchored to assumptions of proximity.

Few college-ready students understand that register variability is a pervasive phenomenon in writing. A common myth among students is to believe that they must leave a world of multiple oral registers to learn a single written register associated with literate communication. True, oral registers are punctuated by a range of nonverbal cues that makes their multiplicity a straightforward perception; written registers lack these nonverbal cues, making register variability a more difficult judgment to the less discerning. Yet register variability is no less true of writing than speaking and much of advanced schooling in writing can be devoted to reinforcing that lesson alone. To increase cultural power, we have suggested, students must learn to address groups of increasing cultural differentiation. These groups and the written documents used to sustain them convey information about the registers that mark their ritualistic patterns of communication. To learn to address these groups, students must learn how to inquire into a group's characteristic registers and to employ them in their practice as they address it.

Variable Personae.   Personae refer to the particular image of self created by a speaker through the message. Is the speaker friendly, hostile, cautious, intelligent, reckless? These are attributions of persona. Some of these attributions may already be prescribed as part of the tone required by a particular register. However, register refers to patterns that are triggered by recurring situations of communication within groups, whereas persona is designed to mark traits of an individual that are proffered as more enduring than either the situation of communication or the group in which the specific communication is structured (even though these "enduring" traits are often still register specific).

College-ready students are adept at manipulating persona in their everyday speech behavior and at understanding the need for varying persona according to the occasion of speech. They know, for example, what to do to make the parent of a friend think them responsive and dependable and how to discourage the same judgments if they are trying to get out of a chore assigned to them by a parent. Yet, as is the case with register, students are less likely to see persona variability as a regularity of writing in the manner of speech. They are less likely to understand that an academic scientist not only can but must read like a person with one set of traits when writing formally to peers and another, in some cases, incompatible set when talking about the results informally or writing a popular account to general audiences. Some periodicals require the writer to be "defiant," whereas others require an air of "calm" and "detachment." A student practicing writing for both will break down if he or she is not trained to see how readers can come so decisively to these "enduring" traits without even the evidence of the writer's physical presence.

Public Dimension

Yet a third dimension along which writing may be taken to benefit students through advanced schooling is the public dimension. This dimension, in the sense we discuss here, is less examined in the literature than the other two but is of equal importance. Viewed as rhetorical behavior, writing, like public speaking, is designed to address a public. The notion of a public, public address, and a "public" discourse involved in this address are as old as ancient Greece. In all these contexts *public* is often used as a synonym for mass audience, which effectively collapses the social and public dimensions. For us, this is a mistake. We believe public has a meaning quite different from physical audiences.

A synonym for our conception of public is "on the record" in the sense of speaking or writing on the record. To speak or write on the record is to make a statement about the permeability of what one says and the contexts in which one means it to be applicable. It is to make a commitment that what one says, on the record, will survive, intact, into future contexts. In other words, the public dimension accounts for the function served by on-the-record discourse in constructing contexts, as well as the roles and positions a writer or speaker can assume within those contexts, for future courses of actions.

Public discourse would be unthinkable if the words of a speaker in one context could not be used to hold the same speaker to account in future contexts. Regardless of the specific coherence of the reasoning or the formality of the register of its speakers, the status of a group as an entity seeking to impact the larger culture would be jeopardized if its members were not held to some standard of on-the-record accountability, if their words could not be used as social tissue to tie them across time and space and to the larger culture, if they had no project to achieve a public identity beyond the identity of a physical group. Taking the writing classroom both as a working group and an emergent public (seeking an internal focus and ties with the culture beyond the classroom), it is the implicit standard underlying why teachers expect the chains of reasoning students and peers produce in one draft to predict in whole or part what they will say in others on the same or a related issue. Without such accountability, teachers cannot sustain the idea that consensus within the classroom can be used both as a window and a writer's lever to the writers and writings of the outside world.

Despite their writing experiences prior to college, students seldom have formal exposure or practice in on-the-record accountability. Earlier, we observed that students are accustomed to writing to audiences with a face, not anonymous groups. This face-to-face expectation is due, in no small part, to the legacy of composition studies and curricula, which has limited the rhetorical nature of writing to "audience awareness": What information do you and your reader share? What information do you need to provide to your reader? Yet the abstraction of a "public" created by on-the-record discourse requires a step beyond writing to a faceless audience. It further requires assuming a strategic involvement within a group that itself operates within a larger cultural matrix. It requires assuming that the writer is at once seeking to increase consensus within a group and to move the larger culture closer to the group consensus.

The public dimension of writing utilizes the cognitive and social dimensions in order to assign writers strategic projects for discovery and action. These strategic projects assume, atypical of most of the undergraduate curriculum, that students are already deeply immersed, as cultural insiders, in the groups where the public dimension plays itself out: civic, professional, and academic groups. These assumptions are notoriously false, however, for higher education in the United States. They are false for two reasons.

First, college-ready students are seldom immersed in culturally strategic projects as insiders. Nor, for the lion's share of undergraduate education, need they be. Students find they can master most of the undergraduate curriculum without culture-specific goals, interests, and values and involved membership in the groups that seek to move the culture according to their internal consensus. They can be "perfect" students while maintaining little or no cultural awareness or sense of cultural agency. Yet a writing class that takes the conception of writing as rhetorical behavior seriously necessarily interrupts this quiet by acting as if the student has been involved as an insider all along. Students rebel against the disruption of this quiet and many administrators and faculty across the university follow suit. They mistake the insistence on cultural involvement in the writing classroom with the writing teacher's force-feeding a particular politics down students' throats. The only thing the teacher need preach is that mature writers see what they do as part of their cultural involvements. To teach writing apart from these involvements is to teach a sterile activity that has no scalability beyond the classroom.

There is a second reason why the assumption of the students' cultural immersion is false. Authority is more than a problem of establishing credentials one does not already have. It is also, and perhaps more importantly, a problem of tying newly learned authorities with the experiences over which one already commands authority. Students do not come to the classroom as tabula rasa, needing only to embark in patterns of reasoning and register that are not yet learned. No public students seek to enter flatly rejects the reasoning and registers of everyday living. Civic, professional, and even academic publics would never have succeeded in the general culture to the extent they have were their patterns of reasoning and register not highly sensitive and adaptive to much of our everyday patterns. These elitist publics, far from rejecting everyday reasoning and register, rather build on, filter, and transcend them according to the requirements of particular involvements.

Because of the complex interdependence between the publics to which we try to acculturate students and their current experience, it is insufficient to think we can teach membership in these publics as a body of new and entirely unfamiliar propositions or conventions. They must rather be taught in interaction with the ways in which students already think of reason and registers. Yet it is very hard to teach this interaction explicitly.

It is much easier, in the manner of various writing across the curriculum texts, to teach academic publics as strange and exotic cultures, to get students to think of what are essentially historically rooted involvements as conventions that can be sliced apart from the history of involvements that gave rise to them. Such slicing suggests a lack of understanding and appreciation of the complexities of writing as rhetorical behavior.

By elaborating the dimensions of writing that should be provided through a college writing program, we have brought to the fore the complexities of writing as a multidimensioned rhetorical act. These are complexities that we as professionals relish but that our students have yet to understand or appreciate. Rather than embrace the richness of writing as an intellectual endeavor, writing programs ignore or suppress them, teaching writing as a set of conventions that can be learned and understood independent of content or context. If we want to continue in our project of teaching students how to write, we clearly need to devote more attention and resources to what writing (and more generally, language use) is and how it functions in real social and historical contexts. For this reason, reflection on language use in such contexts must be an integral part of college writing curricula.

KNOWLEDGE DESIGN: BOOTSTRAPPING STUDENTS' CULTURAL INVOLVEMENTS THROUGH REFLECTIVE PRACTICE

Reflection on the conventions of academic writing, we have suggested, needs to be an integral part of students' productive practices. Writing conventions approached unreflectively, as mere tools of production, are only just that: decontextualized rules and formats that can be learned and imitated but will not lead to effective performance. As such, fostering a reflective stance in our students requires that our pedagogical approach embraces reflection as indispensable to productive practice. Without reflection, instruction in production remains words about alien worlds. For example, it is one thing to tell students that academic discourse is "direct about the 'position'—the argument and reasons and claim" but is "shy, indirect or even evasive about the texture of feelings or attitudes" underlying that position (Elbow, 1991, p. 145); it is an entirely different task for students to realize this convention in their own writing. The problem may be that the vocabulary we use for talking about conventions, although seemingly clear and direct to us, is not a performative vocabulary for our students. Rather, this concrete and specific instruction is all too often heard as high-level abstractions and platitudes. As such, our pedagogies of telling students what to do must be supplemented with a pedagogy of helping students develop their reflective skills. Such an approach would help students see what academic conventions look like in actual practice and what is required to realize those conventions in their own writing. In short, we view reflective practice that is focused on the historically constituted and constitutive nature of conventions as a pedagogical approach that can help students bootstrap their way out of the realm of idiosyncratic experience and into the realm of authorship.

In this portion of the chapter, we present a brief overview of the freshman writing program currently in place at Carnegie Mellon University. We open with a general overview of the goals and purposes that motivated the original conception of our curriculum and how student performance has generally fallen short in realizing those goals and purposes. Our primary interest here, however, is to present our current project of rethinking our theoretical and pedagogical approach toward the goals and purposes underlying our freshman curriculum. Specifically, we present a general framework for a curriculum that weds reflection and production.

Our Curriculum: The Original Conception

As originally conceived, our freshman curriculum was meant to challenge students' naïve belief that language and knowledge are unrelated, with knowledge holding a priori status, and language being merely the mechanism through which knowledge is neutrally and unproblematically conveyed. This received understanding of the relationship between knowledge and language has led students to seeing their primary task as presenting decontextualized, "accurate" descriptions of the authors they read. It further has encouraged students to mistake the linguistic constructions and rhetorical devices comprising their texts as the "output" of objective decisions based on rules of grammar and composition. Students come away with the idea that the "best" writing does not engage the subjective interests or passions of the writer or reader.

Rather, our curriculum has introduced students to a conception of our language and our knowledge of the social world as constructed to express ongoing orientations and commitments that are far from value free, but that may have remained outside students' awareness. Our curriculum has challenged students to conceive of the authors as knowledge constructors. Students have been expected to critique the lines of arguments underlying the authors' positions on an issue in order to find a "gap" in these arguments, and subsequently to develop their position as an attempt to fill that gap. For example, in articles discussing the literacy concerns of an African American community, a student may notice that none of the authors attend to gender issues in their arguments about the causes of and solutions for low literacy rates. The student further realizes that these positions hold the assumption that men and women within this community have the same experiences and concerns. However the student's experience strongly suggests otherwise and thus she develops a perspective that argues for gender as a central concern in discussions of literacy in the African American community. This analytical process requires that students attend both to positions and positioning as necessary components of knowledge design. By position we mean a unique response to an issue (i.e., a topic—literacy—that raises a tension within a community or generates a dissatisfaction with the status quo—essentialist definitions of literacy) that is elaborated through a line of argument detailing the points that constitute that position. By positioning, we mean the rhetorical act of arguing for that position relative to others addressing the same issue; students must strategically place themselves into a conversation by articulating the complex ways in which their position relates to the those offered by the authors. In other words, our curriculum has challenged students to engage in a dialogical process whereby they hold the author's theories and methodologies accountable to their experience while also holding their experience accountable to the authors' theoretical frameworks and methodologies. Such an approach is needed for moving students toward a view of knowledge as positioned and interested and, as such, accessible to their critique.

Although our original conception seemed theoretically sound, the reality of student performance proved unsatisfying as, all too often, students performed at a level below teachers' expectations. Rather than positioning themselves within a community of authors, our students have remained outside that community, operating at the level of idiosyncratic, autobiographical experience. Specifically, they have resisted taking a rhetorical approach to knowledge. Their texts suggest that knowledge is the province of expert writers whereas descriptions of and opinions toward that knowledge is the province of student writers.

Rethinking Our Curriculum

This theory–performance gap has recently caused us to step back and consider ways we can refine our ideas and approach toward teaching students about positions and critique. What is the absolute starting point needed if we are to effectively move students toward performing the intellectually mature activities involved in analytic writing? What is the minimum unit of intellectual activity students need to grasp if they are to glimpse the entire intellectual activity involved in analytic writing? Knowledge design is our answer. It is our response to the nagging frustration we have felt in teaching (or attempting to teach) analytic writing as part of our freshmen writing course. That is, to teach analytic writing we need to focus more of our attention, and that of our students, directly on the idea that knowledge is not found in the world out there, but rather is designed through texts that actively construct, rather than passively reflect, knowledge about the social world. Similar to Givon's (1982) argument, we want students to see that the propositions constituting an argument do not reflect knowledge about the true state of the social world; rather the subjective interests of the writers and readers of these text are (consciously or unconsciously) inextricably involved in the textual presentation of knowledge.

Our present interest, then, lies in laying out a framework for a curriculum that would provide students with the tools they need for understanding how historical context both enables and constrains positions that can be argued and actions that can be taken within that context. Likewise, we want students to understand that texts are designed not only to be heard within that context, but also to alter and redefine it. In other words, the importance of a reflective pedagogy based on the concept of knowledge design arises from the need for students to recognize the material effects brought to bear by some texts and the inability of other texts to realize similar effects. We hope that, in the end, students will internalize the reflective sensitivities they have learned to apply to authors' texts so that they can apply the same sensitivities to their own texts. In short, we want students to approach their writing as knowledge designers.

So what exactly are we asking students to do when we challenge them to become knowledge designers? In the following, we illustrate what knowledge design looks like by examining an author's text, focusing on how she designed the text and what function(s) are served by the design. We begin with the opening paragraph from Scribner's (1984) essay, "Literacy in Three Metaphors."

> Although literacy is a problem of pressing national concern, we have yet to discover or set its boundaries. This observation made several years ago by a leading political spokesman (McGovern, 1978) echoes a long-standing complaint of many policy makers and educators that what counts as literacy in our technological society is a matter "not very well understood" (Advisory Committee on National Illiteracy, 1929). (p. 6)

At first glance, this paragraph simply shows Scribner following fairly standard text conventions for academic writing: She provides the reader with a description of an existing problem and a statement explaining what aspect of that problem still requires the attention of her academic community. However, taking a closer look, we begin to see traces of the sophisticated design decisions that were involved in realizing these conventions in practice.

Notice, for example, how Scribner designed the first sentence so that it objectifies the information it presents; that is, "literacy is a problem" and "we have yet to discover or set its boundaries," removing it from the world of interested, contested positions and locating it in the world out there. Scribner began this relocation process in the first clause of her opening sentence. By placing "literacy is a problem" in a subordinate clause relative to the main focus of the sentence, Scribner presented that information as a presupposed fact that does not require further elaboration, debate, or proof. Further, the entire proposition is reified as a statement of fact by the way the information is presented in the sentence. That is, the information is presented through impersonal projection (Halliday, 1985). Rather than presenting the information as having originated in the thoughts or statements of an individual (e.g., Joe said that it will rain), the information is projected impersonally (e.g., It is the case that it will rain) and, thereby, all traces of the mental and verbal processes generating the information are removed from the statement. In addition to these syntactic design decisions, Scribner also made lexical choices to further objectify the content of her text. By using "to discover" and "boundaries," she characterized literacy not as a concept, but rather as a material entity possessing discrete, discernible features.

This objectifying process continues in the second sentence through Scribner's design of the citations incorporated into her text. In the first clause Scribner constructed the information in the first sentence as a speaker's perception and classification of an action or event. However, she designed this clause such that the speaker's role in this process is minimized. That is, contrary to the first sentence, this sentence provides the information as originating in a speaker's statement; however, this "personal projection" is designed to maintain the factual characterization established in the first sentence. Focusing on the McGovern citation we note two things. To begin with, Scribner used a nominalized form—"This observation"—of a verbal action—"to observe"—to attribute the information presented in the first sentence to its source. Using a nominal form enabled Scribner to remove the verbal act from the immediate context of the specific individual engaged in the act and to place it into the category of timeless situations. In other words, in the sentence form of a nominalization (*McGovern observed that the boundaries of literacy are ill-defined*) the action or event expressed in the sentence is presented by a verb and thus is temporally situated. When the nominal form is used, however, the action or event is presented by a noun and thus is not located in time or attributed to a specific actor (Kress, 1983). Second, Scribner used a visual metaphor to characterize the information presented in the opening sentence and the manner in which that information was acquired. As such, Scribner presented the information as gained through and supported by perceptual (empirical) evidence and, thus, characterized the information, not as a mere statement or claim someone made, but as something someone witnessed. In sum, the nominal form and visual metaphor contained in "This observation" transform what was originally a statement made by a specific individual into an atemporal, discernible entity.

Finally, Scribner's use of nominal form combines with her technique for identifying and naming her sources. As noted earlier, one consequence of using a nominal form for expressing actions and events is to suppress the specific identities of the participants while highlighting the general type or category of person involved in the event or action. This is what we see happening in Scribner's text. "This observation" is attributed to a general type of person at a vague point in the past, and the specific individual and time of the observation are incorporated into the text parenthetically. Thus, although Scribner named the individual who made the observation—"McGovern"—she subordinated this specific name to the general type of person—"a leading political spokesman"—she wanted the reader to align the observation with. The significance of this design move is that it presents the information, not as a statement made by McGovern, but rather as a discernible fact that any "leading political spokesman" would have made.

So, not only does Scribner's design of her citations remove the information presented from her idiosyncratic position; Scribner's design also removes the information from the interested position of its original source. Furthermore, although the first sentence presents a concrete problem currently plaguing the academic community, this problem actually needs to be understood as one that exceeds the bounds of both time and historical circumstance. By the end of this first paragraph, Scribner's academic community is faced with a problem that transcends both personal and historical context.

So far we have discussed how Scribner designed the opening remarks of her text to provide a platform from which she could launch her position and line of argument. She did this, we argued, by objectifying a particular problem within the literacy issue, which she needed the academic community to accept for her argument to be effective. However, what would these opening remarks have looked like if Scribner had been insensitive to the need to anchor her text in a world of material entities and objective information? Or, what if her design focused on highlighting, rather than suppressing the interests and positions underlying her text? In the following rewrite of Scribner's text we offer one alternative design.

> Several years ago, in September of 1978, Democratic Senator George McGovern argued that literacy should be understood as a problem of pressing national concern and that educators and policymakers needed to develop and agree on a definition for the concept "literacy."

When compared to the original text, notice how this design locates the information "literacy is a problem" and "literacy as an ill-defined concept" within the realm of interested, contested positions. Again, the choice of citation format and type of projection play key roles. To begin with, the information is directly attributed as an argumentative point made by a specific person, with specific political affiliations, at a specific time. Of particular interest here is how this attribution leaves the information vulnerable to criticism and debate. First, labeling the speech act an argumentative point characterizes the information as an assertion open for debate. More significant, however, is the shift from attributing the information to a category type, as Scribner did, to attributing the information to a specific person. Scribner's design suggests that she expects readers to infer the attribute "knowledgeable about pressing national concerns" to the category type "leading political spokesman." By identifying her source as first and foremost a general type of spokesman, Scribner used that source as a warranting device that makes her claims relatively resilient to criticism (Potter & Halliday, 1990). However, the redesign of this attribution allows the reader to infer a wider range of characteristics about this specific political spokesman and the motivations behind his argument. For example, rather than categorizing McGovern as a "leading political spokesman," some readers may categorize him as a "tax and spend liberal" and thus challenge his credibility as a source of information concerning "pressing national concerns."

Moreover, the type of projection, sentence form, and lexical choices contained in the clause "Democratic Senator George McGovern argued that . . . " further situate the information in the speaker's position. Again, the information in the foregoing text is constructed as a speaker's perception and classification process. However, the event perceived and classified in this text is not something someone observed, but rather is an individual's speech act. Further, this text foregrounds the speaker's role in this process. Using a verbal, rather than nominal form allows the specific identity of the actor and his temporal context to be included in the text. Combining personal projection with a "saying" verb is also an important design decision for characterizing the manner in which the information was acquired. Specifically, the use of "argued that" (vs. "observed that") characterizes the information as originating in the speaker's thoughts and statements rather than in a world external to those thoughts and statements.

Up to this point we have considered how the author situates the information about the literacy issue in the tenuous and interested position of its original source, but what about the author's position? How can the text be examined for traces of the author's interests and attitude? We have so far explained personal projection as a device for locating information in the position of its original source, but the form in which this projection is incorporated into the text is also important to the author's text design. That is, an author can present speaker statements in one of two forms: as *quoted speech* ("I think it will rain," Joe said.) or as *reported speech* (Joe said that he thinks it will rain.). This choice is not simply a matter of stylistic preference; it is a stylistic choice that yields important semantic consequences. Whereas quoted speech is used to represent a statement in the speaker's original wording, reported speech only claims to present the "essential meaning" of the speaker's original statement (Halliday, 1985). As such, presenting McGovern's statements in the form of reported speech allows the author greater discretion in designing the "essential meaning" of that statement. The author can subtly alter the meaning of the statement through lexical choices (argued vs. stated), variations in syntax (two independent clauses vs. a dependent and independent clause), and changes in modality (literacy is a problem vs. literacy should be understood as a problem). As such, what may at first glance appear to be an independent statement corroborating an author's argument may be better understood as a subtle design move meant to blur the boundaries between independent and interested statements.

In addition to designing the introductory remarks of her argument, Scribner was also faced with the design task of presenting her position relative to the positions previously argued within her academic community. In the following we see how Scribner translated this convention into practice.

> What lies behind the definitional difficulties this statement decries? The authors themselves provide a clue. They suggest that literacy is a kind of reality that educators should be able to grasp and explain. . . .
>
> Without denigrating its contribution, I would like to suggest, however, that conflicts and contradictions are intrinsic to such an essentialist approach.
>
> Consider the following. Most efforts at definitional determination are based on a conception of literacy as an attribute of individuals;. . . . But the single most compelling fact about literacy is that it is a social achievement; individuals in societies without writing systems do not become literate. . . . It follows that individual literacy is relative to social literacy. (Scribner, 1984, p. 7)

In this excerpt we again see Scribner following fairly standard conventions for academic writing as she positioned herself within her community. She synthesized previous positions argued within the community, critiqued those positions, and presented her position as an alternative that will enable the community to address its issues more effectively. Similar to her opening remarks, the design of this segment and the possible functions served by that design can be examined.

In sum, Scribner designed this portion of her argument to bring the audience into the conversation, letting them listen to the competing positions so that they can judge the merits of each case for themselves. Meanwhile, Scribner stood on the sidelines, briefly rejoining the conversation to interject her critique but then quickly moving aside again, allowing the audience an independent view of the situation. Of particular interest here is how Scribner designed this scene of competing positions so that she subtly directed the audience's attention and impression of these positions.

In the first paragraph, Scribner presented her synthesis of the positions held within her community and her critique of those positions. However, she designed this information to suppress her presence in these synthesizing and critiquing tasks, giving the reader unmediated access to an alternative position. In other words, Scribner's characterization and critique were not motivated by her project and interests; rather, she was merely responding to problems belonging to the very nature of the authors' approach. After posing a question to her audience, she told them that the cause of the "definitional difficulties" facing the community can be found by listening to what the authors have to say about the nature of literacy. This directional cue is immediately followed by a presentation of what the authors themselves suggest is the nature of literacy. Scribner then politely reentered the conversation and modestly presented her critique of this "essentialist" approach. Although she clearly marked this criticism as her own, she was quick to point out that her critique was a response to the essential nature of the authors' approach, to a flaw intrinsic to their approach. Her critique is one anybody would make had they carefully considered the foundations of both positions. At the end of this excerpt, Scribner let the reader to do this.

In the final paragraph, Scribner presented the two competing positions to the audience for their consideration. Notice, however, how she varied the design of each presentation such that the essentialist approach is located in the realm of interested projects and assumptions whereas the social approach is located in the realm of empirical observation and logical reasoning. Specifically, Scribner characterized the essentialist approach as originating in efforts (presumably those of researchers, policymakers, and educators) that are based on ideas and notions about the nature of literacy. In contrast, the social approach, the approach Scribner advocated, is not based on conceptions but rather encompasses what literacy is, its essential nature. That is, the social approach originates, not merely in a fact, but in "the single most compelling fact about literacy." By characterizing the information "literacy is a social achievement" as a "fact," Scribner presented a statement that is true by definition (i.e., if writing is the property of society and if literate behavior refers to the written word, then literacy is a social phenomenon) as a truth based in empirical observation and/or direct experience. Further, understanding the factual nature of literacy will ultimately lead the reader to the logical conclusion that "individual literacy is relative to social literacy."

As with her opening remarks, this text is only one of several possible designs Scribner could have used for positioning herself within her academic community; so, let us consider an alternative design in which the primary linguistic and rhetorical tasks are concerned, not with objectifying Scribner's argument, but with highlighting the subjective interests underlying it.

> What lies behind the definitional difficulties this statement decries? A close reading of several authors' arguments suggests that their positions advocate an essentialist approach to literacy. According to this approach literacy is a kind of reality that educators should be able to grasp and explain. . . .
>
> My position, however, contends that individual researchers and educators will experience conflicts and contradictions in their efforts to implement this approach.
>
> As an alternative, I argue for an approach based on a conception of literacy as social achievement. Because writing systems are developed by societies, literacy is, by definition, a social phenomenon. Therefore, because literacy is the outcome of cultural transmission, individual literacy should be understood as relative to social literacy.

In this rewrite of Scribner's text, the pretense of engaging the audience in a conversation with the authors has been discarded; the authors no longer speak for themselves and the readers no longer listen for themselves. Rather, the writer's interpretative practices and academic project are foregrounded as the filters through which the competing positions are presented. Relatedly, the social approach is no longer privileged as the fact-based approach; it is presented as merely grounded in a different conception of literacy than that underlying the essentialist approach. The function of this text, then, is not to present the true nature of literacy for the audience to see; rather, this design presents the literacy debate as an argument about definitions with the central concern being to define the concept of literacy in a way that will most effectively promote the writer's project.

WHERE DO WE GO FROM HERE?

In the preceding section we demonstrated how an author designed her text to realize some of the conventions required by academic writing. Although this design process is in itself a complex and sophisticated intellectual activity, it does not account for all that an author does in developing and arguing a position within an academic community. Clearly, then, in challenging our students to become knowledge designers, authors, we set ambitious goals not only for them, but for ourselves as well.

To play our part in meeting this challenge and thereby help students play their part, we need to further refine our theoretical framework for a reflective pedagogy by pursuing three areas of inquiry. First, we need to conduct case study analysis to understand more concretely how students translate the conventions of authorship into their own writing. What does the design of students' texts suggest about their attitudes toward knowledge, language, argument, and authorship? Second, to help students better meet the challenges posed by our curriculum, we need to develop a more effective approach toward providing feedback. This feedback must involve the students in developing a reflective stance toward their own texts, teaching them to look at, rather than through their writing. The tenor of this feedback would not be corrective, focusing on how students fell short in their attempts to meet our challenge; rather, this feedback would be interactive, focusing students' attention on the design of their texts and what functions are (are not) served by that design. Finally, we need to consider the long-term impact such a pedagogy would have on our students' performance: Where would such a curriculum lead our students? Would it foster improved writing performance? Would it foster improved reflection? Would it do both, enabling students to internalize an approach to their writing that weds reflective practice with performative results? These are only some of the questions we need to answer but, for now, cannot.

REFERENCES

Elbow, P. (1991). Reflections on academic discourse: How it relates to freshmen and colleagues. *College English, 53*(2), 135–155.

Geisler, C., & Kaufer, D. (1989). Making meaning in a literate conversation: A teachable sequence for reflective writing. *Rhetoric Society Quarterly, 19*, 229–244.

Giddens, A. (1984). *The constitution of society*. Cambridge, MA: Polity Press.

Givon, T. (1982). Evidentiality and epistemic space. *Studies in Language, 6*(1), 23–49.

Halliday, M. A. K. (1985). *Introduction to functional grammar*. London: Arnold.

Kaufer, D., & Geisler, C. (1990). Structuring argumentation in a social constructivist framework: A pedagogy with computer support. *Argumentation, 4*, 379–396.

Kaufer, D., Geisler, C., & Neuwirth, C. (1989). *Arguing from sources: Exploring issues through reading and writing*. San Diego: Harcourt Brace Javonovich.

Kaufer, D., & Young, R. (1993). Writing in the content areas: Some theoretical complexities. In L. Odell (Ed.), *Theory and practice in the teaching of writing: Rethinking the discipline* (pp. 71–104). Carbondale & Edwardsville: Southern Illinois University Press.

Kennedy, A. (1992). Committing the curriculum and other misdemeanors. In J. A. Berlin & M. J. Vivion (Eds.), *Cultural studies in the English classroom* (pp. 24–45). Portsmouth, NH: Boynton/Cook.

Kennedy, A., Neuwirth C., Straub K., & Kaufer, D. (1994). Integrating rhetorical theory, cultural studies, and creative writing in the design of a first-year writing curriculum. In D. Dowling (Ed.), *Curriculum innovations* (pp. 235–262). Bloomington: Indiana University Press.

Kress, G. (1983). Linguistic and ideological transformation in news reporting. In H. Davis & P. Walton (Eds.), *Language, image, media* (pp. 120–138). New York: St. Martin's.

Potter, J., & Halliday, Q. (1990). Community leaders: A device for warranting versions of crowd events. *Journal of Pragmatics, 14,* 905–921.

Scribner, S. (1984). Literacy in three metaphors. *American Journal of Education, 93,* 6–21.

(Dis)Missing Compulsory First-Year Composition

Lil Brannon
The University at Albany, SUNY

Until 1986, The University at Albany, SUNY, like most universities across the country, mandated that every first-year student be required to take composition. In 1986, after the writing program faculty built coalitions with faculty across the disciplines and drew up a new writing-intensive curriculum, they convinced the University Senate to abolish compulsory first-year composition. The story of the change in Albany's writing program is an interesting one to tell, but not so much for its plot; "what happened," although intriguing, is very much dependent on the local contingencies and so can, at best, only offer images of possibility. Rather, the story of Albany provides a way of seeing how ideas of literacy shape what is possible for students. At Albany prior to 1986 (and at most colleges today), for example, composition was required because the faculty believed in a commonsense, "functional" idea of literacy. My colleagues' rationale for requiring composition at that time would certainly sound familiar to anyone involved in a writing program: "Students simply don't know how to write." "Students can't write a sentence, much less say put two sentences together." "They can't spell." "They can't read." "It is the English department's responsibility, seeing that the high schools have failed, to teach students how to write prior to taking other courses." The faculty required composition because they accepted the university's responsibility for its students' literacy, believing that writing was something basic, a skill to be mastered, a technology to be applied. Our entering student placement exam for writing involved constructing assessments of student writing that my colleagues thought "discovered" (but that in fact *produced*) a population of students who were not proficient and who were in need of remediation—students who would be required to take our first-year writing course.

In the mid-1980s, the writing faculty on our campus set out to argue for a different idea of literacy, as, in effect, a critique of the functionalist conception. We argued against "testing" our students as "outcomes" of instruction and placing them in courses designed to remedy perceived deficiencies. Instead we wanted our colleagues to construct our students as developing writers and to evaluate them "formatively," within the ongoing, necessarily never-ending, projects of literacy teaching and learning on our campus. After much discussion and debate, in 1986, the University at Albany boldly abolished compulsory first-year composition, a move away from ghettoized general writing skills instruction. This was possible because a group of faculty from across the curriculum understood that their reason for requiring composition of all students was based on a "skills" concept of writing that was losing professional currency; indeed, that it worked against the idea of writing that the English department faculty responsible for the program and the major researchers in the field found credible.

In place of compulsory first-year composition, the University Senate required that all students take a minimum of two writing-intensive courses, at least one of which was an upper division course, ideally in the major. In effect, this requirement repositioned writing within the University, making it a broad faculty responsibility, at the same time foregrounding the inappropriateness of a general writing skills model of composing. The writing-intensive program was designed to enable our students to gain immediate access to the university curriculum *as writers* and therefore makers of knowledge in the disciplines. The faculty turned to their composition specialists for direction and advice about this new program. The Writing Center was given part of the responsibility for writing instruction and for assessing the needs of a diverse student body and offering individualized instruction in writing for all those who sought their counsel. The writing-intensive program, which a professor of economics directs, was given responsibility for classroom instruction. These twin agencies of the writing program are mutually founded on the idea that writing is not a mechanical system of isolated skills that can be mastered either sequentially or once and for all. Writing courses and tutorials do not, cannot, offer one-shot "inoculations" against the "ills" of incorrectness.

The act of writing is a complex sociocognitive interaction with the world that entails, beyond mechanical control, such subtle practices as establishing and maintaining social positions, adapting to variable discursive conventions, and constructing ideas and relationships for oneself and others. It is not separate from one's life or from one's culture. Our faculty's responsibility then was to ensure not that students receive some essentially alien technology, some "correct" set of language practices, in order to proceed through the university, but rather that they learn to use, with greater subtlety and control, the language they bring with them, adjusting the register, the cadences, the vocabulary, the social codes, the nuances, and the intellectual moves, as they confront the demands of writing in academic disciplines.

The most important assumption on which our new writing program is based is that our instructional concern is to open up the disciplinary conversations of the academy to students whose "voices" and language experiences had not yet been included in academic discourse. Writing-intensive courses, we believe, offer students a means of understanding the concepts and arguments of particular fields by writing, under the guidance of disciplinary practitioners, in the very discourses that have produced those concepts and arguments. Meanwhile, for students whose educational experiences had not prepared them adequately for advanced study, The University at Albany offers an array of programs—the Writing Center among them—that give students support, additional instruction, and ways of positioning their ideas within the University.

Our writing program has had to challenge the skills model—the idea that writing is essentially a technology rather than a social practice, that it "comes" in discrete mechanical parts that people learn to assemble, and that what is typically "wrong" with student writing is mechanical breakdown in grammar, structure, and usage. We want, instead, to see writing as the students' way of "knowing" the concepts and conventions of particular fields. We understand that the language practices that students bring to Albany are part of their cultural, ethnic, class, and regional heritage. Part of our work, then, is to help students position their voices within the University, a positioning that is richly complicated by the diversity of experiences of our students. We do not believe that an impersonal diagnostic measure will help us locate students in need, nor will it help us to understand a particular student's problems in confronting academic discourse. We depend, rather, on our faculty and professional staff to locate those students and explain the resources available. We also depend on students themselves to seek out the assistance they need, particularly at the Writing Center, which has always avoided mandatory referral and emphasized voluntary visits. The Writing Center sees hundreds of students every year by these means, a tribute to their maturity and self-awareness.

The Writing Center tutors offer tutorial instruction to students on their work in progress for their regular courses. Although no one is required to use the Writing Center, many members of our faculty urge their students to do so and support their efforts to grow and learn in this environment. Students come on their own because they feel the disparity between their accustomed ways of thinking and writing and those that they are now required to learn. They want professional opinions about their work before they turn it in; they want another reader who will challenge them to do their best work. The Writing Center provides the additional instruction necessary for some students to make the transition from the language of their home, their local communities, and their previous schooling to the language demanded by their new public and intellectual surroundings.

It is important to emphasize that the practices of teaching writing and assessing students' needs that have been adopted at the University at Albany are not the accidental possibilities that come with a privileged population of students (who would "make it" in any educational environment). These practices are possible in virtually any collegiate setting and with virtually any population. What is at stake is not student ability but a competition of educational assumptions, including competing notions about what language is, what writing is, and what the responsibilities of teaching and assessment are. The skills model closes off access to the university by marking certain uses of language as "deficient" and in need of remediation, as hurdles to overcome before learning can profitably happen. A different conception of literacy constructs the very same acts of language, not as errors to be avoided, but as social practices to be examined, valued in the contexts from which they derive, and used in the process of learning other practices better suited to the demands of a different social environment. This conception of literacy understands educational background, social experience, and intelligence differently. It opens up the University to all students, working with them to position their work within the discourses of the academy.

We cannot overlook the cultural power of the notion of functional literacy, and we must remind ourselves that this idea of literacy, like all ideas, are human constructions. Functional literacy constructs the ways teachers see their students and their needs, which in turn shapes the forms of assessment that they or others choose and the programs that are designed to assist the students. Although functional programs, featuring sequential progressions of skill, create the illusion of progress by documenting how a student is mastering each distinctive competence, in fact it allows few students ever to escape the programs to which they are assigned. The slow learner in grade school enters the remedial program of high school and the basic-skills program of the junior college, effectively maintaining the power structures now in place. Although such superficial "progress" from grade to grade and school to school fails to move most people beyond the literal-mindedness that remediation is designed to encourage, it does prepare them for a life of obedience, of following orders, and of repetitious work. Meanwhile, the overwhelming majority of gifted and talented students in high school, who come primarily from middle-class and upper class families, go on to the top colleges and universities, and finally take their place in middle and top management positions. In short, functional literacy does not produce a nation of critically alert readers and writers because it is not intended to do so. The outcome of functional priorities is that students who enter school already practicing the uses of language sanctioned by schools move ahead, whereas those who happen to use less prestigious dialects of English or come from homes where the activities of reading and writing are not particularly valued are channelled into remedial or vocational programs. This sorting system is then rationalized by the testing industry, which appeals to U.S. confidence in objectivity and technical know-how in order to "explain" why some students do very well, whereas others seem not to prosper no matter how many "second chances" they receive or no matter how many times they make another try at mastering "the basics." In this fashion, schools maintain the status quo, albeit at the cost of leaving unfulfilled their extravagant promises of offering opportunity for all students to reach their intellectual potential.

Because of the self-interested complexity of our educational system, its "commonsensical" dependency on functionalism, and the elaborate testing mechanisms in place to ensure that functional priorities are enforced, students who depend on schooling to acquire the abilities to read and write are carefully prohibited from the independence of mind alternative forms of literacy might encourage. This is what is wrong with, or at least limiting about, functionalism and much of the basic skills testing industry and the composition programs designed to support it. Students' inability to perform well on functional tasks appears rooted in their own ignorance, not in a conceptual system that not only stifles their capacities as readers and writers but also fails to demonstrate to them the power that such practices might have in their lives. Limiting literacy to grammatical competence and designing a sequential curriculum based on the mastery of skills, although it appears streamlined, efficient, and accountable, does not offer students insight into how writers and readers actually use those abilities when composing, nor does it give them the motive to want to learn to read and write—which stems, in large part, from a critical understanding of the potentially transforming power that literacy can have. For students whose home environments have already encouraged reading and writing abilities, functional curricular rituals are harmful enough, creating exasperation and boredom, but they become a serious problem, indeed, for students who are dependent on schooling to provide their context for literacy, particularly when the curriculum seldom asks them to participate in literate activities. For them, skills become an illusory means to an end—and for too many of them, these skills become their barriers to literacy rather than their access.

The conceptual innovations in literacy instruction over the last two decades that have begun to define alternative educational goals and methods are based on a competing definition of what constitutes language learning. Critical literacy offers a challenge to the traditional functional view of reading and writing by conceiving of literacy as a transforming process, a political act of naming the world for oneself, an ability to think critically by using reading and writing as a means of intervening in one's own social surroundings. Reading and writing are not mere technologies enabling the transfer of information, but are sociocognitive practices enabling critical inquiry about and intervention in "the world" on one's own behalf. Reading and writing are symbolic acts, not merely the processes of decoding and encoding, but the ability to comprehend and create texts that manifest new ways of being and perceiving the world.[1] Yet for critical literacy to have much impact on the ways students are taught to read and write will mean a fundamental reconceptualizing not only of the everyday world of the classroom but of the social role that schools have typically played. The most important change is in conceiving of knowledge as an activity, not a condition or state. If one believes that the act of knowing is the engagement of the individual mind in the making of connections among the materials of her experience, the classroom must be a place for dialogue and the pursuit of individual needs and concerns. Teaching, then, can no longer be a one-way transmitting of ideas, but must become a conversation, an interaction among peers and teacher, an exploration, and a process of learning. Literacy defined in these terms, where dialogue and inquiry become the dominant metaphors for teaching, would have to be the concern of all faculty members rather than the domain of the first-year compulsory composition teacher, for the act of composing is part of the activity of coming to know a subject.

If one believes that writing and reading are not prior to the understanding of content but integrally connected with it, the difficulty of teaching within a functionalist conception becomes apparent. When composing means the constructing and organizing of ideas in order for writers to express something that matters to them to someone who matters to them, teachers would need the opportunity and time to read and respond to student work and to write to and interact with their students (within a functionalist perspective, English teachers can work with 100 to 150 students, simply because they are to lecture and correct).

When literacy becomes the ability to create and understand symbolic meanings constructed as verbal texts, critical literacy is the ability to construct the world through written language and the ability to reconstruct the world through reflection and critique. Critical literacy moves beyond narrowly prescribed incremental instruction by redefining ethnic and class dialect variation as "difference" rather than "error," offering students the power to speak about that difference while they also learn about alternative practices, requiring that they engage in the active construing and constructing of their world, including an inspection of how distinctions

---

[1]For a full discussion of critical literacy, see Freire (1975), Giroux (1983), and Tuman (1987).

between privileged and subordinated dialects have worked to separate them from opportunity. Such acts of composition also require individuals to reflect on the statements they make, to be accountable for the material of their experiences, and to see that they structure and are structured by their encounters with language. Critical literacy opens up to all students the imaginative, the creative, and the critical; it offers them the possibility of engaging with ideas and people whom they can only encounter through the medium of text. In this perspective, they are no longer restricted to the here and now and the immediate idea, but are required to explore, to expand, to push beyond the ordinary, and to critique the complexity of their experiences. Literate individuals in this perspective do not simply encode and decode, but come to know that texts are situated historically, and therefore can be interpreted and reinterpreted, examined and challenged. In this model of literacy, texts and the construction of texts become powerful means of knowing and changing the world.

Teachers who advocate critical literacy meet a predictably intense resistance. Yet through the work of teachers like those at the University at Albany, educational priorities are being redirected, and the institutional realities that support functional literacy are being deliberately critiqued. What happened in my department and the University as a result of abolishing compulsory first-year composition has been both intellectually exciting and politically interesting and might serve as an example of possibilities. When we abolished compulsory first-year composition, we did not abolish writing or our commitment to students as writers. Those who had traditionally taught first-year composition were redeployed into writing-intensive literature courses, upper division writing courses, lower division creative writing courses, literature courses, courses in rhetoric and poetics, in teaching within the Writing Center, or working as consultants to various disciplines. Our students began writing more as a result of this curricular change. Before the institution of writing-intensive courses, students wrote little before entering compulsory first-year composition and little after they left, but now it seems we cannot offer enough writing-intensive courses: More than three quarters of our students take more than the required two. Our new writing sequence within the English major must turn away students because we cannot offer enough places for them. There has not been any increase in the numbers of students from the general student population who have failed or left the university (and those who have left have not indicated that they failed because they were unable to write). Let me say as well that the average combined SAT scores of students entering The University at Albany last year was 1100. We have a 17% enrollment of minority students.

Just as important, what has happened at Albany is that the idea of writing and literacy both within English studies and across the curriculum is continually being negotiated.

To begin with English studies, the contestation over "writing" in the English Department has led to a reexamination of the undergraduate major and graduate program by challenging the literary historical emphasis that used to shape them. Those in rhetoric and composition allied themselves with those in creative writing, in critical theory, and in more radical literary criticism to develop a new PhD in writing/teaching/and theory, which argues for the continual contestation of those terms and the interplay of discourses that purport to define and elaborate them. Out of the conversations over the successful PhD initiative, the writing faculty has developed a writing track within the undergraduate English major with an emphasis on theories of composing, rhetorical and critical theory, and poetics. As we have worked to develop the curriculum for the undergraduate program and our new PhD, the idea of writing is the key term of debate that brings into focus ways of reading that are employed in our department as well as constructions of knowledge, methods of inquiry, and concepts of teaching and learning. For example, one debate within the department is over the idea of writing to learn. Those who take an expressive literacy position argue that the students' experience is the ground for learning, the classroom—a safe haven for the students to explore their own response to course material, to read and offer their ideas to each other. This expressive position is contested by postmodern feminists who see expressive concepts as reasserting the humanist subject and its reliance on the myth of individual consciousness. This group argues that the classroom is a contested place—its discomfort an important starting place for creating critiques of the status quo. "The personal," "experience," and "comfort" are critiqued and challenged.

We are, I am convinced, able to have these extensive and probing debates precisely because we can turn our attention to them. We are no longer working from an embattled position, trying to argue for the need for writing over technical accuracy (correct spelling, commas and semicolons) that our colleagues long to see in their students' work. We no longer have to dust off those long rehearsed and now weary arguments against drill and skill, or worse, the five-paragraph theme so that we can offer our students a humane, transforming pedagogy. When we do not have to justify our own existence, we can hear arguments that are traditional or radical as ways of understanding better what we believe and as ways of questioning why we believe the things we do.

In departments across the curriculum, the faculty associated with the Writing Program in English have been asked to facilitate discussions within departments about the ways writing constructs knowledge within the disciplines. This consulting has included the English writing faculty actually taking undergraduate courses in various fields and researching the language practices that are both implicitly and explicitly enforced within various subject areas. This inquiry into the ways we and our students learn has opened new lines of questioning among the faculty. For example, Spanier (1992), a molecular biologist on our faculty, wrote in the MLA volume on writing across the curriculum on how concepts of gender impact on the language practices of the biological sciences. In her forthcoming book, she expanded this idea to include the construction of the field itself, demonstrating how feminists in the sciences have shown how concepts of cell reproduction are limited by masculine imagery: Sperm, for example, are characterized as acting on the egg, the egg a passive recipient—the same phenomena could be more accurately described and understood if the field used different language. Although the sperm does move toward the egg, fluids within the woman's body move the sperm toward the egg; that is, the woman's body works in collaboration with the sperm. Rather than the sperm penetrating the egg, one might just as convincingly argue that the egg reacts with the sperm. Examining how language is used to constitute a discipline—to develop disciplinary concepts—changes how writing is conceived and practiced.

As a result of our work with colleagues and students across the university, the Writing Center has become the place where faculty discuss their teaching and the role that language plays in it. Although the Writing Center continues to offer individual tutorial instruction that helps students position their ideas into the debates of the fields, we have been able to extend the idea of writing into classes that do not require it. We helped to develop special study groups for students who are in large lecture courses with large failure rates (the killer courses on campus) so that students can talk and write together about the course material. Writing-intensive faculty have also brought about a new general education program that features active learning as a requirement for course approval.

Having faculty involved in the Center as coinvestigators has not only generated important innovations on our campus, but have extended to professional arguments within composition studies—Mahala's (1991) *College English* essay "Writing Utopias: Writing Across the Curriculum and the Promise of Reform" and Kalamaras' (1994) SUNY Press book *Reclaiming the Tacit Tradition: Symbolic Form in the Rhetoric of Silence* began as they were working in the Writing Center and the writing-intensive program on our campus.

Of course, the University at Albany is not without its struggles. Change is slow and the arrangements of curricula still need to be rearticulated; the uses of resources still need to be reassessed; such "basic" yet persistently insoluble problems as class size, teacher workload, classroom materials, access to technology, funding of the Writing Center, the education of faculty and tutors need to be addressed. In other words, the supplanting of functionalist priorities with those of a critical literacy requires systemic change, an imaginative restructuring of the current practices of schools in the context of a reexamination of the realities of U.S. life. Writers like Freire (1975), Berthoff (1981), Knoblauch (Knoblauch & Brannon, 1993), North (1987), Shor (1980), Johnston (1992), and Goswami (Goswami & Stillman, 1986), to name a few, have spoken strongly and effectively about alternative possibilities for literacy and writing programs and their work has provided images for us as we have undertaken to develop our new writing program. We hope that other college and university faculty will join with us in critiquing functionalist ideas of literacy and offering better, more comprehensive programs for our students. In our letting go our hold on compulsory first-year composition, we have opened up possibilities for writing that have invigorated our teaching and transformed our undergraduate and graduate programs, indeed the university at large. It just may be time for more of us to abolish compulsory first-year composition.

REFERENCES

Berthoff, A. (1981). *The making of meaning*. Portsmouth, NH: Heinemann Boynton/Cook.
Freire, P. (1975). *Pedagogy of the oppressed*. New York: Seabury.
Giroux, H. (1983). *Theory and resistance in education: A pedagogy for the opposition*. South Hadley, MA: Bergin & Garvey.
Goswami, D., & Stillman, P. (Eds.). (1986). *Reclaiming the classroom*. Portsmouth, NH: Heinemann Boynton/Cook.
Johnston, P. (1992). *Constructive evaluation of literate activity*. New York: Longman.
Kalamaras, G. (1994). *Reclaiming the tacit tradition: Symbolic form in the rhetoric of silence*. Albany: State University of New York Press.
Knoblauch, C. H., & Brannon, L. (1993). *Critical teaching and the idea of literacy*. Portsmouth, NH: Heinemann Boynton/Cook.
Mahala, D. (1991). Writing utopias: Writing across the curriculum and the promise of reform. *College English 53*, 773–789.
North, S. M. (1987). *The making of knowledge in composition*. Portsmouth, NH: Heinemann Boynton/Cook.
Shor, I. (1980). *Critical teaching and everyday life*. Chicago: University of Chicago Press.
Spanier, B. (1992). Encountering the biological sciences: Ideology, language, and learning. In A. Harrington & C. Moran (Eds)., *Writing, teaching, and learning in the disciplines* (pp. 193–212). New York: Modern Language Association.
Tuman, M. (1987). *A preface to literacy*. Tuscaloosa: University of Alabama Press.

Response: Curricular Responsibilities and Professional Definition

Charles Bazerman
University of California, Santa Barbara

The essays in this volume pose three questions for the profession of writing. The first two are fully explicit, the last less so:

1. How should we understand writing?
2. Given our understanding of writing, should first-year writing courses continue in their current form or in any form?
3. Given an understanding of writing that extends far beyond the bounds of the first-year writing course, should the profession remain so tied to and defined by that curricular responsibility?

The first is, on the face of it, a typical and nondisruptive question, part of the regular debate of the profession. The conclusions from that debate might direct our thoughts and empirical investigations in one direction or another. Our conclusions may also lead us to new ways to organize the classroom and new things to do and say during class hours. Nonetheless, debate over our object of investigation and our consequent approach to the classroom does not on the face of it require major changes in the institutional arrangements of the profession or the curricular space where we meet students.

However, almost every essay in this volume argues that what we now understand compels us, if we are honest, to give up a curricular space that is not only grounded in a wrong set of concepts (here labeled as GWSI) that no matter how reconceived, is a curricular space that just will not work. A few of the authors offer less radical alternatives, but almost all say that first-year writing, in its current form, must go.

249

The last issue, of professional identity, although it arises explicitly in only a few of the essays, seems to permeate most, as first-year writing is treated as distracting us from the full range of our subject and denying us full citizenship as an academic discipline.

Professional identity, curricular space, and reigning beliefs about writing clearly are related. Although rhetoric has a long history that predates first-year writing courses or even the university by thousands of years, our current configuration of the profession has grown out of the pedagogic responsibilities of a particular curricular site invented in the 1890s and rapidly expanded in the middle of this century. Accordingly, much of our research and theory has been focused on first-year composition and its remedial extensions. However, recent developments in research and theory have reminded us to look beyond the first-year writing course to notice writing is pervasive in the academy and world beyond; moreover, in those manifold sites of writing we have seen practices and commitments that are not locatable within the specific curricular setting of first-year writing courses.

Although the distinction between writing in composition courses and writing at other sites in the academy has been recurrently observed and has inspired various reformist movements, as noted by Connors and Russell, in recent years research in disciplinary, professional and nonacademic settings has created a wider ranging intellectual and professional basis to reconsider writing. The new research and related theorizing have revived and reinterpreted classical rhetorical concepts such as rhetorical situation and genre, but have also reached toward new ideas from sociology, cognitive psychology, science studies, linguistics, organizational theory, and other disciplines that map the complexity of people's actions in the world.

This exploration of the meaning of writing in the world has gone hand in hand with a pedagogic reaching out through business, legal, technical, and other professional writing, as well as writing across the curriculum. When successful, the dynamics of that pedagogic reaching out become almost irresistible: As teachers and researchers we become more intimately aware of the specialized literacy practices; students seeking the tools of participation in their chosen disciplinary and professional fields are highly motivated, focused, and knowledgeable; the faculty members of those disciplines and professions we work with come to appreciate both the value of our teaching and the rhetorical expertise and perspective we bring to bear on the communicative workings of their profession and the development of their students. We find research projects that engage us as intellectual equals with colleagues in many departments. Institutional authority often increases with this heightened sense of reality and value. As teachers and researchers of writing we find a professional respect that has been hard to come by when we have been solely associated with a required first-year course (such are the morals of Brannon's narrative.) It is hardly an accident that those writing programs that have achieved some degree of programmatic autonomy and institutional respect frequently have strong technical communication or writing across the curriculum components.

SITUATEDNESS AND ENGAGEMENT

So there are powerful and good reasons to want to define the research and pedagogic scope of our field broadly, reaching far beyond first-year writing courses. These powerful and good reasons are all built on a pair of observations hammered home in almost every one of the chapters in this volume: Effective writing speaks to its situation and effective writing is a deeply engaged form of participation. Petraglia sums these two up as a sense of the genuinely transactive—a sense that incorporates both the writer's perception of the consequentiality of the circumstances and the writer's commitment to influencing the unfolding events.

These observations are not new to this decade, or this century, or even this millennium, as Goggin, Connors, and Russell remind us, but recent research and scholarship have given us many more reasons for believing them and much more detailed pictures of how these two principles of situatedness and engagement work themselves out in a wide and differentiated set of cases and circumstances. The analyses of this volume draw together much of this recent work and advance the investigation into the operations of engaged participation through literate interaction within concrete situations; particularly important in this regard are Hill and Resnick's invocation of the work in situated cognition, Petraglia's drawing on the resources of cognitive psychology, Russell's presentation of activity theory, Freedman's application of linguistics and genre theory, and Royer's explication of Whitehead's pragmatic phenomenology. Each of these extend our ability to look into situation and the engaged self in significant ways.

As we deepen our understanding of situated engagement, pedagogic practices based on a generalized model of writing skills seem increasingly thin and pale. The recurrent critique against generalized writing instruction, which, as Connors retells, is often directed against the first-year writing course gains a new force and credibility. The essays in this volume, following that tradition, both make the larger critique against the teaching of unsituated writing skills and call into question the viability of an across the board first-year course. First-year writing as currently designed, almost all the authors suggest, is neither sufficiently situated in meaningful and complex activities that provide the real challenges of writing (Hill & Resnick concentrate most fully on this argument) nor sufficiently engaging to evoke the deep commitment and creativity from which serious writing flows (Royer most fully articulates this). Although a few of the authors suggest ways to raise issues of located engagement (particularly Kaufer and Dunmire and Russell) in the first-year composition class or to restructure the classroom so as to increase the actual engagement (particularly Jolliffe and Kemp), current practices in first-year writing courses are largely dismissed as being versions of GWSI with the strong implication that any across-the-board course taught to all students will be enmired in GWSI. Several of the essays, including the introductory essay, explicitly raise arguments for the abolition of first-year composition (e.g., Connors, Brannon, Hill & Resnick, Petraglia, and Freedman).

THE CURRICULAR REALITY OF GWSI

Although I thoroughly agree that situatedness and engagement are central to all good writing and all effective writing pedagogy, I think we need to be much more careful about characterizing both the range of practices currently enacted in the composition classroom and the possibilities for situated engagement in writing as we come to understand the curricular space of the first-year class more fully. Composition encompasses a complex history and a wide range of current practices that need to be observed before we adopt totalizing rejections.

Certainly there are large and visible GWSI elements in the institutional mandate that has created the first-year writing course. Institutional motives for creating massive (although usually underfunded) compulsory writing courses for this past century are almost always based on something like a GWSI set of assumptions. Administration and faculty usually want their students able to write sufficiently well to participate competently in the undergraduate curriculum. The desired competence is often described in general writing skills terms, and the charge to those delegated to teach composition is to instruct students in these general skills.

This curricular charge of GWSI has created one of the central problems for the profession: to put meaning and life into an unpromising curricular space. Just because we have been funded with a reductionist notion of our task has not meant that we have been bound to follow through in a reductionist way. Over the years the pages of the composition journals have been filled with ways in which writing teachers have developed to turn their first-year writing classes into situated and meaningful occasions that engage students in motivated writing. As Freedman observes, situatedness and engagement cannot be made up out of whole cloth; students must feel the force of the situation and be drawn into it powerfully before they take seriously any explicit discussion of genres or any writing technique. As the writing begins to matter, the students implicitly orient to the situation, with focal attention on the statements they want to make rather than on the techne by which they bring the statements into being. Nonetheless, as they are struggling with their implicit resources to bring the statement into being, they are most in need of, and receptive to, specific technical instruction that directly helps them. The writing must matter before the reflection on writing matters. This insight elaborates an insight gained by every generation of writing teachers. The problem has always been to bring some compelling sense of reality to the writing classroom.

Because the curricular charge has been so thin and unsatisfactory, successful writing teachers, the ones who stay with it, find their own *modus vivendi*—that is, their mode of bringing life to the tasks of writing. Writing teachers may build engagement around students' personal development—students' increasing self-consciousness and articulateness about themselves and their own histories, their entry into adulthood, and their career concerns. Writing teachers may build engagement around students' excitement over entering a university of ideas; their current concerns about war and peace and ecology and multiculturalism; the power of particular texts; the endless discoveries to be made through library research; reflection on language, culture, advertising, rhetoric, or semiotics; or any subject the teacher's enthusiasm could draw students into. Both Jolliffe and Kaufer and Dunmire's suggestions, despite being placed within the revolutionary context of this volume, fall well within this tradition of finding ways of increasing student involvement in writing.

Each of us might find some of these means of bringing life to the writing class preferable to others. Some we might argue are more important to students or more likely to serve the students' needs in the long run. All of these approaches can and have worked for teachers committed to them. If anything, the great variety of these approaches suggests something of the enormity of writing, that so many aspects of life can be enhanced through writing.

Until each instructor finds a vitality that activates the particular students gathered in each class, the writing course can indeed be lifeless. A writing class that does not elicit motivation, hard work, and attention does little for students' ability to write. At best, you get a coerced, transparent, and unsatisfying imitation of communication. Even when one locates the power, the power is not always with you. I have been there, and I have known, as all writing teachers have known, death at 8 a.m. on Wednesday morning.

STUDENTS' REALITY AND THE REALITY OF THE FIRST-YEAR WRITING COURSE

I also know enough of the life of the first-year course to know the potential importance of the first-year course as a curricular site for writing. In particular, first-year students entering a university and marking a major transition in their life have needs the first-year writing courses can and often do meet. First-year students, as novices in the complex literate environments of the university, are engaged in many transformations in their literacy practices; they can use curricular support.

Surviving and then thriving at the university shape the psychological habitat of students and can motivate writing that engages all that they are at that moment. First-year students are immediately concerned with defining who they are in their new situation, how they can participate successfully as students, and how their new competencies and identity change their view of the world they have just come from. The world of legal briefs or environmental impact statements or corporate reports that they may be writing 5 or 10 years from now may be pretty hazy, but the literature essay and the chemistry lab report due next week are about as real as you can get, followed closely by the sociology paper due the week after. Students reflect on themselves as students in the language of students, as they engage with disciplines in the role of students. Moreover, the tasks they are given as students are student tasks, not the tasks of professionals, even when the assignments consciously attempt to model professional practice. The students write student papers, even when those papers look like corporate reports. The freshman writing course is precisely an introduction into the literacy practices of being a university student.

Indeed to locate the students directly into the specialized discourses of advanced professionalism without giving them a chance to mediate those discourses with whatever discourses they use to contemplate their lives, values, and goals as students makes it difficult for them to locate themselves as anything but the most trivial actors in specialized discourses. As students they are necessarily only marginal figures, novices, within disciplines and professions. They cannot frame their own agendas for those disciplines, nor can they see the flexibility within the current literate practices that give them the opportunity to move professional discourses to new terrain. To jump directly into professional discourses without that kind of reflective discourse that is often developed in first-year writing may leave students alienated or cynical about discourses that they do not see the sense of. For those that survive and succeed within those discourses, their accomplishment and satisfaction are limited by passivity, unarticulated ambivalences, and inability to frame creative personally committed agendas. When they are cast in fully professional roles, only a few discover the means to address the full creative possibilities of their nominally empowered roles. A number of the difficulties in contemporary professional life are I believe traceable to the nonreflective and unempowered way many people are introduced to their disciplinary discourses.

If we start analyzing the first-year writing course we find it is a very real place. We need to look at the students, at the institution, at the undergraduate curriculum, at the issues of the time and place, and a thousand other factors that might come to bear on locating the course. Every generation, every college, and every group of students gathered in the class is different, and we must attend to those differences. There is no simple prescription for locating where this class is, but with that analysis we can create the engaged situation that will make the writing real, important, and challenging.

WHERE ARE THE STUDENTS?

Given the concern of the authors in this volume for situatedness and engagement, and their obvious desire to engage students in more meaningful discourse, I would have hoped there would have been more concrete analysis of the situation and engagement of students, who they are, what drives them, what puzzles them, what they need, and what they perceive they need. Only Freedman and Geisler turn to those issues with energy, but still only from the perspective of locating the situations that discourage engagement.

Perhaps composition classes are everywhere unengaging and sterile, and it is not worth inquiring into what engagements students have found there. However, I doubt that, and I would want extensive wide-ranging empirical evidence before I would believe it. One of composition's continuing strengths, at times to a fault, has been its attention to the students. Often composition is the only course where students find any attention, the one course where they can start to reflect on who they are and how they can best participate in their new situation. In almost every institution I have been at, students have said that their first-year writing teacher is the only teacher that knew them. Moreover, because first-year students are so concerned about their new literate environment in the university, they are often more ready to work on developing their writing than institutionally savvy sophomores and juniors who have already settled on a way to deal with college writing requirements. Before we cast off or entirely redesign first-year writing, we have some obligation to understand the role of the course in the lives of first-year students and the kinds of successes it has had that have encouraged it to move in the directions it has.

Nor do the essays in this volume provide much analysis of the situation of higher education, which they, for the most part, dissolve simply into preprofessionalism. Although the authors in this volume, if asked directly, would likely assert their belief in the importance of the university as a formative experience for each student and as an important institution in contemporary life and would likely deny any simplistic distinction between the real world outside the university walls and an insubstantial unreality within, the discursive priorities expressed in some of these essays would seem to indicate otherwise. Where preferences are expressed, the language of the workplace is preferred to any personal, developmental, educational, reflective, philosophical, cultural, or other discourse usually associated with the university experience. I certainly believe the discourses of the disciplines and professions are extremely important and not adequately understood. I have devoted much of my research career to explicating them and much of my pedagogic career in advancing their teaching at all levels. I do not, however, believe they simply ought to displace all the other discourses in which we engage.

The failure to analyze concretely the wide range of discourses that make up university life is especially disappointing given the deep historical and institutional understanding of the university that several of the authors in this volume have expressed elsewhere. The undergraduate years are a time of moving from prior assumptions into a broader, more reflective view of life and a growing commitment to particular ways of being and acting in world, integrating greater learning and literacy. Geisler points to the absence of this reflective literate activity in secondary education. The first-year writing course has often served as precisely a place that introduces students to the critical reflective discourse that provides the medium for the undergraduate experience.

The university is a real and special place. It is one of the most influential of institutions in the modern world in defining substantial parts of our culture and in producing knowledge and opinions that shape public, cultural, and technological agendas. Moreover, it increasingly provides a compulsory passage for those who will participate most fully and powerfully in our society. In the past the culture of the university may have reflected a class ideal and a university education served as a class marker, but in this half century the university has increasingly formed the cultural engine for all of society. (This I take as the ultimate consequence of Russell's observation about the appropriation of academic discourses in public discourse.) Students standing at the front door of this unusual culture can use some early guidance to its literate practices and in finding their individual ways to find engagement in this important life passage. They need to take part fully in the literate activities of the university before they can take part fully in the activities of any profession or discipline.

DISCURSIVE DIFFERENCES, TRANSFERABILITY, AND FLEXIBILITY

In setting out this argument for the value of a first-year writing course I need to take up one final point: the transferability of literate practices (raised most explicitly by Petraglia and Russell). If, as I agree with the authors, discourses vary one from another and competence in one is no guarantee of competence in another, of what value is a writing course not geared directly to the practices the student will ultimately participate in? A student may have the most engaged and exciting time writing papers on the social psychology of being a Generation X unemployable, but how much will that help to write the architectural proposal that will get him or her a job and will have an impact on society? In fact, becoming skilled in such a culturally critical discourse may teach counterproductive habits and commit students to discursive styles that will be inappropriate in their later professional encounters. The student may come to believe that there is only one valued way of writing and their entire identity may become bound up with it, so that they would spurn other discourses. Although this scenario may sound far fetched, we have all observed discursive chauvinism among some of our colleagues and their students.

The answer, however, is not to avoid teaching any discourse that may not ultimately be useful. After all, how can we know which practice or practices will be most essential 5 or 10 years from now for an 18-year-old? Even if we could know, how good is it to be able to write only legal briefs and nothing else? In any event, how can we restrain our own impulses to urge those discourses each of us may individually value?

The answer cannot be to shelter students from discourses and limit their experience to what we imagine might be useful to them. The answer is to make visible and real over the period of a student's education a variety of discourses, so that the students can reorient to and evaluate new discourses as they become visible and relevant. A course that spans boundaries and sits precisely at a juncture in the discursive lives of students, as the first-year course does, is a place that can effectively make that point. Moreover, if the first-year course is combined with upper division writing instruction in relation to the major, students can experience and reflect on the multiplicity of discourse.

The best way to learn the power of writing is to write and become engaged in a compelling discourse. Then you learn that the hard work of writing well is worth it. The best way to learn flexibility in writing is to become engaged in a second discourse, and perhaps a third. When you experience the rewards of writing well in one domain, you are likely to demand of yourself that same high level of participation in any discourse you will engage in the future. The lesson that it is worth working hard at writing is perhaps the most important lesson, and it is the one most transferable. The lesson only goes wrong if you cannot differentiate the nature of the second discourse and keep trying to reassert the strategies of the first. More integrations, more fully, into more discursive systems is the answer, not fewer. Rhetorical flexibility is further increased if students are given the tools of rhetorical analysis that allow them to explicitly recognize, analyze, and respond to the particularities of the discursive systems and situations that they may move into, as Russell suggests. Although as Petraglia notes, cognitive studies indicate that transferability is hardly to be taken for granted, studies also suggest that transferability is increased when specific skills of recognizing and comparing situations are taught along with criteria for adapting procedures to meet the new situation.

ONE SITE AMONG MANY, BUT NOT ONE TO BE AVOIDED

Seeing the activities of composition courses within the complex of all the writings of the academy and the world reveals the first-year course as a major site of instruction and support, but not the only site. Moreover, the kinds of writing appropriate to the first-year course are particular, and do not define good writing in other situations. I agree with many of the contributors that our understanding of writing has been held back by too close an association with issues framed around the first year course, only the more basic forms of writing, and the earlier stages of writing development. If we wish to understand writing and support practices at all levels, we need to take a broad view of writing in all locations of society, from the earliest developmental practices through the most skilled and specialized writings in philosophy, the law, international negotiations, corporate management, political journalism, or literature.

However, taking this broad view still allows us to remain responsible to a major social need that provides much of the social and institutional support for the profession. Because law is now engaged in complex corporate dealings and regulation of many aspects of government and society, this does not mean lawyers have stopped basic criminal and contract practice. Because medicine is developing a complex understanding of the human organism in biological, genetic, environmental, social, and psychological contexts and is learning to deal with complex and rare conditions this does not mean that it can disown family medicine, as it has discovered to its chagrin. Rather, the knowledge that both fields have developed in the more esoteric parts of their practice provide new resources and contexts for the traditional points of contact with most people.

The base of the writing profession in first-year composition has proven remarkably productive in the last 25 years, reinvigorating writing instruction at all levels, from kindergarten to graduate school. Knowledge of writing processes, journals, invention, and drafting techniques has pervaded almost every primary and secondary school in this country and is influencing educational practice around the world. Collaborative learning, although starting in writing laboratories, proved so successful when brought to the freshman writing course, that it is now found at all levels of education in a wide range of disciplines. Writing across the curriculum, with all its multiple impacts, was born as an extension of the first-year writing program. As we now begin to learn more of the specialized nature of writing practices that lead us to see limitations to these pedagogical developments, it would be short-sighted to ignore the tremendous educational accomplishment built on freshman writing. How much more productive a pedagogical site will it be as we develop more sophisticated analyses of the situatedness, activities, and local engagement to be found there?

Recognizing the particularity of this site of instruction is part of redefining the profession to be greater than that one site. Drawing first-year writing as part of a much larger picture may grant some dignity to that location, a dignity that will help lift it out of some of the exploitations and oppressions that have regularly meant we have had too many students for not enough trained (or even untrained) staff, who are paid too little.

On the other hand, denying just that site where students, faculty, and administrations recognize and accept a need may remove the basis for the profession. If there were no first-year writing programs to be taught and overseen, how many writing professionals would most English departments support? If there were no first-year writing course, how many of the now-autonomous writing programs could avoid being folded back into other units? If there were no strong first-year writing program, how many writing across the curriculum programs could resist the drift of loosely monitored writing-intensive requirements and the habit of disciplines to make their rhetoric invisible in the service of epistemic authority? If there were no highly visible writing program, how many institutions (other than technical universities) would recognize more advanced writing courses as appropriate college work and how many nominally advanced courses would reformulate to pick up the needs no longer served by the vanished first-year course? If the first-year course did not keep literacy on the university agenda, how much research into issues of literacy would be supported except in colleges of education, and what would happen then to research on the advanced literacy practices of disciplines, professions, and the workplace?

It is not easy to wish away the base on which the profession has been built, just because that base is troublesome, not always well conceived, limiting, and overburdened with too many needs to address simply and with inadequate resources. Nor is it necessarily wise to wish it away; nor right. With our new understandings of writing as they are presented here, let us address the troubles, reconceive the course, place it in relation to our broader view, and find intelligent ways to meet the needs and gather the resources. That is the right thing to do. That will provide the continuing support for our much broader inquiry into the literate workings of all aspects of contemporary social life.

Author Index

Subject Index

267

at CMU, 228
as rhetoricians, 29–30, 37
school, 129–130
skill, 95
in society, 53, 74
as sociocognitive interaction, 240
from sources, 106, 201–203
tasks, 110
on thinking, 113
as a tool, 56, 60, 70
transactional, 103
in the workplace, 73, 129, 132, 139–140,
    152, 156

Writing with no content in particular
    (WNCP), 51, 88, 200–201, 218
Writing with specific content, 51
Writing intensive curriculum, *see* Writing,
    intensive courses
Written arguments, 136
Wyoming Resolution, 21

Z

Zones of proximal development, 54, 56, 70